Learning Cocoa with
Objective-C

D1456010

Related Mac OS X Titles from O'Reilly

SECOND EDITION

Learning Cocoa with Objective-C

James Duncan Davidson and Apple Computer, Inc.

O'REILLY®

Beijing · Cambridge · Farnham · Köln · Sebastopol · Taipei · Tokyo

Learning Cocoa with Objective-C, Second Edition
by James Duncan Davidson and Apple Computer, Inc.

Copyright © 2002, 2001 O'Reilly Media, Inc. All rights reserved.
Printed in the United States of America.

Published by O'Reilly Media, Inc., 1005 Gravenstein Highway North, Sebastopol, CA 95472.

O'Reilly Media, Inc. books may be purchased for educational, business, or sales promotional use. On-line editions are also available for most titles (*safari.oreilly.com*). For more information, contact our corporate/institutional sales department: (800) 998-9938 or *corporate@oreilly.com*.

Editor:	Chuck Toporek
Production Editor:	Brian Sawyer
Cover Designer:	Emma Colby
Interior Designer:	David Futato

Printing History:

May 2001:	First Edition. Originally published under the title *Learning Cocoa*.
September 2002:	Second Edition.

RepKover™ This book uses RepKover™, a durable and flexible lay-flat binding.

ISBN: 978-0-596-00301-2
[M]   [7/08]

Table of Contents

Part V.   Appendixes

Preface

Like a finely tuned BMW, Mac OS X is the ultimate programming machine.

Under the hood lies a powerful Unix engine, named Darwin, developed via Apple's open source initiative and based on FreeBSD 4.4 and the Mach 3.0 microkernel. On the outside is a highly polished graphical user interface (GUI) whose usability can't be touched by any desktop environment on the planet, including GNOME and KDE for Linux, as well as Windows XP.

The newest cat on the block—Mac OS X 10.2 (code-named Jaguar)—takes desktop and network computing to a new level. Jaguar, first introduced to developers as a pre-Alpha release at Apple's Worldwide Developer Conference (WWDC) in May 2002 and later released to the public on August 24, 2002, brings many changes and improvements to the legacy set forth by the previous Mac OS X releases. These changes include several additions to the Cocoa application programming interfaces (APIs), known as the Cocoa frameworks, arguably the best GUI application development environment on the face of the planet. An integrated set of libraries and runtime, Cocoa provides a rich infrastructure on which to build great user applications.

On Codenames and Cats

As mentioned earlier, Mac OS X 10.2 was code-named Jaguar during its development and testing phase. Earlier releases of Mac OS X included Puma (Mac OS X 10.1) and Cheetah (Mac OS X 10.0). Software developers like to give their projects names that evoke some emotion or theme for the release being worked on. A little research shows that the cheetah is the world's fastest land mammal, while the jaguar, unlike many other big cats, has no predators save for man. Worthy goals indeed.

Apple became so enamored of the Jaguar name that they ended up putting it onto the box in which Mac OS X 10.2 is released, complete with a jaguar fur motif.

When it comes to building Cocoa applications, developers can choose from three languages to work with the Cocoa APIs: Objective-C, Java, and AppleScript. This new edition of *Learning Cocoa*, retitled as *Learning Cocoa with Objective-C* and thoroughly revised and updated for Jaguar, shows you how to get started with building Cocoa applications for Mac OS X using the Objective-C binding to the Cocoa frameworks.

As an introductory book on Cocoa development, *Learning Cocoa with Objective-C* accomplishes the following:

- Introduces you to the concepts of object-oriented programming with Objective-C
- Shows you how to use Apple's Developer Tools, in particular, Project Builder and Interface Builder
- Introduces you to Cocoa's frameworks—Foundation and the Application Kit— by having you build simple applications along the way

The concepts learned in one chapter spill over to the next, and the sample programs you build while reading along get more complex as you go deeper into the book. By the end of the book, you will have learned enough about Cocoa and Objective-C to set you on your way to higher learning, and for that, there are plenty of other books available:

- *Building Cocoa Applications: A Step-by-Step Guide*, by Simson Garfinkel and Michael K. Mahoney (O'Reilly & Associates, Inc.)
- *Cocoa Programming for Mac OS X*, by Aaron Hillegass (Addison-Wesley)
- *Cocoa Programming*, by Scott Anguish, Erik Buck, and Donald Yacktman (Sams)

While these books also deal with Cocoa programming with Objective-C, each book takes a slightly different approach. Programming is a funny art, and sometimes it is invaluable to see several approaches to the same subject matter. To be a true master of the craft, you'll probably want to read each of these books and glean from each what you can.*

In addition to this and the previously listed books, you also have a vast resource of information at your fingertips in the form of Apple's own documentation. Installed on your system along with the Developer Tools, Apple's docs can be found in */Developer /Documentation* in both PDF and HTML format. If you have a fast or constant link to the Internet, you can save some space on your hard drive by dumping these docs in the Trash and using the online documentation found at *http://developer.apple.com*.

 When Apple updates their documentation, they often first post the revisions online, so you might want to keep that URL handy.

---

* Learn the ways of the Force, Luke—just stay away from the Dark Side.

Additionally, there are some online resources—mailing lists and web sites—that you should subscribe to and read frequently. A listing of these resources can be found in Appendix B, *Additional Resources*, located at the back of this book.

Audience

As the title implies, this is a "Learning" book—a book for newcomers to Cocoa and Objective-C. This book assumes you have a basic knowledge of ANSI C and that you're open to learning the concepts of object-oriented programming. If you're not familiar with C and you haven't programmed with Java or some other compiled language, you might want to hold off on reading this book just yet. Likewise, if you're already familiar with Objective-C or have programmed for NeXTSTEP, chances are this book will be too basic for your liking. Not that you can't pick something up from reading it, but this book is better suited for newcomers.

Who Should Read This Book

As mentioned earlier, this book was written for programmers who are interested in learning how to develop Cocoa applications using the Objective-C language. It assumes that you have some experience with C programming, as well as a basic understanding of computer-science concepts. If you're familiar with C or Java, you should have no problem picking up Objective-C.

Who Should Not Read This Book

Of course, one book can't be everything to everyone. Some people will find this book too basic or too advanced for their liking. For example:

Novice programmers
> If you have never programmed before and want to learn the basics of programming, you should start off reading an introductory programming text. To learn C, the language upon which Objective-C is based, we recommend the following books:
>
> - *The C Programming Language*, by Brian W. Kernighan and Dennis M. Ritchie (Prentice Hall)
> - *Practical C Programming*, by Steve Oualline (O'Reilly)
>
> These books will introduce you to the concepts of programming with C, giving you the foundation you need before reading this book.

Experienced NeXT developers
> If you have worked with OpenStep or NeXTSTEP, you will probably find the material in this book too basic. You might use this book as a refresher to come up to speed, but it probably won't be the Nirvana you're searching for.

Java developers

This book covers Cocoa using the Objective-C language. If you are a Java developer and don't mind learning a new language (learning new languages is always good for you!), then you will do fine with this book. However, if you want a strict treatment of Cocoa with Java, this book is not for you.

What You Need to Know

Extensive programming experience is not required to complete the examples in this book. Since the Objective-C language is a superset of ANSI C, experience with the C programming language is helpful. If you have experience with an object-oriented programming language such as Java or Smalltalk, you should find the concepts of Objective-C easy to comprehend. If you don't have experience with object-oriented concepts, don't worry; we will try our best to guide you through the terminology and to give you pointers to other texts and reference material.

No prior experience programming on Mac OS X is necessary to complete the tutorials in this book. We'll show you how to use the Developer Tools that come with Mac OS X and show you how to build your first Cocoa application in no time.

At some point you should explore the wealth of developer documentation that Apple installs with the Developer Tools. This documentation covers the Mac OS X system architecture, developer tools, release notes, the Objective-C language, the Cocoa API references, and so on. There are four places you can access Apple's developer documentation:

- The */Developer/Documentation* folder on your system. Specifically, most of the Cocoa documentation is located in the */Developer/Documentation/Cocoa* folder.

- The Help menu in Project Builder (*/Developer/Applications*), which is one of the development tools you will use as you work your way through this book.

- Mac Help from the Finder. After launching Mac Help and clicking on the "Help Center" toolbar item, you'll be able to find the Developer Help Center link.

- Online at *http://developer.apple.com*. As mentioned earlier, Apple often posts updates to its documentation online first, so you should check here if a document on your system doesn't have the answer for which you're looking.

About the Example Code

You will find many examples in this book. The code for these examples is contained within the text, but you may prefer to download a disk image (*.dmg*) of the examples rather than typing all that code in by hand. You can find the code online and packaged for download at *http://www.oreilly.com/catalog/learncocoa2.** You may also want to visit this site for any important notes or errata about the book.

All of the examples have been tested using Mac OS X 10.2, Project Builder 2.0, and Interface Builder 2.1. If you use this book with a later release of any of these products, the user interface and features may be different from those shown in the book, but everything should work. However, because the examples utilize many features first introduced with Jaguar, such as GCC 3† and the AddressBook APIs, you should not use an earlier release of Mac OS X with this book.

In some of the examples, we put a number (or letter, depending on the other elements on the page) on the right side of any line of code that we explain in detail. Numbered explanations appear below a listing, as shown in the following example:

```
int row = [itemList selectedRow];                                    // 1
NSString * newName = [[itemList selectedCell] stringValue];          // 2
```

1. The index of the row is obtained by passing the selectedRow message to the itemList object.

2. The newName string is obtained from the cell by using the stringValue message.

How This Book Is Organized

This book consists of 17 chapters and 3 appendixes, organized into 5 parts. The first three parts are organized so that each chapter builds upon the previous one. You should start at the beginning and proceed sequentially until you've read through the last chapter.

Most chapters contain example applications for you to work through, as well as exercises that build upon the material covered. Each chapter's applications and exercises are self-contained and do not spread across chapters.

Part I, *Cocoa Overview and Foundation*

Cocoa Overview and Foundation introduces the Cocoa frameworks and describes the high-level features they provide application programmers, as well as how they fit with other Mac OS X frameworks. It also includes a brief introduction to object-oriented programming, the Objective-C language, and Apple's development tools.

---

* This book does not come with a CD-ROM. Bundling a CD would increase the cost of production and the cost to you. It is our belief that anyone reading this book has access to an Internet connection and would rather save money by simply downloading the example code off the Web.

† GCC 3 introduces support for the C 99 standard, allowing us to make our example code more readable and easier to understand.

Chapter 1, *Introduction to Cocoa*
> Places Cocoa in the context of the Mac OS X programming environment and introduces the frameworks and classes that make up the Cocoa API.

Chapter 2, *Cocoa Development Tools*
> Introduces Project Builder and Interface Builder, Apple's tools for Mac OS X development. The chapter then goes on to describe the wide array of tools and utilities available to assist in building, debugging, and performance-tuning applications on Mac OS X.

Chapter 3, *Object-Oriented Programming with Objective-C*
> Explains the benefits of object-oriented programming practices (as compared to procedural programming) and provides an introduction to the terminology and core concepts needed to use the Cocoa frameworks effectively. It also includes a primer on the Objective-C programming language.

Chapter 4, *The Cocoa Foundation Kit*
> Provides a series of mini-tutorials to introduce the Cocoa Foundation, including strings, arrays, collections, utility functions, and memory management.

Part II, *Single-Window Applications*

Single-Window Applications covers the basic building blocks of any Cocoa application that displays a single GUI window to the user. This section uses a series of examples to illustrate the concepts presented. The techniques and concepts you learn in each chapter will lay the foundation for the next chapter.

Chapter 5, *Graphical User Interfaces*
> Introduces the Model-View-Controller (MVC) pattern and how Cocoa programs are structured and developed. You will also learn about nib files and how to use them in your applications.

Chapter 6, *Windows, Views, and Controls*
> Goes into detail about how the windowing system works, as well as how to create View and Controller objects to present a user interface.

Chapter 7, *Custom Views*
> Cocoa's default set of controls covers most of the common UI needs that applications have, but they can't cover everything. Your application may need to present a specialized view onto a data source or simply draw arbitrary content to the screen. This chapter shows how to create these custom views.

Chapter 8, *Event Handling*
> Introduces the event loop and explains how events propagate along the responder chain. It also covers how events are queued and dispatched, as well as how event delegation works.

Chapter 9, *Models and Data Functionality*

Shows how to work with the data-bearing objects of an application. The chapter also shows how this information can be utilized with the Controllers and Views of an application and how it can be read from and written to storage.

Part III, *Document-Based Applications*

Many applications today, such as word processors and web browsers, are built around the concept of a document. Creating an application that can handle multiple documents is tedious in the best of times. Luckily, Cocoa provides the ability for an application to handle multiple documents with ease. *Document-Based Applications* shows how to use Cocoa's document architecture.

Chapter 10, *Multiple Document Architecture*

Presents the basic concepts of the document-handling architecture and how documents are managed. The chapter guides you through the process of creating an application that takes advantage of the architecture.

Chapter 11, *Rich-Text Handling*

Shows advanced text-handling abilities of Cocoa, such as handling fonts, working with layout managers, enabling rulers, and working with attachments.

Part IV, *Miscellaneous Topics*

Miscellaneous Topics covers a variety of Mac OS X and Cocoa features that are important to delivering finished applications and giving them their finishing touches. The chapters in this part of the book cover diverse topics and can be read in any order.

Chapter 12, *Printing*

This chapter shows you how to add printing functionality to your application.

Chapter 13, *Bundles and Resources*

Here we describe how bundles, application or otherwise, are structured, how icons and document types are defined, and how application signatures work.

Chapter 14, *Localization*

Once you build an application, there are several ways to customize the interface to accommodate users in different parts of the world.

Chapter 15, *Defaults and Preferences*

Mac OS X provides comprehensive management of user preferences. This chapter explains how to work with this system to store information that can be used across multiple invocations of your application.

Chapter 16, *Accessory Windows*

Applications will often have more than just one interface component. Inspectors and palettes abound in modern applications. This chapter shows in detail how to store your user interface in multiple nib files to improve performance and ease maintainability and localization.

Chapter 17, *Finishing Touches*

Once you build an application, there are several important things you should do to make it ready for distribution. Cocoa provides default copyright strings and About boxes that need to be edited, and you should probably create some sort of Help documentation for the application. Finally, this chapter shows how to create an icon for your application and add that to the application bundle as well.

Part V, *Appendixes*

The *Appendixes* include quick-reference material for learning more about Cocoa's Objective-C classes and list resources that are beyond the scope of this book for expanding your Cocoa development horizon.

Appendix A, *Exercise Solutions*

Provides solutions to all of the exercises found at the end of each chapter.

Appendix B, *Additional Resources*

Provides a valuable list of Cocoa-related resources and where to find them, including Mac OS X's "built-in" developer documentation, books, mailing lists, and web sites.

Appendix C, *Using the Foundation and Application Kit API References*

Provides a guide to the various API references available to you as a developer, as well as some tools that will help you search and browse the available documentation.

How to Use This Book

Our recommendation is that you read this book from cover to cover, particularly if you're new to Cocoa and need to learn more about object-oriented programming (OOP). As you read through the book, you should work on the sample programs along the way. Doing so will give you the foundation you need to understand what Objective-C is (and isn't) and the concepts of OOP, most notably the MVC paradigm that aids in GUI application design. We try to take the approach of teaching you small things first and then building on those small concepts throughout the rest of the book.

If you have experience with Java or Smalltalk, we recommend that you read this book from front to back as well. Since you have experience with object-oriented concepts and programming, there are some sections that you will be able to skim. However, be careful not to skim too fast, as you might miss some important details.

Conventions Used in This Book

The following is a list of the typographical conventions used in this book:

Italic

> Used to indicate new terms, URLs, filenames, file extensions, directories, commands and options, program names, and to highlight comments in examples. For example, a path in the filesystem will appear as *Developer/Applications*.

`Constant Width`

> Used to show code examples, the contents of files, or the output from commands.

`Constant Width Bold`

> Used in examples and tables to show commands or other text that should be typed literally.

`Constant Width Italic`

> Used in examples and tables to show text that should be replaced with user-supplied values.

Menus/Navigation

> Menus and their options are referred to in the text as File → Open, Edit → Copy, etc. Arrows are used to signify a navigation path when using window options; for example, System Preferences → Login → Login Items means that you would launch System Preferences, click the icon for the Login control panel, and select the Login Items pane within that panel.

Pathnames

> Pathnames are used to show the location of a file or application in the filesystem. Directories (or folders) are separated by a forward slash. For example, if you see something like, "... launch Project Builder (*/Developer/Applications*)" in the text, that means that the Project Builder application can be found in the *Applications* subdirectory of the *Developer* directory.

↵

> A carriage return (↵) at the end of a line of code is used to denote an unnatural line break; that is, you should not enter these as two lines of code, but as one continuous line. Multiple lines are used in these cases due to printing constraints.

%, #

> The percent sign (%) is used in some examples to show the user prompt from the *tcsh* shell; the hash mark (#) is the prompt for the root user.

Menu Symbols

> When looking at the menus for any application, you will see some symbols associated with keyboard shortcuts for a particular command. For example, to cre-

ate a new project in Project Builder, you would go to the File menu and select New Project (File → New Project), or you could issue the keyboard shortcut, Shift-⌘-N.

You should pay special attention to notes set apart from the text with the following icons:

This is a tip, suggestion, or general note. It contains useful supplementary information about the topic at hand.

This indicates a warning or caution. It will help you solve and avoid annoying problems.

How to Contact Us

We have tested and verified the information in this book to the best of our ability, but you may find that features have changed (or even that we have made mistakes!). As a newcomer to Cocoa and a reader of this book, you can help us to improve future editions by sending us your feedback. Please let us know about any errors, inaccuracies, bugs, misleading or confusing statements, and typos that you find anywhere in this book.

Please also let us know what we can do to make this book more useful to you. We take your comments seriously and will try to incorporate reasonable suggestions into future editions. You can write to us at:

O'Reilly & Associates, Inc.
1005 Gravenstein Highway North
Sebastopol, CA 95472
(800) 998-9938 (in the U.S. or Canada)
(707) 829-0515 (international/local)
(707) 829-0104 (fax)

You can also send us messages electronically. To be put on the mailing list or to request a catalog, send email to:

info@oreilly.com

To ask technical questions or to comment on the book, send email to:

bookquestions@oreilly.com

The web site for *Learning Cocoa with Objective-C*, Second Edition lists examples, errata, and plans for future editions. You can find this page at:

http://www.oreilly.com/catalog/learncocoa2

For more information about this book and others, see the O'Reilly web site:

http://www.oreilly.com

Acknowledgments

First and foremost, I'd like to thank my editor, Chuck Toporek, who talked me into writing the new edition of this book (twice even) and alternately utilized the editor's whip and kind words of encouragement to guide me toward its completion. Without him, his advice, and his faith in me to get the job done, this book would not have happened. Also at O'Reilly, I'd like to thank Jeff Holcomb, the copyeditor for this book; David Chu, who assisted Chuck in pulling this book together for production; Brenda Miller, who produced the index; Derrick Story, who encouraged my early efforts with Cocoa by letting me write for the O'Reilly Network; and finally Tim O'Reilly, Michael Loukides, and Bob Eckstien, who always knew that I would write a book for O'Reilly & Associates some day.

Thanks as well to all the people at Apple, especially to the original NeXT and Apple documentation teams. For this new edition, we've changed the title, stripped the book down to bare metal, and built it back up. Without the foundation provided by the original documentation teams, the job would have been much harder. Also thanks to the many Cocoa engineers at Apple for taking the time to hash over the outline for the revision, and for reviewing drafts of the manuscript along the way. You guys know who you are.

Many thanks to the independent reviewers of this book, including Jo Davidson (who gave up part of the Memorial Day weekend to help us meet our deadlines) and Mike Barron.

Special thanks to Jason Hunter, who gave me an author's insight into the writing process, for helping me find the right metaphors in Chapter 3, and for always being there when needed. In addition, many thanks to Wilfredo Sánchez Vega, who got me hooked on Mac OS X in the first place after my Windows laptop went through one of its periodic meltdowns.

Music from many creative and talented people fueled the writing of this book. Among the artists in heavy rotation in iTunes and on the iPod: Tori Amos, Bedrock, Blue Man Group, BT, The Chemical Brothers, The Crystal Method, Darude, DJ Amber (from the San Francisco Bay rave scene), DJ Dragn'fly (from the Sacramento rave scene), Brian Eno, Fatboy Slim, The Future Sound of London, Juno Reactor, Moby, New Order, The Orb, Orbital, Mario Piu, Prodigy, Rinocerose, Sasha, Squarepusher, Underworld, Paul van Dyk, and many others.

And finally, thanks to all my family and friends who lent support to the book writing process and who encouraged me to chase my dreams: Dad, who taught me everything I needed to know after all; Mom, who brought me into the world; Mahaila, who probably never expected that I—of all the people in the family—would write a book; my sisters Susan, Illona, Joli, and Heather, as well as my friends Justyna Horwat and Jim Driscoll. Last, but not least, I want to thank Eleo, who ended up thoroughly addicted to the wireless network I installed at her place so that I could work on her couch, tapping away on my Titanium PowerBook until late in the night.

PART I

Cocoa Overview and Foundation

This part of the book introduces the Cocoa frameworks (Foundation and Application Kit) and describes the high-level features they provide application programmers, as well as how they fit with other Mac OS X frameworks. It also includes a brief introduction to object-oriented programming, the Objective-C language, and Apple's Developer Tools.

Chapters in this part of the book include:

CHAPTER 1

Introduction to Cocoa

Cocoa provides a rich layer of functionality on which you can build applications. Its comprehensive object-oriented API complements a large number of technologies that Mac OS X provides. Some of these technologies are inherited from the NeXTSTEP operating system. Others are based on the BSD Unix heritage of Mac OS X's core. Still others come from the original Macintosh environment and have been updated to work with a modern operating system. In many cases, you take advantage of these underlying technologies transparently, and you get the use of them essentially "for free." In some cases, you might use these technologies directly, but because of the way Cocoa is structured, they are a simple and direct API call away.

This chapter provides an overview of the Mac OS X programming environment and Cocoa's place in it. You will then learn about the two frameworks—Foundation and Application Kit (or AppKit)—that make up the Cocoa API, as well as the functionality that they provide.

The Mac OS X Programming Environment

Mac OS X provides five principal application environments:

Carbon

A set of procedural APIs for working with Mac OS X. These interfaces were initially derived from the earlier Mac OS Toolbox APIs and modified to work with Mac OS X's protected memory environment and preemptive task scheduling. As a transitional API, Carbon gives developers a clear way to migrate legacy applications to Mac OS X without requiring a total rewrite.* Adobe Photoshop 7.0 and

---

* Contrary to what you may have heard elsewhere, Carbon is not doomed to fade away over time. This erroneous opinion seems to be caused by a misinterpretation of the word "transitional" to mean that the API itself will be going away, rather than meaning it is the API to use to transition older applications. Moving forward, it will remain one of the core development environments for Mac OS X. In fact, Apple engineers are striving to enable better integration between Carbon and Cocoa.

Microsoft Office v. X are both examples of "Carbonized" applications. For more information on Carbon, see */Developer/Documentation/Carbon* or *Learning Carbon* (O'Reilly).

Cocoa

A set of object-oriented APIs derived from NeXT's operating-system technologies that take advantage of many features from Carbon. Programming with the Cocoa API is the focus of this book. Many applications that ship with Mac OS X, such as Mail and Stickies, are written in Cocoa. In addition, many of Apple's latest applications, such as iPhoto, iChat, and iDVD2, are built on top of Cocoa.

Java

A robust and fast virtual-machine environment for running applications developed using the Java Development Kit. Java applications are typically very portable and can run unchanged, without recompilation, on many different computing environments.

BSD Unix

The BSD layer of Mac OS X that provides a rich, robust, and mature set of tools and system calls. The standard BSD tools, utilities, APIs, and functions are available to applications. A command-line environment also exists as part of this layer.

Classic

The compatibility environment in which the system runs applications originally written for Mac OS 8 or Mac OS 9 that have not been updated to take full advantage of Mac OS X. Classic is essentially a modified version of Mac OS 9 running inside a process that has special hooks into other parts of the operating system. Over time, Classic is becoming less interesting as more applications are ported to run natively in Mac OS X.

To some degree, all of these application environments rely on other parts of the system. Figure 1-1 gives a layered, albeit simplified, illustration of Mac OS X's application environments and their relationship to the other primary parts of the operating system.

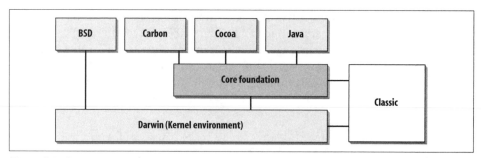

Figure 1-1. Cocoa as part of Mac OS X's programming environment

As you can see from Figure 1-1, each of Mac OS X's application environments relies upon functionality provided by deeper layers of the operating system. This functionality is roughly broken into two major sections: Core Foundation, which provides a common set of application and core services to the Cocoa, Carbon, and Java frameworks, and the kernel environment, which is the underlying Unix-based core of the operating system.

Cocoa Defined

Cocoa is an advanced object-oriented framework for building applications that run on Apple's Mac OS X. It is an integrated set of shared object libraries, a runtime system, and a development environment. Cocoa provides most of the infrastructure that graphical user applications typically need and insulates those applications from the internal workings of the core operating system.

Think of Cocoa as a layer of objects acting as both mediator and facilitator between programs that you build and the operating system. These objects span the spectrum from simple wrappers for basic types, such as strings and arrays, to complex functionality, such as distributed computing and advanced imaging. They are designed to make it easy to create a graphical user interface (GUI) application and are based on a sophisticated infrastructure that simplifies the programming task.

Cocoa-based applications are not just limited to using the features in the Cocoa frameworks. They can also use all of the functionality of the other frameworks that are part of Mac OS X, such as Quartz, QuickTime, OpenGL, ColorSync, and many others. And since Mac OS X is built atop Darwin, a solid BSD-based system,[*] Cocoa-based applications can use all of the core Unix system functions and get as close to the underlying filesystem, network services, and devices as they need to.

The History of Cocoa

Cocoa has actually been around a long time—almost as long as the Macintosh itself. That is because it is, to a large extent, based on OpenStep, which was introduced to the world as NeXTSTEP in 1987, along with the elegant NeXT cube. At the time, the goal of NeXTSTEP was to, as only Steve Jobs could say, "create the next insanely great thing." It evolved through many releases, was adopted by many companies as their development and deployment environment of choice, and received glowing reviews in the press. It was, and continues to be, solid technology based on a design that was years ahead of anything else in the market.

---

[*] BSD stands for *Berkeley Software Distribution*. For more information about BSD and its variants, see *http://www.bsd.org/*.

NeXTSTEP was built on top of BSD Unix from UC Berkeley and the Mach microkernel from Carnegie-Mellon University. It utilized Display PostScript from Adobe—allowing the same code, using the PostScript page description language—to display documents on screen and to print to paper. NeXTSTEP came with a set of libraries, called "frameworks," and tools to enable programmers to build applications using the Objective-C language.

In 1993 NeXT exited the hardware business to concentrate on software. NeXTSTEP was ported to the Intel x86 architecture and released. Other ports were performed for the SPARC, Alpha, and PA-RISC architectures. Later, the frameworks and tools were revised to run on other operating systems, such as Windows and Solaris. These revised frameworks became known as OpenStep.

Fast forward to 1996. Apple had been working unsuccessfully on a next-generation operating system, known as *Copland*, to replace the venerable Mac OS 7. Their efforts were running amok and they decided to look outside for the foundation of the new OS. The leading contender seemed to be BeOS, but in a surprise move, Apple acquired NeXT, citing its strengths in development software and operating environments for both the enterprise and Internet markets. As part of this merger, Apple embarked on the development of *Rhapsody*, a development of the NeXTSTEP operating system fused with the classic Mac OS. Over the next five years, Rhapsody evolved into what was released as Mac OS X 10.0. As part of that evolution, OpenStep became Cocoa.

Mac OS X remains very much a Unix system; the Unix side of Mac OS X is just hidden from users unless they really want to use it. Its full power, however, is available to you, the programmer, to utilize. Not only can you take advantage of the power, you can actually look under the hood and see how it all works. The source code to the underpinnings of Mac OS X can be found as part of Apple's Darwin initiative (*http://www.developer.apple.com/darwin*).

Cocoa's Feature Set

At its foundation, Cocoa provides basic types such as strings and arrays, as well as basic functions such as byte swapping, parsing, and exception handling. Cocoa also provides utilities for memory management, utilities for archiving and serializing objects, and access to kernel entities and services such as tasks, ports, run loops, timers, threads, and locks.

On top of this foundation, Cocoa provides a set of user-interface widgets with quite a bit of built-in functionality. This functionality includes such expected things as undo and redo, drag and drop, and copy and paste, as well as lots of bonus features such as spell checking that can be enabled in any Cocoa component that accepts text. You will see how much of this functionality works while you work through the tutorials in this book.

Imaging and printing

Mac OS X's imaging and printing model is called *Quartz* and is based on Adobe's Portable Document Format (PDF). Unlike previous versions of Mac OS, the same code and frameworks are used to draw the onscreen image and to send output to printers. You'll get firsthand experience drawing with Quartz in Chapter 7, and with printing in Chapter 12.

Apple's color management and matching technology, *ColorSync*, is built into Quartz, ensuring that colors in documents are automatically color-corrected for any device on which they are printed or displayed. Any time an image is displayed in a Cocoa window or printed, its colors are automatically rendered correctly according to any color profile embedding in the image along with profiles for the display or printer.

Internationalization and localization

Cocoa's well-designed internationalization architecture allows applications to be localized easily into multiple languages. Cocoa keeps the user-interface elements separate from the executable, enabling multiple localizations to be bundled with an application. The underlying technology is the same that is used by Mac OS X to ship a single build of the OS with many localizations.* This technology is covered in Chapter 14.

Because Cocoa uses Unicode as its native character set, applications can easily handle all the world's living languages. The use of Unicode eliminates many character-encoding hassles. To help you handle non-Unicode text, Cocoa provides functionality to help you translate between Unicode and the other major character sets in use today.

Text and fonts

Cocoa offers a powerful set of text services that can be readily adapted by text-intensive applications. These services include kerning, ligatures, tab formatting, and rulers, and they can support text buffers as large as the virtual memory space. The text system also supports embedded graphics and other inline attachments. You'll work this text system firsthand in Chapter 11.

Cocoa supports a variety of font formats, including the venerable Adobe PostScript (including Types 1, 3, and 42), the TrueType format defined by Apple in the late 1980s and adopted by Microsoft in Windows 3.1, and the new OpenType format, which merges the capabilities of both PostScript and TrueType.

---

* Mac OS X 10.2 ships with localizations in the following languages: English, German, French, Dutch, Italian, Spanish, Japanese, Brazilian, Danish, Finnish, Korean, Norwegian, Swedish, and both Simplified and Traditional Chinese. Apple might add to or modify this list at any time.

Exported application services

Cocoa applications can make functionality available to other applications, as well as to end users, through two mechanisms: scripting with AppleScript and via Services.

AppleScript enables users to control applications directly on their system, including the operating system itself. Scripts allow even relatively unskilled users to automate common tasks and afford skilled scripters the ability to combine multiple applications to perform more complex tasks. For example, a script that executes when a user logs in could open the user's mail, look for a daily news summary message, and open the URLs from the summary in separate web-browser windows. Scripts have access to the entire Mac OS X environment, as well as other applications. For example, a script can launch the Terminal application, issue a command to list the running processes, and use the output for some other purpose.

Services, available as a submenu item of the application menu, allow users to use functionality of an application whenever they need to. For example, you can highlight some text in an application and choose the "Make New Sticky Note" service. This will launch the Stickies application (*/Applications*), create a new Sticky, and put the text of your selection into it. This functionality is not limited to text; it can work with any data type.

Component technologies

One of the key advantages of Cocoa as a development environment is its capability to develop programs quickly and easily by assembling reusable components. With the proper programming tools and a little work, you can build Cocoa components that can be packaged and distributed for use by others. End-user applications are the most familiar use of this component technology in action. Other examples include the following:

- Bundles containing executable code and associated resources that programs can load dynamically
- Frameworks that other developers can use to create programs
- Palettes containing custom user-interface objects that other developers can drag and drop into their own user interfaces

Cocoa's component architecture allows you to create and distribute extensions and plug-ins easily for applications. In addition, this component architecture enables Distributed Objects, a distributed computing model that takes unique advantage of Cocoa's abilities.

The Cocoa Frameworks

Cocoa is composed of two object-oriented frameworks: Foundation (not to be confused with Core Foundation) and Application Kit. These layers fit into the system as shown in Figure 1-2.

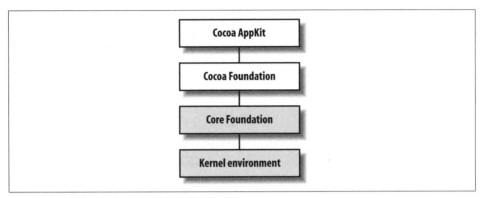

Figure 1-2. The Cocoa frameworks in the system

The classes in Cocoa's Foundation framework provide objects and functionality that are the basis, or "foundation," of Cocoa and that do not have an impact on the user interface. The AppKit classes build on the Foundation classes and furnish the objects and behavior that your users see in the user interface, such as windows and buttons; the classes also handle things like mouse clicks and keystrokes. One way to think of the difference in the frameworks is that Cocoa's Foundation classes provide functionality that operates under the surface of the application, while the AppKit classes provide the functionality for the user interface that the user sees.

Languages

You can build Cocoa applications in three languages: Objective-C, Java, and AppleScript. Objective-C was the original language in which NeXTSTEP was developed and is the "native language" of Cocoa. It is the language that we will work with throughout this book. During the early development of Mac OS X (when it was still known as Rhapsody), a layer of functionality—known as the Java Bridge—was added to Cocoa, allowing the API to be used with Java. Support has been recently added for AppleScript in the form of AppleScript Studio, which allows AppleScripters to hook into the Cocoa frameworks to provide a comprehensive Aqua-based GUI to their applications.

Objective-C

The brainchild of Brad Cox, Objective-C is a very simple language. It is a superset of ANSI C with a few syntax and runtime extensions that make object-oriented programming possible. It started out as just a C preprocessor and a library, but over time developed into a complete runtime system, allowing a high degree of dynamism and yielding large benefits. Objective-C's syntax is uncomplicated, adding only a small number of types, preprocessor directives, and compiler directives to the C language, as well as defining a handful of conventions used to interact with the runtime system effectively.

Objective-C and C++

Starting with Mac OS X 10.1, the Objective-C compiler allows C++ and Objective-C code to be mixed in the same file. This is called Objective-C++ and allows you to access functionality easily in C++ libraries from Cocoa programs. This hybrid does not add C++ features to Objective-C, nor does it add Objective-C features to C++. The object models and hierarchies between Objective-C and C++ remain distinct and separate.

For more information about Objective-C++, see Apple's web site at *http://developer. apple.com/techpubs/macosx/ReleaseNotes/Objective-C++.html*.

You can also mix standard C code with Objective-C code, allowing you to choose when to do something in an object-oriented way and when to stick to procedural programming techniques by defining a structure and some functions, rather than a class. Combining Objective-C code with standard C code also lets you take advantage of existing C-based libraries. This is useful when you need functionality that is not available in Objective-C, are using libraries provided by a third party, or even reusing some of your own old code.

Objective-C is a very dynamic language. The compiler throws very little information away, which allows the runtime to use this information for dynamic binding and other uses. We'll be covering the basics of Objective-C in Chapter 3. Also, there is a complete guide to Objective-C, *Inside Mac OS X: The Objective-C Language*, included as part of the Mac OS X Developer Tools installation. You can find this documentation in the */Developer/Documentation/Cocoa/ObjectiveC* folder.

Java

Java is a cross-platform, object-oriented, portable, multithreaded, dynamic, secure, and thoroughly buzzword-compliant programming language developed by James Gosling and his team at Sun Microsystems in the 1990s. Since its introduction to the public in 1995, Java has gained a large following of programmers and has become a very important language in enterprise computing.

Cocoa provides a set of language bindings that allow you to program Cocoa applications using Java. Apple provides Java packages corresponding to the Foundation and Application Kit frameworks. Within reason, you can mix the APIs from the core Java packages (except for the Swing and AWT APIs) with Cocoa's packages.

AppleScript

For many years, AppleScript has provided an almost unmatched ability to control applications and many parts of the core Mac OS. This allows scripters to set up workflow solutions that combine the power of many applications. AppleScript combines an English-like language with many powerful language features, including list and record manipulation. The introduction of AppleScript Studio in December 2001, as well as its final release along with Mac OS X 10.2, allows scripters the ability to take their existing knowledge of AppleScript and build Cocoa-based applications quickly using Project Builder and Interface Builder.

Coverage of AppleScript Studio is beyond the scope of this book. To learn more about AppleScript Studio, see *Building Applications with AppleScript Studio* located in */Developer/Documentation/CoreTechnologies/AppleScriptStudio/BuildApps_AppScrpt-Studio*.

The Foundation Framework

The Foundation framework is a set of over 80 classes and functions that define a layer of base functionality for Cocoa applications. In addition, the Foundation framework provides several paradigms that define consistent conventions for memory management and traversing collections of objects. These conventions allow you to code more efficiently and effectively by using the same mechanisms with various kinds of objects. Two examples of these conventions are standard policies for object ownership (who is responsible for disposing of objects) and a set of standard abstract classes that enumerate over collections. Figure 1-3 shows the major groupings into which the Foundation classes fall.

The Foundation framework includes the following:

- The root object class, `NSObject`
- Classes representing basic data types, such as strings and byte arrays
- Collection classes for storing other objects
- Classes representing system information and services

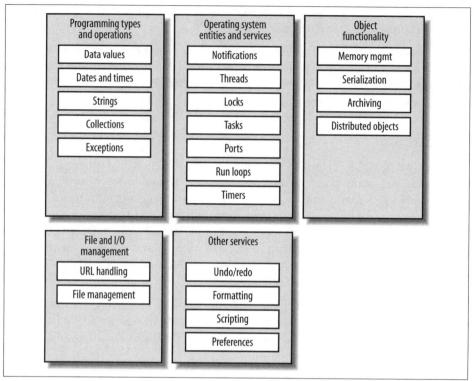

Programming types and operations	Operating system entities and services	Object functionality
Data values	Notifications	Memory mgmt
Dates and times	Threads	Serialization
Strings	Locks	Archiving
Collections	Tasks	Distributed objects
Exceptions	Ports	
	Run loops	
	Timers	

File and I/O management	Other services
URL handling	Undo/redo
File management	Formatting
	Scripting
	Preferences

Figure 1-3. Features of the Foundation framework

Programming Types and Operations

The Foundation framework provides many basic types, including strings and numbers. It also furnishes several classes whose purpose is to hold other objects—the array and dictionary collections classes. You'll learn more about these data types—and how to use them—throughout the chapters in this book, starting in Chapter 4.

Strings

Cocoa's string class, NSString, supplants the familiar C programming data type char * to represent character string data. String objects contain Unicode characters rather than the narrow range of characters afforded by the ASCII character set, allowing them to contain characters in any language, including Chinese, Arabic, and Hebrew. The string classes provide an API to create both mutable and immutable strings and to perform string operations such as substring searching, string comparison, and concatenation.

String scanners take strings and provide methods for extracting data from them. While scanning, you can change the scan location to rescan a portion of the string or to skip ahead a certain number of characters. Scanners can also consider or ignore case.

Collections

Collections allow you to organize and retrieve data in a logical manner. The collections classes provide arrays using zero-based indexing, dictionaries using key-value pairs, and sets that can contain an unordered collection of distinct or non-distinct elements.

The collection classes can grow dynamically, and they come in two forms: mutable and immutable. Mutable collections, as their name suggests, can be modified programmatically after the collection is created. Immutable collections are locked after they are created and cannot be changed.

Data and values

Data and value objects let simple allocated buffers, scalar types, pointers, and structures be treated as first-class objects. Data objects are object-oriented wrappers for byte buffers and can wrap data of any size. When the data size is more than a few memory pages, virtual memory management can be used. Data objects contain no information about the data itself, such as its type; the responsibility for how to use the data lies with the programmer.

For typed data, there are *value objects*. These are simple containers for a single data item. They can hold any of the scalar types, such as integers, floats, and characters, as well as pointers, structures, and object addresses, and allow object-oriented manipulation of these types. They can also provide functionality such as arbitrary precision arithmetic.

Dates and times

Date and time classes offer methods for calculating temporal differences, displaying dates and times in any desired format, and adjusting dates and times based on location (i.e., time zone).

Exception handling

An exception is a special condition that interrupts the normal flow of program execution. Exceptions let programs handle exceptional error conditions in a graceful manner. For example, an application might interpret saving a file in a write-protected directory as an exception and provide an appropriate alert message to the user.

Operating System Entities and Services

The Foundation framework provides classes to access core operating-system functionality such as locks, threads, and timers. These services all work together to create a robust environment in which your application can run.

Run loops

The run loop is the programmatic interface to objects managing input sources. A run loop processes input for sources such as mouse and keyboard events from the window system, ports, timers, and other connections. Each thread has a run loop automatically created for it. When an application is started, the run loop in the default thread is started automatically. Run loops in threads that you create must be started manually. We'll talk about run loops in detail in Chapter 8.

Notifications

The notification-related classes implement a system for broadcasting notifications of changes within an application. An object can specify and post a notification, and any other object can register itself as an observer of that notification. This topic will also be covered in Chapter 8.

Threads

A thread is an executable unit that has its own execution stack and is capable of independent input/output (I/O). All threads share the virtual-memory address space and communication rights of their task. When a thread is started, it is detached from its initiating thread and runs independently. Different threads within the same task can run on different CPUs in systems with multiple processors.

Locks

A lock is used to coordinate the operation of multiple threads of execution within the same application. A lock can be used to mediate access to an application's global data or to protect a critical section of code, allowing it to run atomically—meaning that, at any given time, only one of the threads can access the protected resource.

Tasks

Using tasks, your program can run another program as a subprocess and monitor that program's execution. A task creates a separate executable entity; it differs from a thread in that it does not share memory space with the process that creates it.

Ports

A port represents a communication channel to or from another port that typically resides in a different thread or task. These communication channels are not limited to a single machine, but can be distributed over a networked environment.

Timers

Timers are used to send a message to an object at specific intervals. For example, you could create a timer to tell a window to update itself after a certain time interval. You can think of a timer as the software equivalent of an alarm clock.

Object Functionality

The Foundation framework provides the functionality to manage your objects—from creating and destroying them to saving and sharing them in a distributed environment.

Memory management

Memory management ensures that objects are properly deallocated when they are no longer needed. This mechanism, which depends on general conformance to a policy of object ownership, automatically tracks objects that are marked for release and deallocates them at the close of the current run loop. Understanding memory management is important in creating successful Cocoa applications. We'll discuss this critical topic in depth in Chapter 4.

Serialization and archiving

Serializers make it possible to represent the data that an object contains in an architecture-independent format, allowing the sharing of data across applications. A specialized serializer, known as a Coder, takes this process a step further by storing class information along with the object. Archiving stores encoded objects and other data in files, to be used in later runs of an application or for distribution. This topic will also be covered in depth in Chapter 4.

Distributed objects

Cocoa provides a set of classes that build on top of ports and enable an interprocess messaging solution. This mechanism enables an application to make one or more of its objects available to other applications on the same machine or on a remote machine. Distributed objects are an advanced topic and are not covered in this book. For more information about distributed objects, see */Developer/Documentation/Cocoa/TasksAndConcepts/ProgrammingTopics/DistrObjects/index.html.*

File and I/O Management

Filesystem and input/output (I/O) functionality includes URL handling, file management, and dynamic loading of code and localized resources.

File management

Cocoa provides a set of file-management utilities that allow you to create directories and files, extract the contents of files as data objects, change your current working location in the filesystem, and more. Besides offering a useful range of functionality, the file-management utilities insulate an application from the underlying filesystem, allowing the same functionality to be used to work with files on a local hard drive, a CD-ROM, or across a network.

URL handling

URLs and the resources they reference are accessible. URLs can be used to refer to files and are the preferred way to do so. Cocoa objects that can read or write data from or to a file can usually accept a URL, in addition to a pathname, as the file reference.

Other Services

The Foundation framework provides the ability to manage user preferences, the undo and redo of actions, data formatting, and localization to many languages. Cocoa applications can also be made responsive to AppleScript commands.

The Application Kit Framework

The Application Kit framework (or AppKit, as it's more commonly called) contains a set of over 120 classes and related functions that are needed to implement graphical, event-driven user interfaces. These classes implement the functionality needed to efficiently draw the user interface to the screen, communicate with video cards and screen buffers, and handle events from the keyboard and mouse.

Learning the many classes in the AppKit may seem daunting at first. However, you won't need to learn every feature of every class. Most of the AppKit classes are *support classes* that work behind the scenes helping other classes operate and with which you will not have to interact directly. Figure 1-4 shows how AppKit classes are grouped and related.

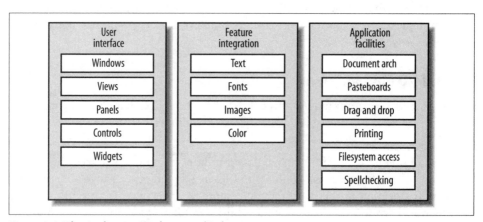

Figure 1-4. The Application Kit framework's features

User Interface

The user interface is how users interact with your application. You can create and manage windows, dialog boxes, pop-up lists, and other controls. We'll cover these topics in depth starting in Chapter 6.

Windows
> The two principle functions of a window are to provide an area in which views can be placed and to accept and distribute to the appropriate view events that the user creates through actions with the mouse and keyboard. Windows can be resized, minimized to the Dock, and closed. Each of these actions generates events that can be monitored by a program.

Views
> A view is an abstract representation for all objects displayed in a window. Views provide the structure for drawing, printing, and handling events. Views are arranged within a window in a nested hierarchy of subviews.

Panels
> Panels are a type of window used to display transient, global, or important information. For example, a panel should be used, rather than a window, to display error messages or to query the user for a response to remarkable or unusual circumstances.
>
> The Application Kit implements some common panels for you, such as the Save, Open, and Print panels. These common panels give the user a consistent look and feel for performing common operations.

Controls and widgets
> Cocoa provides a common set of user-interface objects such as buttons, sliders, and browsers, which you can manipulate graphically to control some aspect of your application. Just what a particular item does is up to you. Cocoa provides menus, cursors, tables, buttons, sheets, sliders, drawers, and many other widgets.

As you'll find throughout this book, the Cocoa development tools provide quite a lot of assistance in making your applications behave according to Apple's Human Interface Guidelines. If you are interested in the details of these guidelines, read the book *Inside Mac OS X: Aqua Human Interface Guidelines*, commonly known as the "HIG." You can find a local copy of the HIG in */Developer/Documentation/Essentials/Aqua-HIGuidelines/AquaHIGuidelines.pdf*.

Feature Integration

The AppKit gives your applications ways to integrate and manage colors, fonts, and printing, and it even provides the dialog boxes for these features.

Text and fonts

Text can be entered into either simple text fields or into larger text views. Text fields allow entry for a single line of text, while a text view is something that you might find in a text-editing application. Text views also add the ability to format text with a variety of fonts and styles. We'll see the text-handling capabilities of Cocoa in action in Chapter 11.

Images

Images encapsulate graphics data, allowing you easy and efficient access to images stored in files on the disk and displayed on the screen. Cocoa handles many of the standard image formats, such as JPG, TIFF, GIF, PNG, PICT, and many more. We'll work a bit with images in Chapter 13.

Color

Color is supported by a variety of classes representing colors and color views. There is a rich set of color formats and representations that automatically handle different color spaces. The color support classes define and present panels and views that allow the user to select and apply colors.

Other Facilities

The AppKit provides a number of other facilities that allow you to create a robust application that takes advantage of all the features your users expect from an application on Mac OS X.

Document architecture

Document-based applications, such as word processors, are some of the more common types of applications developed. In contrast to applications such as iTunes, that need only a single window to work, document-based applications require sophisticated window-management capabilities. Various Application Kit classes provide an architecture for these types of applications, simplifying the work you must do. These classes divide and orchestrate the work of creating, saving, opening, and managing the documents of an application. We'll cover the document architecture in depth in Chapter 10.

Printing

The printing classes work together to provide the means for printing the information displayed in your application's windows and views. You can also create a PDF representation of a view. You'll see how to print in Chapter 12.

Pasteboards

The pasteboard is a repository for data that is copied from your application, and it makes this data available to any application that cares to use it. The pasteboard implements the familiar cut-copy-paste and drag-and-drop operations. Programmers familiar with Mac OS 9 or Carbon will recognize this functionality as the "Clipboard."

Drag-and-drop

With very little programming on your part, objects can be dragged and dropped anywhere. The Application Kit handles all the details of tracking the mouse and displaying a dragged representation of the data.

Accessing the filesystem

File wrappers correspond to files or directories on disk. A file wrapper holds the contents of a file in memory so it can be displayed, changed, or transmitted to another application. It also provides an icon for dragging the file or representing it as an attachment. The Open and Save panels also provide a convenient and familiar interface to the filesystem.

Spellchecking

A built-in spell server provides spellchecking facilities for any application that wants it, such as word processors, text editors, and email applications. Any text field or text view can provide spellchecking by using this service. We'll enable spellchecking in an application we build in Chapter 10.

CHAPTER 2

Cocoa Development Tools

Getting started with Cocoa requires that quite a few concepts be presented at once. Since a book is a linear construction, we have had to make some choices as to what pieces to present first. In order to get your hands dirty using the tools, we chose to introduce Apple's Development Tools first as a way to get you started in building your first Cocoa application. You'll see some concepts here that will be glossed over. Don't worry; we will revisit them as we go. For now, though, just go along for the ride and try not to pay too much attention to the details we're saving for later.

Installing the Developer Tools

When Apple released Mac OS X, they made a really great decision. They decided to provide their development tools to every Mac user for free. These tools allow development of Carbon- and Cocoa-based applications, system libraries, BSD command-line utilities, hardware device drivers, and even kernel extensions. We'll be focusing on two of these tools to develop Cocoa-based applications throughout the book: Project Builder for editing, compiling, and debugging source code, and Interface Builder for laying out the graphical user interface (GUI) components for the application.

By default, the tools aren't installed, as most *users* won't use them and probably want the almost 500 MB of disk space for something else. But *developers* can easily find them and install them from a variety of sources. And, since they are free, any user who wants to try developing software can do so by investing only the time it takes to learn.

You can quickly check to see if you have the Developer Tools installed. If you have a */Developer/Applications* folder on your hard drive, as shown in Figure 2-1, you are ready to go. If not, you'll need to install the tools from either the Developer Tools CD that came with your copy of Mac OS X or from a disk image you can download from the Apple Developer Connection (ADC) site.

Figure 2-1. Apple's development tools in the filesystem

Installing from the Developer Tools CD

A CD containing the Developer Tools comes with every boxed set of Mac OS X (including Mac OS X Server). To install the tools, simply find the CD (it's the gray one), put it into your CD-ROM drive, and double-click the *Developer.mpkg* file that appears in a Finder window, as shown in Figure 2-2.

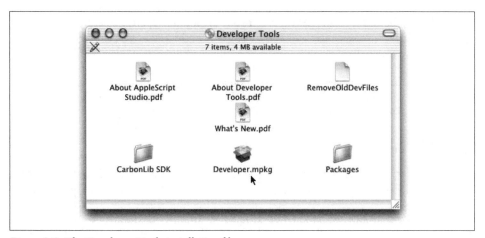

Figure 2-2. The Developer Tools installation file

Installing from the ADC Site

If you can't find your Developer Tools CD, or if you received a Mac OS X upgrade package that didn't include it, you will need to go to the ADC member web site at *http://connect.apple.com* and download a disk image.

To download the tools, log in to the ADC Member web site, click on Download Software in the navigation bar, then click on the Mac OS X subcategory link that appears. From this page you can download the Developer Tools either in segments or in one big chunk. If you download the Tools in segments, simply double-click on the first segment. Stuff-It will launch and put all the segments together into one file.

 Membership in the Apple Developer Connection has its privileges. There are many levels of membership available. The free online membership gets you a good range of benefits, including access to the latest version of the Developer Tools and the ability to track bugs that you submit. You can register, free of charge, for online membership at *http://connect.apple.com*.

Upgrading Your Tools

Apple provides regular updates to the Developer Tools through the ADC Member web site. These updates, which have been appearing at a rate of two to three times a year, introduce new features, fix bugs, and improve the available documentation. The only downside is that updates can be rather large. For example, the Developer Tools release that came with Jaguar weighed in at 285 MB. Despite the size, you should budget some time to download and use the latest versions from the ADC web site.

 Because of the large size, updates to the Developer Tools are not available through Mac OS X's Software Update tool (part of the System Preferences pane). You should be aware of this if you're thinking that you can use Software Update as a way to ensure that you have the latest set of Tools.

If you don't have a high-speed connection, you can get Apple to send you the latest copy of the Developer Tools CD at a nominal charge. Log in to the ADC member web site, and go to the Purchase section.

Project Builder

Project Builder is the hub application of Apple's Developer Tools. It manages software-development projects and orchestrates and streamlines the development process. Project Builder's key features include the following:

- A project browser that manages all the resources of a project, allowing you to view, edit, and organize your source files.

- The ability to invoke the build system to build your projects and run the resulting program.
- A graphical source-level debugger that allows you to walk through the code, set breakpoints, and examine call stacks.
- A code editor that supports language-aware keyword highlighting, delimiter checking, and automatic indentation for many languages, including C, Objective-C, C++, Java, and AppleScript.
- Project search capabilities that allow you to find strings anywhere in a project.
- Source control management integration using the Concurrent Version System (CVS). CVS enables development teams (local or distributed) to work together easily on the same source code base.

Project Builder's main window is shown in Figure 2-3.

Say "Hello, World"

To introduce you to Project Builder and to tip our hat to almost every introductory tutorial ever written on programming, we are going to build a very simple working program that prints "Hello, World!" Building and running this program will also verify that you have a working development environment.

Open Project Builder

Before you can start building applications with Project Builder, you will need to launch the application.

1. Find Project Builder in */Developer/Applications*.
2. Double-click the icon.

If this is the first time that you have started Project Builder, you will be presented with an Assistant to set up your application preferences.

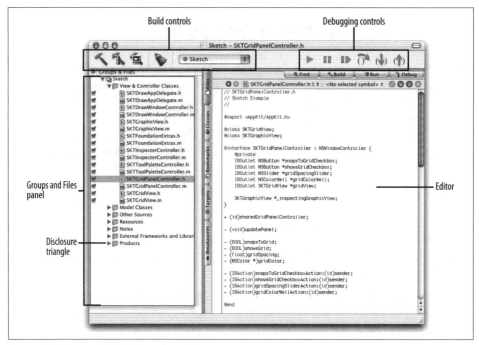

Figure 2-3. Project Builder's main window

1. Click Next on the Assistant's welcome page.

2. Choose where the components of your programs will be placed when they are built. We recommend that you go with the default, although you can change this at any time via Project Builder's preferences. Click Next to move on.

3. Next, you'll be presented with a Window Environment configuration option, as shown in Figure 2-4. This configuration sets how Project Builder's interface is presented to you. Choose between having everything in one window and having everything occupy its own window.

   The figures in this book use the Single Window environment, because this is the environment that we personally use. If you have used another IDE, such as CodeWarrior, that uses many windows and are comfortable with that approach, you may want to select one of the other two options.

4. When you have finished the first-time configuration, Project Builder displays the Release Notes for the particular version you are using. Important information often shows up in these release notes. After the first time you run Project Builder, you can access this information using the Help → Show Release Notes menu.

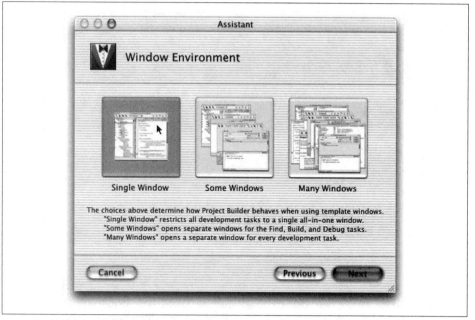

Figure 2-4. Window Environment configuration

Creating a new project

To create the "Hello, World" project, select File → New Project. Project Builder then displays the New Project Assistant, shown in Figure 2-5, which takes you through a few simple steps to create a new project.

The New Project Assistant lets you choose a project type. Based on the type of project you select, your Project will be created with files that serve as a useful starting point. When you select a type of application here, Project Builder creates it for you with a skeleton of the files that you will need for that particular application type. The application types are as follows:

Application
> Starting points for creating Cocoa applications (Objective-C- and Java-based), as well as Carbon- and AppleScript-based applications

Bundle
> Starting points for creating bundles that link against the Cocoa, Carbon, or Core Foundation frameworks

Framework
> Starting points for creating frameworks that link against either Cocoa or Carbon

Java
> Starting points for developing Java applets or applications using either the AWT or Swing APIs

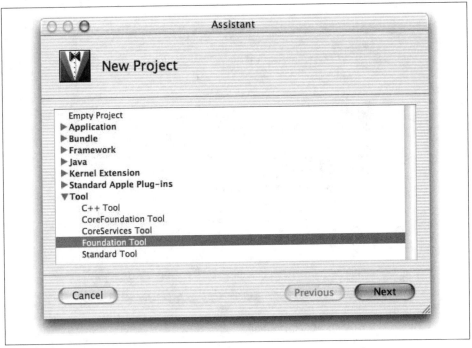

Figure 2-5. Project Builder's New Project Assistant

Kernel Extension
> Starting points for developing both generic kernel extensions and IOKit drivers

Standard Apple Plug-ins
> Starting points for developing palettes for Interface Builder, preference panes for the System Preferences application, and screen savers

Tool
> Starting points for creating command-line applications that link against the Core Foundation, Cocoa Foundation, or Core Services frameworks

Throughout this book, we focus almost exclusively on two categories of applications: simple tools with no GUI (called Foundation Tools) and applications with GUI windows. For this example, we will build a simple tool that doesn't have a graphical interface. Proceed as follows:

1. Scroll down to the list of Tool choices, and select Foundation Tool from the list, as shown in Figure 2-5, and click Next.

2. The Assistant gives you an opportunity to name your new project and choose a location in the filesystem in which to save it. Type *hello* in the Project Name field, as shown in Figure 2-6.

3. If you Tab to the location field, you will see that Project Builder gives you the option of saving the project in *~/hello*. This will create a new directory in your

home directory named "hello". However, for the purpose of working through the examples in this book, we recommend that you change this to *~/LearningCocoa /hello*. That way, all of the projects you create with this book can be saved in the *~/LearningCocoa* directory.

4. Click Finish.

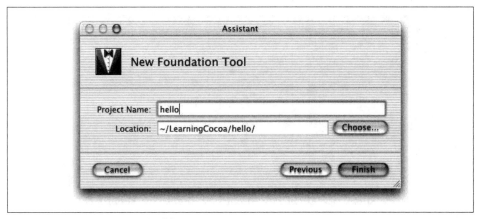

Figure 2-6. Naming a Project Builder project

When you finish creating the project, the main project window opens, as shown in Figure 2-7.

Notice that Project Builder uses hierarchical groups to organize the various parts of a project. In this project, these groups are the following:

Source
> This group contains *main.m*, the file that contains the main function that is the entry point for your application.

Documentation
> This group contains a prototype Unix manpage for the program.[*]

External frameworks and libraries
> This group contains references to the frameworks that the application imports to gain access to system services.

Products
> This group contains the results of project builds and is automatically populated with references to the products created by each target in the project.

---

[*] Manpages are the standard form of Unix documentation for command line utilities and are written as plain text files with nroff macros. See *http://www.opensource.apple.com/projects/documentation/howto/html /man_page_HOWTO.html* for more information.

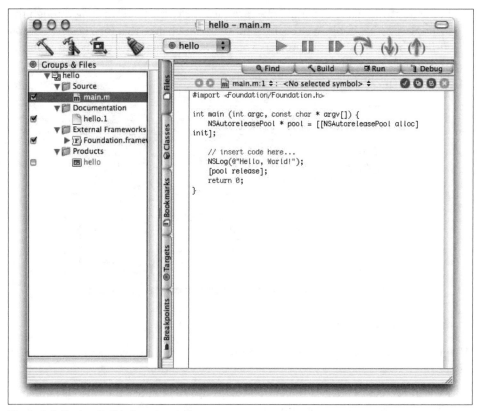

Figure 2-7. Project Builder's main window

These groups are very flexible in that they do not necessarily reflect either the on-disk layout of the project or the manner in which the build system handles the files. Their sole purpose is to help you organize the files in your project. The default groups created for you by the templates can be used as they are or rearranged however you like.

To see the source code for the application's entry point as shown in Figure 2-7:

1. In the Groups & Files list of Project Builder's main window, click the disclosure triangle to the left of the Source group.

2. Click on the icon for the *main.m* file. You will see the contents of the file in the code editor.

The *main.m* file contains the entry point for the application. The Foundation Tool project template provides a standard main function that prints "Hello, World!", so we don't even need to add any code.

```
import <Foundation/Foundation.h>                                    // 1

int main (int argc, const char * argv) {                            // 2
    NSAutoreleasePool * pool = [[NSAutoreleasePool alloc] init];     // 3
```

```
    // insert code here...
    NSLog(@"Hello, World!");                                      // 4
    [pool release];                                               // 5
    return 0;                                                     // 6
}
```

Now let's walk through the code, line-by-line, so you can get a feeling for what's going on here:

1. Imports the Foundation framework. This directive is similar to #include, except that it won't include the same file more than once.

2. Declares the standard C main function for a program. This function is where execution starts when the program is started.

3. The NSAutoreleasePool is one of Cocoa's memory-management tools. We'll cover more about how memory management works in Chapter 4.

4. The NSLog function works very much like printf in the C language. The difference is that NSLog takes an NSString object instead of a C string. The @"..." construct is a compiler directive that creates an NSString object using the characters between the quotation marks.

5. This line contains another part of Cocoa's memory housekeeping that we will explain in depth later.

6. A return from the main function indicating a normal program exit.

> Why does NSLog have the NS prefix? Simple: NS stands for NeXTSTEP. All of the classes and functions in the Cocoa frameworks start with NS to help protect the namespace in which all functions and classes exist from collisions. The continued use of NS is a vestige that shows Cocoa's heritage.

Building the project

To build the project, click the Build button in the main window. It's the one that looks like a hammer on the far left side of the toolbar. A dialog box will appear, asking you to "Save before building?" Click Save All, or hit Return, to save and build the project. As the project builds, Project Builder's build pane opens to reveal detailed information about the build as it progresses. When Project Builder is finished—and encounters no errors along the way—it displays "Build succeeded" in the lower-left corner of the project window, as shown in Figure 2-8.

> If you don't want Project Builder to question you to save files each time you try to buid a project, you can change this option in Project Builder's Preferences. Select Project Builder → Preferences → Building, and then select Always Save from the pul-down menu next to Unsaved files.

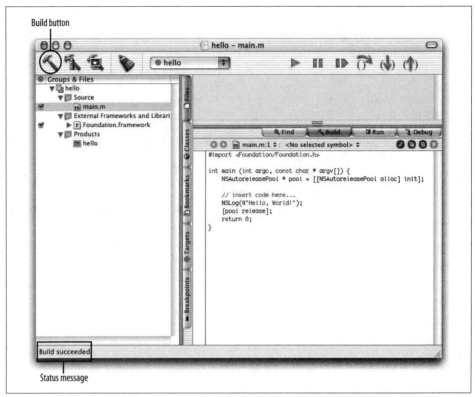

Figure 2-8. *Project Builder after successfully building the project*

Solving build problems

The code for this program should compile without a problem, since Project Builder generated it. However, when you write code yourself, you won't always be so lucky. To see how Project Builder notifies you of build problems, let's create one. Remove the semicolon right after the NSLog(@"Hello, World!") statement; then try building the project. You'll see a build failure notice, as shown in Figure 2-9.

Project Builder tells you that there was a syntax and parse error. To see where the error is, click on the syntax error message, and Project Builder highlights the line about which the compiler is complaining. Unfortunately, the compiler is not smart enough to figure out that we don't have a semicolon in the right place; it just notices that it has run across some syntax that it did not expect. This is typical with syntax errors. If you don't see the problem at first, look at the line of code above the reported line.

Add the missing semicolon back in after the NSLog function, and recompile by clicking the Build button to get a working program again.

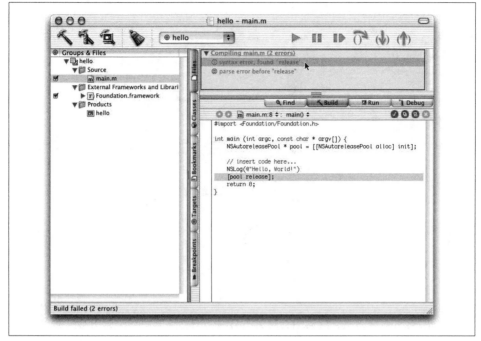

Figure 2-9. Build failed

Running the application

Congratulations! You've just created your first Cocoa application and didn't even have to type in any code. All that is left to do is click the Build and Run button, as shown in Figure 2-10. When the application launches, the Run pane of Project Builder's main window will enlarge to display the output of the NSLog function.

 Since building and running is a straightforward process, in future chapters we don't tell you how to "build and run" your application—we just say "build and run your application."

In addition to the string, the NSLog function prints the current date and time, the program name, and the process ID number (PID) of the program. Since this is a tool application with no GUI, you might want to see the behavior of this program on the command line.

1. Open up a Terminal window, found in the */Applications/Utilities* folder.

 As with Project Builder, you may want to add the Terminal application to your Dock for easy access, if you haven't already done so.

Build and Run

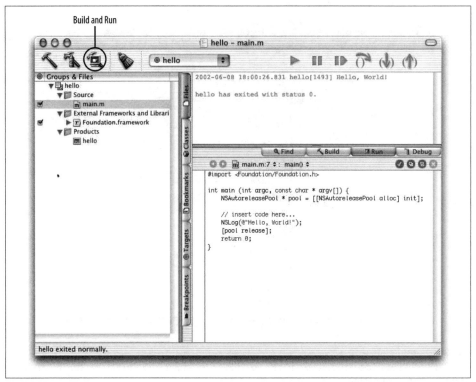

Figure 2-10. Project Builder's main window after running Hello World

2. The *hello* executable is built into a subdirectory of your project. To run it, enter the following into the Terminal window:

```
[localhost:~] duncan% LearningCocoa/hello/build/hello
```

When the program is run, you should see something similar to the following output:

```
2002-06-08 23:23:29.919 hello[490] Hello, World!
```

The timestamp and process ID information come in handy when you are looking for the output from a program that was launched from the Finder, but not from inside of Project Builder or from the command line. In those cases, the output from NSLog will show up in the system's message log. You can easily view these messages using the Console application, also found in the */Applications/Utilities* folder.

If you have spaces in the folder in which you saved your program, the Terminal shell will complain. The reason is that spaces are used to separate the arguments in a shell command and must be escaped. If you saved your project into a *~/Learning Cocoa* directory (notice the space), your command would need to look like this:

```
[localhost:~] duncan% Learning\ Cocoa/hello/build/hello
```

The backslash in front of the space tells the shell that the space is part of the path of the program.

Console Versus the Terminal

The Terminal application is the command-line interface to Mac OS X. It presents an interface to what old-school Unix users call the "shell." In a shell, you can issue any command line you want and see it executed. In contrast, the Console is a simple log of messages printed to STDOUT by various programs, which do not end up anywhere else. In the Console, you will typically see messages from various background processes and, sometimes, debug statements from GUI programs.

Using the Debugger

Project Builder provides an easy-to-use interface to the system's debugger that lets you step through code line-by-line, set breakpoints (places to pause the execution of the program), and view variables and threads. The following steps allow you explore the debugger.

1. Set a breakpoint in your code by clicking into the left margin of the code editor near the main method declaration, as shown in Figure 2-11. Notice that where you click, a marker appears.

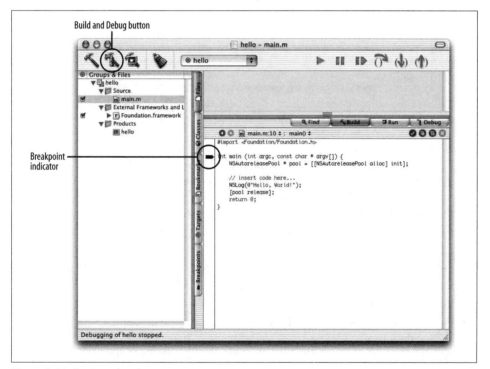

Figure 2-11. Setting a breakpoint

2. Now click the Build and Debug button. This will start the debugger and then load the hello program into it. Execution will stop at the first statement after the breakpoint. In this case, it will stop at the first line of our main method, as shown in Figure 2-12.

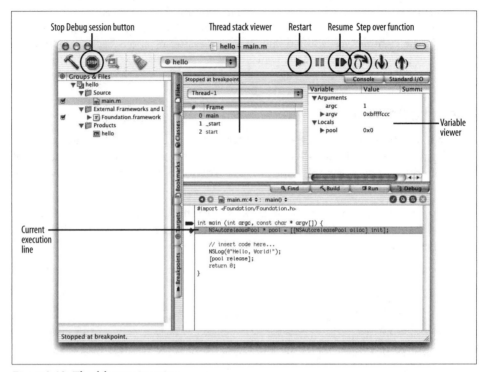

Figure 2-12. The debugger in action

Notice that Project Builder shows both a thread stack viewer and a variable viewer. The thread stack viewer shows execution stack. The main method is at the top of the stack, indicating that this is the method within which execution is stopped. The variable viewer gives the values of all the arguments and variables that are applicable in the function. Notice the value of the pool variable.

3. Click once on the Step over Function button (called out in Figure 2-12). Note that the current execution highlighter moves to the next valid line of code. Also notice that the value of the pool variable is highlighted in red. This means that the pool variable was just set. The value is actually a pointer to the contents of the object in memory.

4. Click the Step over Function button once again. The NSLog function was called. To see the output, click the Console tab above the variable viewer, as shown in Figure 2-13. Also notice tht the value of the pool variable is no longer red. This highlighting lasts only one step after the contents of a variable change.

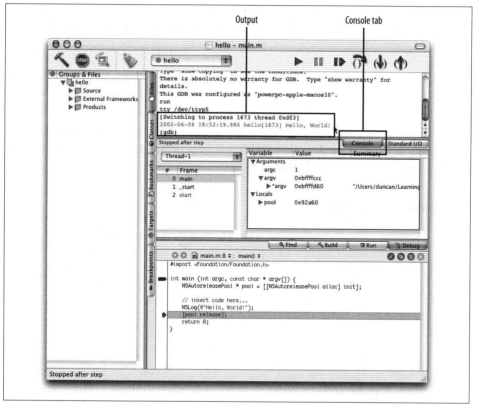

Figure 2-13. Console output in the debugger

5. Click the Continue execution button to let the program execute as normal. You can click the Restart button (called out in Figure 2-12) to restart the program at the beginning of execution.

6. Click the Stop button in the toolbar to exit the debugger.

Now that we have explored how to say "Hello, World!" to the console, let's take a look at building a GUI application that says hello in a much different way.

Interface Builder

Interface Builder is where you create the graphical user interfaces (GUIs) for your applications. Instead of typing code by hand to lay out the interface components, you drag objects from palettes and drop them onto the GUI you are creating. Objects can be connected to one another and with instances of classes that you provide as part of your application.

Interface Builder generates *nib*[*] files that are an archive of object instances and are packaged up with your built application. Unlike the product of many user interface–building systems, *nib* files are not generated code—they are true archived (also known as "freeze-dried") objects consisting of related user interface objects and supporting resources, along with information about how the objects are related. The objects in the *nib* file are created and manipulated using Interface Builder's graphical tools.

Interface Builder's standard palettes hold an assortment of AppKit components. Other palettes can include Cocoa objects from other frameworks, third-party objects, and custom-compiled objects.

Graphical "Hello, World"

To introduce you to Interface Builder, we are going to create a program that says "Hello, World" in a window on the screen instead of as a text message in a Terminal window. To begin, we need to make a new project of a type different than our previous Hello World application. Choose New Project from the File menu. Project Builder then displays the New Project Assistant. This time, create a project of type Cocoa Application, as shown in Figure 2-14.

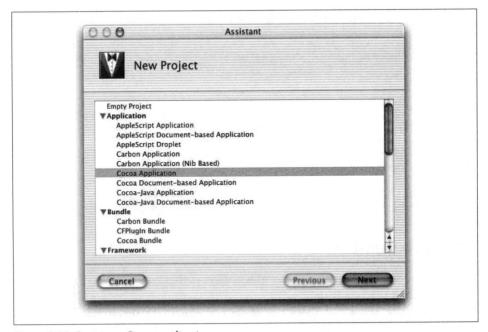

Figure 2-14. Creating a Cocoa application

---

[*] The name "nib" is an acronym for "NeXT Interface Builder," yet another vestige of Mac OS X's heritage.

This will create a project that is set up as a simple Cocoa application. Go ahead and create the project, giving it the name *Hello World* and saving into your *~/LearningCocoa* folder. When you have created the project, you will see a window similar to that shown in Figure 2-15.

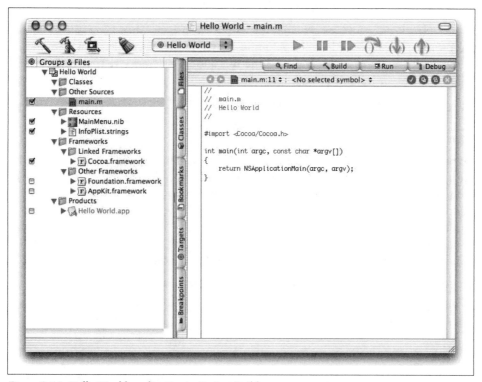

Figure 2-15. Hello World application in Project Builder

The Cocoa Application project type uses a different set of groups to organize projects than those used in the Foundation Tool example. The groups in this project type are as follows:

Classes

This group is empty at first, but is used to hold the implementation (*.m*) and header (*.h*) files for your project's classes.

Other Sources

This group contains *main.m*, the file containing the main function that loads the initial set of resources and runs the application. In Cocoa applications with graphical interfaces, you typically don't have to modify this file.

Resources

This group contains the *nib* files and other resources that specify the application's GUI.

Frameworks
> This group contains references to the Frameworks (Foundation and AppKit) that the application imports to gain access to system services.

Products
> This group contains the results of project builds.

To see what Project Builder provides for you by default, go ahead and build and run the project. A blank window should appear once Project Builder is done compiling everything. Play with this window a little bit, and you'll notice that you can resize, minimize, and maximize it.

Now, to finish our application, we should make it say "Hello, World" to us!

Open the main nib file

To begin constructing a user interface using Interface Builder, the first step is to open the application's main *nib* file. Double-click *MainMenu.nib* in the Resources group of the Groups & Files list of Project Builder's main window. This will launch Interface Builder (if it is not already running) and open the *nib* file, as shown in Figure 2-16. A lot of windows will appear. You might want to hide your other running applications so that you can concentrate on just the windows that belong to Interface Builder. You can do this by using the Interface Builder → Hide Others menu.

These are the various parts of Interface Builder (called out in Figure 2-16):

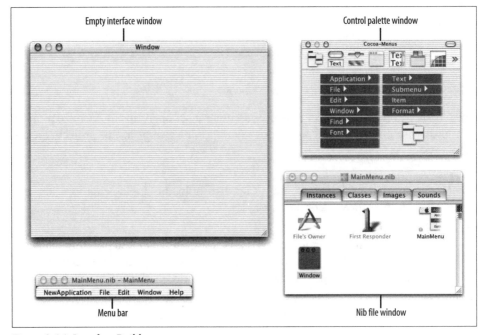

Figure 2-16. Interface Builder

Nib file window

This window is where the various objects that are part of your *nib* file are defined and manipulated. We'll explain more about the various parts of this window in Chapter 5.

Control palette window

This window contains all the controls that you can add to an interface. We'll explore many of these controls throughout the book.

Menu bar

The menu-bar window contains the menu bar that will be active when your application is running.

Empty interface window

This is the window that will be displayed when your application is run. Notice that it is the same size and in the same location on screen as when you Built and Ran the application.

Interface Builder stores all kinds of information about user-interface objects in an application's *nib* files. For example, you can set both the size and initial location of an application's main window by simply resizing and moving the window in Interface Builder.

1. Move the window near the upper-left corner of the screen by dragging the title-bar.

2. Make the window smaller by using the resize control at the bottom-right corner of the window.

To create our application, we need to add a text label to the window.

1. Select the Cocoa-Views by clicking the second button from the left top of the Cocoa objects palette window, as shown in Figure 2-17. If you don't see the Cocoa palette window for some reason, select Palettes from the Tools menu to bring it forward.

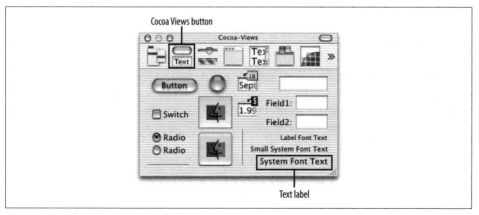

Figure 2-17. The Cocoa-Views palette

2. Drag a System Font Text label from the palette onto the window.

3. Double-click on the new label and change the text to "Hello World".

4. Resize the interface window to a smaller size, and move the text label to the center of the window. You should have something that looks similar to Figure 2-18.

Figure 2-18. Our finished Hello World interface

Next, save your interface, as we are now done with Interface Builder. Some people refer to saving the interface as "freeze-drying" it. All the various parts of the interface—definitions about how they are related and connected—are saved in a form that can be quickly built up at runtime. This process is also called "archiving" or "serialization."

To see the application in action:

1. Return to Project Builder.

2. Click the Build and Run button.

When the application runs, it opens up a window containing the Hello World text. Note that you can resize the window (although the text doesn't stay centered, we'll learn how to do that in later chapters), minimize it, maximize it, and close it. You can even quit the application using the menu or the standard ⌘-Q keyboard shortcut. All of this functionality is simply "built-in" to Cocoa, allowing you to spend more time writing your applications and less time taking care of details you shouldn't have to.

Other Tools

In addition to Project Builder and Interface Builder, there are other applications that you can use in the Cocoa development process. Development tools that feature a GUI are listed in Table 2-1. Except where noted, these applications are installed in the */Developer/Applications* folder.

Table 2-1. Other development tools

Name	Description
FileMerge	Visually compares the contents of two files or two directories. You can use FileMerge to determine the differences between versions of the same source-code file or between two project directories. You can also use it to merge changes.
icns Browser	Displays the entire contents of Mac OS X icon files.
IconComposer	Creates Mac OS X icons from source art.
IORegistryExplorer	Provides a hierarchical display of the system I/O registry.
MallocDebug	Measures the dynamic-memory usage of applications, finds memory leaks, analyzes all allocated memory in an application, and measures the memory allocated since a given time.
ObjectAlloc	Tracks and displays all Cocoa and Core Foundation object allocations for a running application. Object-Alloc allows you to view the list of objects, as well as the call stack that resulted in each allocation.
PackageMaker	Creates Mac OS X installer packages.
Pixie	Magnifies the screen area under the cursor, allowing you to see the exact pixels comprising any onscreen object. Magnification is adjustable from 1 to 12 times normal.
Property List Editor	Opens, displays, and/or modifies the contents of a property list (*.plist*) file.
Quartz Debug	Displays a list of all windows known to the system. This program allows you to turn on a Quartz debugging mode that flashes yellow over areas of the screen as the window server updates them.
Sampler	Analyzes performance characteristics of your application by sampling the call stack of your program over a user-specified period of time.
Thread Viewer	Allows you to browse the high-level thread behavior of an application.

Command-Line Tools

There are several command-line tools for compilation, debugging, performance analysis, and so on, installed as part of the Developer Tools package. Many of these tools are ports of standard Unix applications with which you may have prior experience. These tools, listed in Table 2-2, can be found in the */usr/bin* directory.

Table 2-2. Command-line development tools

Name/command	Description
cc, gcc	The GNU C compiler (*gcc*). Compiles C, Objective-C, C++, and Objective-C++ source-code files.
gdb	A source-level symbolic debugger for C extended to support Objective-C, C++, and Objective-C++.
as	Assembles; translates assembly code into object code.
defaults	Reads, writes, searches, and deletes user defaults. The defaults system records user preferences that persist when the application isn't running.
nibtool	Reads the contents of an Interface Builder *nib* file. The nibtool prints classes, the object hierarchy, objects, connections, and localizable strings.
libtool	Creates static or dynamic libraries from specified object binary files.

Table 2-2. Command-line development tools (continued)

Name/command	Description
otool	Displays specified parts of object files or libraries.
nm	Displays the symbol table, in whole or part, of the specified object files.
pbxbuild	Allows Project Builder projects to be built from the command line
fixPrecomps	Creates or refreshes a precompiled header file for each of the major frameworks.
strip	Removes or modifies the symbol table that is attached to assembled and linked output.
cvs	CVS allows teams composed of multiple members to coordinate their work on a common codebase.
sample	Gathers the running behavior of a process and produces a report showing what functions were executed during the run of an application.
leaks	Examines a process for malloc-allocated buffers that are not referenced by the program.

Although the Mac OS X development environment contains many tools, the tutorials in this book focus almost exclusively on the use of Project Builder and Interface Builder. Some tools, such as the compiler, debugger, and linker, are usually invoked indirectly through Project Builder when building a project. Others, such as ObjectAlloc, Quartz Debug, and Sampler, are extremely useful to gain a deeper understanding of an application's inner workings. Feel free to experiment with them at any point while working through the tutorials in this book.

Exercises

1. Locate the Project Builder and Interface Builder applications, and put them into the Dock.

2. Locate the developer documentation, and place a shortcut to it in your Dock or in your browser.

3. Watch the "Accessing API Documentation in Project Builder" movie at *http://developer.apple.com/techpubs/macosx/DeveloperTools/ProjectBuilderAccess /index.html.*

CHAPTER 3

Object-Oriented Programming
with Objective-C

Object-oriented programming isn't rocket science, but you can't learn it overnight either. There is a lot of terminology—composed of words like "encapsulation" and "polymorphism" and phrases like "is-a" and "has-a"—that goes with the territory. The concepts behind these terms are not terribly complicated, but they can be hard to explain. Like most useful fields of study, you must work with it a while before it all clicks together in your mind. As each concept becomes clear, you will gain a deeper understanding of the subject. That said, you don't have to understand everything about object-oriented programming on the first pass to make good use of the concepts.

In this chapter, we present the object-oriented concepts that matter most when working with Cocoa, along with quite a bit of hands-on practice using those concepts. If this is the first time you've approached object-oriented programming, read carefully, but don't worry if you don't get everything at first. Just remember to flip back to this part of the book later if something didn't sink in. If you already know a bit about object-oriented programming, then you should treat this as a refresher and see how Objective-C's implementation of the object-oriented concepts with which you are familiar works.

Introducing Objects

Procedural programming divides the programming problem into two parts: data and operations on that data. Because all of the functionality of a procedural program works on the same set of data, the programmer must be very careful to manipulate the data of a program in such a way that the rest of the program can work correctly. He must be aware of the entire program at a low level of abstraction so as not to introduce errors. As a procedural program grows in size, the network of interaction between procedures and data becomes increasingly complex and hard to manage.

Object-oriented programming (OOP), first developed in the 1960s,[*] restructures the programming problem to allow for a higher level of abstraction. It groups operations and data into modular units called *objects*. These objects can be combined into structured networks to form a complete program, similar to how the pieces in a puzzle fit together to create a picture. In contrast to procedural programming's focus on the interaction between data and functions, the design of objects and the interactions between those objects become the primary elements of object-oriented program design.

By breaking down complex software projects into small, self-contained, and modular units, object orientation ensures that changes to one part of a software project will not adversely affect other portions of the software. Object orientation also aids software reuse. Once functionality is created in one program, it can easily be reused in other programs.

Programming with objects is quite like working with real-world objects. Take an iPod, for example. It embodies both state and behavior. When you operate it, you don't necessarily care how it works, as long as it works in the way that you expect. As long as your iPod plays music when you tell it to and synchronizes your music collection with iTunes when you plug it into your computer, you're happy. Object-oriented programming brings this same level of abstraction to programming and helps remove some of the impediments to building larger systems. To enjoy listening to music, you don't have to know that iTunes and your iPod use the MP3 format; you just put a CD into your computer and import the music into your collection. iTunes and your iPod work together to download the music from your computer when you plug in the iPod. Figure 3-1 shows these components working together.

Classes of Objects

In the real world, there are often many objects of the same kind, or *type*. My iPod is just one of many iPods that exist in the world. In the lingo of object-oriented programming, each iPod is an *instance*. An instance of an object has its own state and leads an existence independent of all other instances. My iPod probably has a very different collection of music than yours does.[†] But just as all iPods have the same set of buttons—allowing the same set of operations (play, stop, etc.)—all instances of a particular object expose the same functionality to the outside world.

You specify an object by defining its *class*. Think of a class as a blueprint for making object instances. It provides all the information needed to build new instances of an object. Each class defines the internal variables that hold the data of an object instance and the ways, or *methods*, by which that data can be manipulated. These

---

[*] SIMULA I and SIMULA 67 were the first two object-oriented programming languages. They were designed and built by Ole-Johan Dahl and Kristen Nygaard in Norway between 1962 and 1967.

[†] There's even a decent chance that you might not like the music on my iPod, and vice versa.

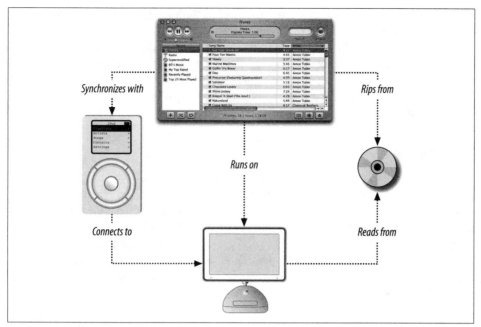

Figure 3-1. Real-world objects interacting together

methods define the *interface* of the object. The interface is how other objects are allowed to use it.

On the back of every iPod is the phrase "Designed by Apple in Cupertino. Assembled in Taiwan." This is a useful analogy for thinking about how classes and objects relate to each other. In its corporate offices in California, Apple defined how an iPod operates and what kinds of data it can store. Apple shipped those definitions to the factory in Taiwan that now creates many unique instances of an iPod to ship to customers around the world. When you create a class, you create a definition from which the *runtime* (the layer of software that enables the object-oriented system to run) can create any number of objects (see Figure 3-2).

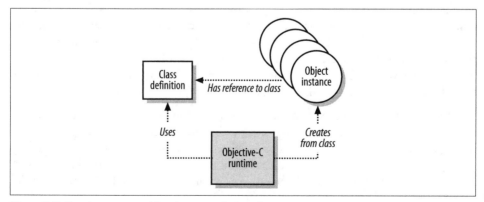

Figure 3-2. Runtime creates object instances from a class

In Objective-C, classes are more than just blueprints. They are actually first-class objects themselves that can have methods associated with the class and not with its instances. These are called *class methods*. Every object created has a reference to its own class. The iPod analogy starts to get a bit stretched here, but imagine that each iPod had a reference to the plans on which it was based and could consult them at any time. This is sort of what it means for an object to look up its class object anytime it needs to do so.

Inheritance

We've defined a class to be a definition, or blueprint, from which object-oriented instances are created. An iPod is an instance of the iPod class. But classes themselves can be defined as specializations of other classes. For example, if you didn't know what an iPod was, you would probably understand if I told you that it was a handheld MP3 player. In fact, all handheld MP3 players share a certain number of characteristics. Like an iPod, a Rio can hold and play MP3 files downloaded from a computer. It can't hold as many songs as the iPod, but at least some of the functionality is the same.

 The iPod is actually much more than a portable MP3 player. It's also a bootable FireWire drive that can hold any kind of data that you want it to hold. People are finding some pretty creative uses for it beyond playing music. In Objective-C, objects that can perform other functions can declare that they obey a particular *protocol*, or way of behaving. We'll talk more about protocols and how they can be used effectively in Chapter 9.

Object-oriented programming lets us collect similar functionalities of different classes and group them into a common parent class through *inheritance*. We can say that an iPod and a Rio are both types of MP3 players. If we define a common MP3Player class, we can gather certain aspects common to both devices into one class, as shown in Figure 3-3.

The iPod and Rio classes are both *subclasses* of the MP3Player class. Likewise, the MP3Player class is the *superclass* of the iPod and Rio classes. Each subclass inherits state (in the form of variable definitions) and functionality from the superclass. In this case, both players inherit the same basic functions (play, stop, fast forward, etc.), but have very different underlying implementations. The iPod uses a high-capacity hard drive while the Rio uses flash memory.

Creating a new class is often a matter of specialization. Since the new class inherits all of its superclass's behavior, you don't need to reimplement the things that work in the way that you want. The subclass merely extends the inherited behavior by adding new methods and any variables needed to support the additional methods. A subclass can alter superclass behavior by overriding an inherited method, reimple-

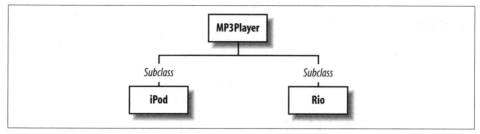

Figure 3-3. Class hierarchy for the MP3Player class

menting the method to achieve a behavior different from the superclass's implementation.

With Objective-C, a class can have any number of subclasses, but only one superclass.* This means that classes are arranged in a branching hierarchy with one class at the top—the root class that has no superclass—as shown in Figure 3-4.

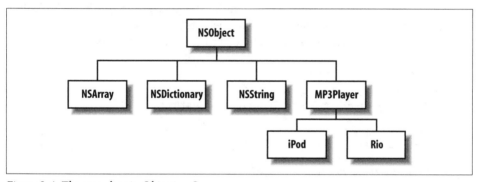

Figure 3-4. The root class in Objective-C

NSObject is the root class of this hierarchy. From NSObject, other classes inherit the basic functionality that lets them work in the system. The root class also creates a framework for the creation, initialization, deallocation, introspection, and storage of objects.

As noted earlier, you often create a subclass of another class because that superclass provides most, but not all, of the behavior that you require. A subclass can have its own unique purpose that does not build on the role of an existing class. To define a new class that doesn't need to inherit any special behavior other than the default behavior of objects, you make it a subclass of NSObject.

---

* Some object-oriented programming languages, such as C++, allow classes to inherit functionality from more than one superclass. This ability, known as multiple-inheritance, can often lead to more problems than it solves. Objective-C provides protocols (discussed in Chapter 9) to provide some of the benefits of sharing behavior (but not implementation) across the class hierarchy.

Inheritance is a powerful concept—one that many people new to object-oriented programming tend to use too much. Used inappropriately, it can lead to fragile software. In Cocoa, it's often easier to use a new set of classes from a new class than to use inheritance. This is called *object composition*. As you work through this book, you'll see many examples of object composition.

Creating and Using Objects

Now that we've introduced a few object-oriented concepts, we are going to dive into some simple code exercises to show how to apply this knowledge. The following steps will guide you:

1. In Project Builder, create a new Foundation tool (File → New Project → Tool → Foundation Tool) project named "objects", and save it in your ~/*LearningCocoa* folder.

2. Next, modify the *main.m* file, located in the "Source" group, so that it looks like Example 3-1. The Foundation tool project template automatically generates some of this code. The lines that you need to add are shown in **boldface** type.

Example 3-1. Creating objects

```
int main (int argc, const char * argv[]) {
    NSAutoReleasepool *pool = [[NSAutoreleasepool alloc] init];

    NSObject * object;                              // a
    object = [NSObject alloc];                      // b
    object = [object init];                         // c
    NSLog(@"Created object: %@", object);           // d

    [pool release];
    return 0;
}
```

Here's what the code that we added does:

a. Declares a variable named object of type NSObject. You should recognize this as a regular C pointer.

b. Creates a new object of type NSObject and assigns it to the object variable. The alloc method reserves (or allocates) memory space for the object and returns a pointer to that space. We'll explain more about methods in just a bit.

c. Before an object is used in any way, it must be initialized. This init call initializes the object so it can be used. The init method returns a fully initialized object ready for use. Since it is possible that the init method will return a different object, we assign the return to the object variable again.

d. Prints a representation of the object to the console using a `printf` style format string with a `%@` token, indicating that the svalue of the object given after the format string should be printed.

There's actually a bit more going on in this code than what we've described. However, we'll fill in the missing pieces as we go to avoid introducing too many concepts at once.

Format String Tokens

There are several methods in Cocoa, such as `NSLog` and `[NSString stringWithFormat]`, that can use format strings with a list of arguments. These format strings can contain all of the normal `printf`-style tokens, as well as a Cocoa-specific token for objects. You'll find the following tokens to be useful:

`%@`
> Print as an object

`%d` *or* `%i`
> Print as a signed decimal

`%o`
> Print as an unsigned octal

`%s`
> Print as a string

`%u`
> Print as an unsigned decimal

`%x`
> Print as an unsigned hexadecimal

In addition to the tokens in this short list, you can add all sorts of modifiers to control precisely how values are printed. See the `printf` manpage for complete information about format strings. You can access the manpage in either of the following ways:

- Open a Terminal window and enter **man printf** at the prompt.
- In Project Builder, use the Help → Open man page... menu item.

---

3. Build and run the program. You should see something like this on the console:

```
2002-06-11 23:17:16.181 objects[477] Created object: <NSObject: 0x5ae90>
```

This tells us that we created an object of type `NSObject` that is located at the memory address 0x5ae90. This isn't the most exciting information that could be printed, and it certainly won't win any user-interface awards, but it shows us that objects are being created in the system by the runtime.

As a Cocoa programmer, you probably won't ever make direct use of the memory location of the object instances you create. But under the hood, Cocoa uses this information to locate and manipulate objects that you reference in code.

Since objects should never be used without proper allocation and initialization, Objective-C programmers tend to combine the methods into one line as shown in Example 3-2. Replace lines a, b, and c from Example 3-1 with the single bolded line in Example 3-2.

Example 3-2. Combing object allocation and initialization

```
int main (int argc, const char * argv[]) {
    NSAutoReleasepool *pool = [[NSAutoreleasepool alloc] init];

    NSObject * object = [[NSObject alloc] init];
    NSLog(@"Created object: %@", object);

    [pool release];
    return 0;
}
```

This shortens the allocation and initialization of an object to one line, ensuring that everything works properly, even in the case where the init method of a class returns a different object than originally allocated. We will use this style of object creation throughout the rest of the book.

Working with Multiple Objects

Working with multiple object instances of the same class is easy, as long as you keep the references to different objects distinct.

1. Edit the code in the project's *main.m* file as shown in Example 3-3.

   Example 3-3. Working with multiple objects

   ```
   int main (int argc, const char * argv[]) {
       NSAutoReleasepool *pool = [[NSAutoreleasepool alloc] init];

       NSObject * object1 = [[NSObject alloc] init];
       NSObject * object2 = [[NSObject alloc] init];
       NSLog(@"object1: %@", object1);
       NSLog(@"object2: %@", object2);

       [pool release];
       return 0;
   }
   ```

2. When built and run, the program will print something similar to the following:

```
2002-06-11 15:59:29.716 objects[370] object1: <NSObject: 0x4ce90>
2002-06-11 15:59:29.717 objects[370] object2: <NSObject: 0x4b410>
```

This example shows that two object instances of NSObject have been allocated, and they occupy two different locations in memory.

Methods and Messages

In our discussion about objects so far, we've been using (and promised to explain) the term *method*. Methods are structured like C functions and can be thought of as procedures; but, instead of being global in nature, they are procedures associated with and implemented by the object's class.

There are two kinds of methods: *class methods* and *instance methods*. Class methods are scoped to the class itself and cannot be called on instances of the class. The alloc method is an example of a class method. Instance methods, on the other hand, are scoped to object instances. The init method is an example of an instance method that is called on an instance of an object returned by the alloc method.

To call a method, send an object a *message* telling it to apply a method. All those square brackets that you have seen in the code are message expressions that result in methods being called. Figure 3-5 shows the various parts of a basic message.

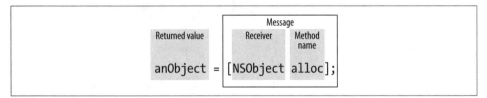

Figure 3-5. Objective-C message expression

In this figure, the message is the expression enclosed in square brackets to the right of the assignment operator (equals sign). The message consists of an object, known as a *receiver*, and the name of a method to call on that object. In this case, the object is the NSObject class, and the method to be called is the alloc method. In response to receiving this message, the NSObject class returns a new instance of the class that will be assigned to the variable anObject.

Arguments in Messages

The message in Figure 3-5 calls a method that doesn't take any arguments. Like procedures, methods can receive multiple arguments. In Objective-C, every message argument is identified with a label (a colon-terminated keyword), which is considered part of the method name. Figure 3-6 shows a message with a single argument.

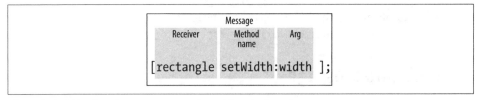

Figure 3-6. Objective-C message expression with a single argument

In this figure, the message tells the runtime to call the `setWidth:` method and pass it the argument `width`. Notice that a colon terminates method names that take an argument, while method names that don't take an argument (like the `alloc` method in Figure 3-5) don't have a colon.

Figure 3-7 shows a multiple-argument message. Here, the message and arguments are used to set the width and height of the rectangle object to `width` and `height`, respectively. This method is called the `setWidth:height:` method.

Figure 3-7. Objective-C message expression with multiple arguments

 Note that `setWidth:height:` refers to one method, not two. It will call a method with two arguments. When using this method, you must pass in two arguments, labeled and formatted as in Figure 3-6. If you haven't used Smalltalk or one of its derivatives, you will find this practice strange at first, but you'll soon appreciate the readability it imparts to code.

Nested Messages

Figure 3-8 shows nested messages. By enclosing one message within another, you can use a returned value as an argument without having to declare a variable for it. The innermost message expression is evaluated first, resulting in a return object. Then the next nested message expression is evaluated using the object that was returned in the inner expression as the receiver of the second message. We saw this in action in Example 3-2 when we combined the `alloc` and `init` methods of `NSObject`.

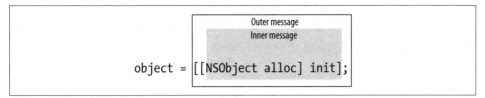

Figure 3-8. Nested Objective-C messages

Nested messages work only when the inner expression returns an object value. If the inner expression returns something else (for example, an int) then a crash will result at runtime. This is because messages can be passed only to objects, not to primitive types.

How Messaging Works

The NSObject class ensures that every object in the system has an instance variable named isa. This variable points to the class that defines how the object works.In addition, every class object has a reference to its superclass. This relationship is illustrated in Figure 3-9.

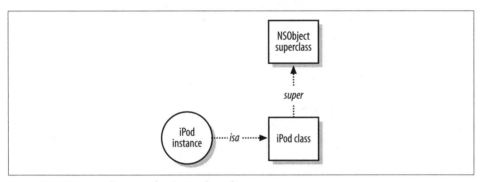

Figure 3-9. Instances have a reference to their class.

The class object contains quite a bit of information about the internals of the class and how it works. Part of this information is a method lookup table that maps *selectors* to methods, as shown in Figure 3-10.

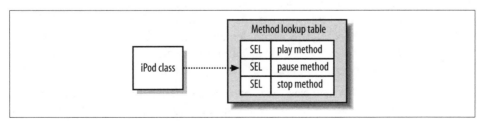

Figure 3-10. Method lookup table

A selector (defined as the SEL type in Objective-C) is a compiler-assigned code that identifies a method to the runtime. When you send a message to an object, the compiler actually creates code to perform a call to an Objective-C-defined function, which uses the selector information to perform a dynamic method lookup at runtime. For more details about how this functionality works underneath the hood, read *Inside Mac OS X: The Objective-C Language*, located in the */Developer/Documentation /Cocoa/ObjectiveC* folder.

Objective-C–Defined Types

So far, we've talked about a few of Objective-C's built-in types, such as SEL. Before we continue, Table 3-1 lists the set of Objective-C–defined types.

Table 3-1. Objective-C–defined types

Type	Definition
id	An object reference (a pointer to its data structure)
Class	A class object reference (a pointer to its data structure)
SEL	A selector (a compiler-assigned code that identifies a method name)
IMP	A pointer to a method implementation that returns an id
BOOL	A Boolean value, either YES or NO
nil	A null object pointer, (id)0
Nil	A null class pointer, (Class)0

The id type can be used to type any kind of object, class, or instance. In addition, class names can be used as type names to type instances of a class statically. A statically typed instance is declared as a pointer to an instance of its class or to an instance of any class from which it inherits.

Creating New Classes

When you want to create a new kind of object, you define a new class. A class is defined in two files. One file, the *header file (.h)*, declares the variables and methods that can be invoked by messages sent to objects belonging to the class. The other file is the *implementation file (.m)*, which actually implements the methods declared by the header file, as well as the private implementation details of the class. The interface defined in the header file is public. The implementation is private and can be changed without affecting the interface or the way the class is used.

To show how to create a new class, we will model songs that would go into an MP3 player. Don't get too scared yet; we're not actually going to write the MP3 player itself.

1. To get started, create a new Foundation Tool in Project Builder (File → New Project → Tools → Foundation Tool) named "songs", and save it in your ~/LearningCocoa folder.

2. Define a header for our song class. Choose File → New File, then select Objective-C class as the file type, as shown in Figure 3-11.

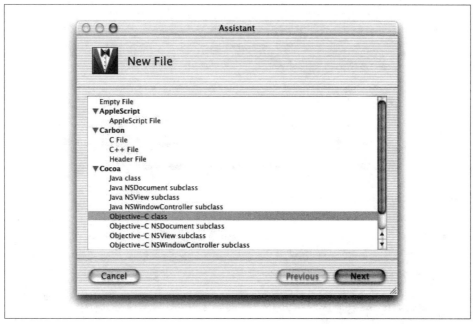

Figure 3-11. New File Assistant

3. Name the file *Song.m*, as shown in Figure 3-12. Make sure that the Also create "Song.h" checkbox is clicked. This creates the header file for the application's interface.

 Be careful not to confuse this use of the word *interface* with the term *Graphical User Interface*. This use of the word refers to how components talk, or know, about each other and doesn't refer to how users will interact with the program.

When you finish, Project Builder should look something like Figure 3-13. If *Song.h* and *Song.m* are not in the Source category of files, you can simply drag them there. (Hint: Use the black insertion indicator that appears in the outline view to guide you as you drag.) Where they appear doesn't matter to Project Builder, but keeping things neat and tidy will help you, especially on larger projects.

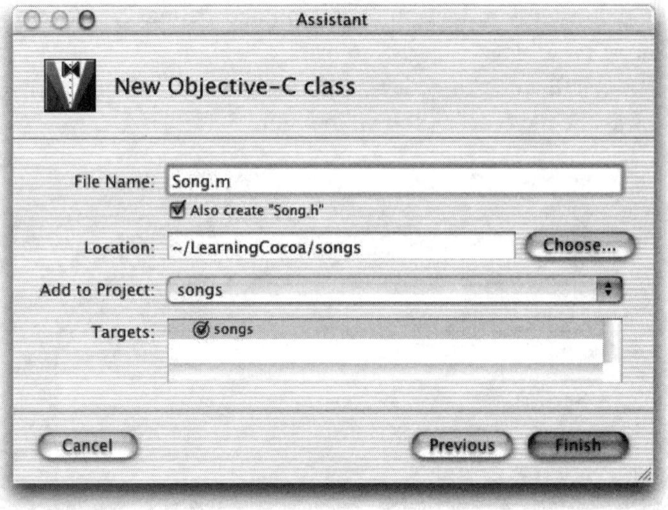

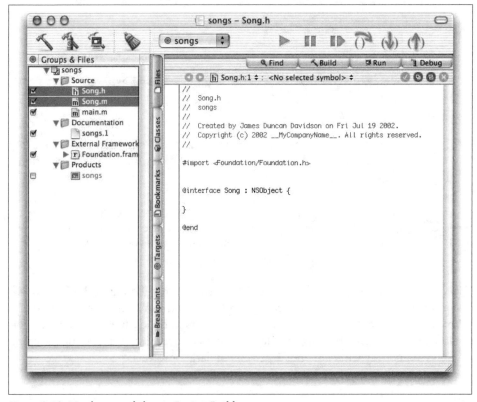

Figure 3-12. New Objective-C class Assistant

Figure 3-13. Newly created class in Project Builder

By creating the class header and implementation files, we have a start on a class that can be used in the rest of the program, including our main function in the *main.m* file. Project Builder creates a basic *Song.h* header file for you. A new class is declared in the header file with the @interface compiler directive. In this case, the directive is the following:

```
@interface Song : NSObject
```

This indicates that we are defining a class called Song that inherits from NSObject. The colon indicates the inheritance. The rest of the file is left for us to complete. All the instance variables used by the class are declared between the brackets. All the methods of the class are declared between the end bracket and the @end directive.

Defining the Song Interface

Edit the *Song.h* file as shown in Example 3-4. Once again, the lines that you need to add are shown in **boldface** type.

Example 3-4. Song.h interface

```
@interface Song : NSObject {
    NSString * name;                              // a
    NSString * artist;                            // b
}
- (NSString *)name;                               // c
- (void)setName:(NSString *)newName;              // d
- (NSString *)artist;                             // e
- (void)setArtist:(NSString *)newArtist;          // f
@end
```

Here's what the additional code does:

a. Declares the name variable that will point to an object of type NSString.

b. Declares the artist variable that will point to an object of type NSString.

c. Declares an instance method, named name, that returns a pointer to an NSString object when called.

d. Declares an instance method, named setName:, that takes a pointer to an NSString object as an argument. The minus sign at the start of the method declaration indicates that it's an instance method, as opposed to a class method. This method will be used to set the name of the song that the object represents. The method does not return anything, so we declare it to return void.

e. Declares an instance method, named artist, that returns a pointer to an NSString object when called.

f. Declares an instance method, named setArtist:, that takes a pointer to an NSString object as an argument. This method will be used to set the artist of the song that the object represents. Once again, this method does not return anything, so we declare it to return void.

In our example so far, we've only defined instance methods using the minus sign (–). Class methods, such as the `alloc` method of NSObject, are defined in code using the plus sign (+).

Properties and Accessor Methods

Notice that in our *Song.h* file we have two methods for each variable, which are named using a simple pattern. The variable is known as a *property*. The methods are known as *accessor methods*. The method that is named after the property returns the value of the property to the caller. The method named setProperty changes the property. In the case of our Song class, the name method gets the name of the Song, and the setName method sets it. Hiding access to the properties of the object is called *encapsulation*; this allows you to change the implementation of how variables are stored inside the object without potentially breaking code elsewhere.

Defining the Song Implementation

Now that we have defined the interface, we actually need to fill in the implementation of the class. Take a look at the *Song.m* file. You will notice that it imports *Song.h*, which is the application's interface. There are also two compiler directives, @implementation Song and @end.

Add the code shown in Example 3-5 between the @implementation and @end directives.

Example 3-5. The Song.m implementation

```
#import "Song.h"

@implementation Song

- (NSString *)name                                          // a
{
    return name;                                            // b
}

- (void)setName:(NSString *)newName                         // c
{
    [newName retain];                                       // d
    [name release];                                         // e
    name = newName;                                         // f
}

- (NSString *)artist                                        // g
```

Example 3-5. The Song.m implementation (continued)

```
{
    return artist;                                      // h
}

- (void)setArtist:(NSString *)newArtist                 // i
{
    [newArtist retain];                                 // j
    [artist release];                                   // k
    artist = newArtist;                                 // l
}
```

@end

Here's what the additional code does:

a. Declares the name method that returns an NSString return value.

b. Returns the NSString object associated with the name instance variable.

c. Declares the setName: method that takes a single NSString argument.

d. Sends the retain message to the newName object. This tells the object that we intend to keep a reference to it. This is part of Cocoa's memory management that will be described in depth in Chapter 4.

e. Sends the release message to the name object. If the name object is not pointing to an NSString object (if it is pointing to nil), then this message will not do anything. However, if name had been set on this Song object before, this message would tell the NSString object that we were not interested in it anymore.

f. Sets the name variable to point to the NSString object to which newName points.

g. Declares the artist method that returns an NSString return value.

h. Returns the NSString object associated with the artist instance variable.

i. Declares the setArtist: method that takes a single NSString argument.

j. Sends the retain message to the newArtist object, telling it that we are interested in keeping a reference to it.

k. Sends a release message to the existing object to which our artist variable points, if any.

l. Sets the artist variable to point to the NSString object to which newArtist points.

Using the Song Class

Now, we need to edit the main function in the *main.m* file, so we can do something with the Song class.

1. Edit the *main.m* file to match Example 3-6.

Example 3-6. Using the Song class

```
#import <Foundation/Foundation.h>
#import "Song.h"                                              // a

int main (int argc, const char * argv[]) {
    NSAutoreleasePool * pool = [[NSAutoreleasePool alloc] init];

    Song * song1 = [[Song alloc] init];                      // b
    [song1 setName:@"We Have Explosive"];
    [song1 setArtist:@"The Future Sound of London"];

    Song * song2 = [[Song alloc] init];                      // c
    [song2 setName:@"Loops of Fury"];
    [song2 setArtist:@"The Chemical Brothers"];

    NSLog(@"Song 1: %@", song1);                             // d
    NSLog(@"Song 2: %@", song2);

    [pool release];
    return 0;
}
```

Here's what the additional code does:

    a. Imports the *Song.h* interface file, so we can use the Song class.

    b. Allocates, initializes, and sets the name (setName) and artist (setArtist) of song1. The alloc and init methods work just the same as they did with NSObject, since Song inherits them from NSObject.

    c. Allocates, initializes, and sets the name and artist of song2.

    d. Prints the song1 and song2 objects, so we can see them.

2. Build and run the program. You should see something like this on the console:

```
2002-06-11 22:05:11.866 songs[7058] Song 1: <Song: 0x50f30>
2002-06-11 22:05:11.867 songs[7058] Song 2: <Song: 0x4f4b0>
```

You will recognize that this output is similar to the output that was printed from the NSObject object instances. This is because the NSLog method actually calls the description method on an object, as defined by the NSObject class. To change this to print something a bit more user-friendly, we somehow need to redefine what the description method prints.

 If you get a compiler error saying that the song2 variable is undeclared, chances are that you are not using Mac OS X 10.2 (Jaguar). This book makes use of many of the new features of Jaguar, including support for the C99 standard in GCC 3.1.

Overriding Methods

A subclass can not only add new methods to the ones it inherits from a superclass; it can also replace, or *override*, an inherited method with a new implementation. No special syntax is required; just reimplement the method in the subclass's implementation file.

Overriding methods doesn't alter the set of messages that an object can receive. It alters the method implementation that will be used to respond to those messages. This ability for each class to implement its own version of a method is known as *polymorphism*.

1. Edit the *Song.m* file as shown in Example 3-7 to add the `description` method.

   Example 3-7. Adding the description method

   ```
   #import "Song.h"

   @implementation Song

   - (NSString *)name
   {
       return name;
   }

   - (void)setName:(NSString *)newName
   {
       [newName retain];
       [name release];
       name = newName;
   }

   - (NSString *)artist
   {
       return artist;
   }

   - (void)setArtist:(NSString *)newArtist
   {
       [newArtist retain];
       [artist release];
       artist = newArtist;
   }

   - (NSString *)description                                    // a
   {
       return [self name];                                      // b
   }

   @end
   ```

The code we added performs the following tasks:

    a. Declares the description method that overrides the method by the same name in the NSObject class. We don't need to declare this method in the *Song.h* interface file, as it is already part of the interface declared by NSObject.

    b. Returns the name of the song as its description, using the special self variable that points to the object under operation. We could have just returned the variable directly from this method, but using the [self name] message means that if the internal implementation of the Song class changes, this method will work correctly with no additional work.

2. Build and run the program. You should see the following output on the console:

```
2002-06-11 22:32:20.435 songs[7096] Song 1: We Have Explosive
2002-06-11 22:32:20.436 songs[7096] Song 2: Loops of Fury
```

Overriding the description method allows us to assign much more meaningful strings for output than NSObject's default class name and memory address output.

Calling Superclass Methods

Sometimes, in a method that overrides a superclass's method, calling the functionality in the superclass's method can be useful. To do this, you can send a message to super, a special variable in the Objective-C language. When you send a message to super, it indicates that an inherited method should be performed, rather than the method in the current class.

For example, if we wanted to print the same information that the NSObject class prints in the description method, we could implement our description method as follows:

```
- (NSString *)description
{
    return [super description];
}
```

If we were to make this change, we would see the following output:

```
2002-06-11 22:37:03.997 Songs[7115] Song 1: <Song: 0x53100>
2002-06-11 22:37:03.998 Songs[7115] Song 2: <Song: 0x530a0>
```

Since this defeats the purpose of overriding the description method, we're not going to add this implementation to our Song class. If you experiment with this, be sure to set it back to return [self description].

Object Creation

One of a class's primary functions is to create new objects of the type defined by the class. As we've seen, objects are created at runtime in a two-step process that first allocates memory for the instance variables of the new object and then initializes those variables. We've said this before, but because it's important, we'll repeat it here: an alloc message should *always* be coupled with an init message in the same line of code. The receiver for the alloc message is a class, while the receiver for the init message is the new object instance:

```
TheClass * newObject = [[TheClass alloc] init];
```

The alloc method dynamically allocates memory for a new instance of the receiving class and returns the new object. The receiver for the init message is the new object that was dynamically allocated by alloc. An object isn't ready for use until it is initialized, but it should be initialized only once. The version of the init method defined in the NSObject class does very little. In fact, it simply returns self, a special variable in Objective-C that is defined to point to the object that is called upon by the method.

After being allocated and initialized, a new object is a fully functional member of its class with its own set of variables. The newObject object can receive messages, store values in its instance variables, and so on.

Subclass versions of the init method should return the new object (self) after it has been successfully initialized. If it can't be initialized, the method should release the object and return nil. In some cases, an init method might release the new object and return a substitute. Programs should therefore always use the object returned by init, and not necessarily the one returned by alloc.

Subclass versions of init incorporate the initialization code for the classes from which they inherit through a message to super. When working with classes that inherit from NSObject, a simple call to the superclass init method, as shown in the following code block, is sufficient.

```
- init
{
    [super init];
    /* class-specific initialization goes here */
    return self;
}
```

Note that the message to super precedes the initialization code added in the method. This ensures that initialization proceeds in the order of inheritance.

However, since extending classes other than NSObject may return a different object than that on which the initializer was called, you must be more careful in these cases and use the following code:

```
- init
{
    if (self = [super init]) {
        /* class specific initialization goes here */
    }
    return self;
}
```

Note that this code checks to see if super returned an object, or nil, before doing any initialization itself. This code will work in any situation; however, none of the classes that we create in this book require these checks.

> If you have been observant, you may have noticed that we have used two kinds of syntax to denote comments. The first is the traditional /* ... */ C-style comment. The second is the newer // style comment that continues to the end of the line. You'll see both forms used quite frequently in Objective-C code. There really aren't any guidelines as to which style should be used where. You should simply use whichever works best, given the context of the comment.

Designated initializers

Subclasses often define initializer methods with additional arguments to allow specific values to be set. The more arguments an initializer method has, the more freedom it gives you to determine the character of initialized objects. Classes often have a set of initializer methods, each with a different number of arguments, to set up objects ahead of time with appropriate information. For example, we could define the following initializer method for our Song class:

```
- (id)initWithName:(NSString *)newName artist:(NSString *)newArtist;
```

This initializer allows us to create new Song objects and set them up with one line of code rather than three. For this to work properly in cases where users of this class don't call this initializer, but simply use the init method, we make sure that the init method calls this initializer with appropriate default arguments. This method is called the *designated initializer* for the class. The other initialization methods defined in this class invoke the designated initializer through messages to self. In this way, all the initializers are chained together. The designated initializer should always call its superclass's designated initializer.

> Typically, though not always, the designated initializer is the one with the most arguments. The only way to determine the designated initializer of a class accurately is to read the documentation for the class.

1. To work with designated initializers, edit *Song.h* and add the initializers, as shown in Example 3-8.

   Example 3-8. Adding a designated initializer

   ```
   #import <Foundation/Foundation.h>

   @interface Song : NSObject {
       NSString *name;
       NSString *artist;
   }
   - (id)initWithName:(NSString *)newName artist:(NSString *)newArtist;
   - (NSString *)name;
   ```

Example 3-8. Adding a designated initializer (continued)

```
- (void)setName:(NSString *)newName;
- (NSString *)artist;
- (void)setArtist:(NSString *)newArtist;

@end
```

The code we added declares an initializer for our Song class that takes the name of the song as well as the artist.

2. Now add the initializer implementations to *Song.m* as shown in Example 3-9.

Example 3-9. Designated initializer implementation

```
#import "Song.h"

@implementation Song

- (id)init                                                      // a
{
    return [self initWithName:nil artist:nil];
}

- (id)initWithName:(NSString *)newName artist:(NSString *)newArtist    // b
{
    [super init];                                               // c
    [self setName:newName];                                     // d
    [self setArtist:newArtist];                                 // e
    return self;                                                // f
}
- (NSString *)name
{
    return name;
}

- (void)setName:(NSString *)newName
{
    [newName retain];
    [name release];
    name = newName;
}

- (NSString *)artist
{
    return artist;
}

- (void)setArtist:(NSString *)newArtist
{
    [newArtist retain];
    [artist release];
    artist = newArtist;
}
```

Example 3-9. Designated initializer implementation (continued)

```
- (NSString *)description
{
    return [super description];
}
```

@end

The code we added in Example 3-9 performs the following tasks:

    a. Overrides the init method provided by NSObject. This overridden method calls the new designated initializer with nil string arguments for the name and artist arguments.

    b. Declares our designated initializer with the same signature we used in *Song.h*.

    c. Calls the init method of the NSObject superclass.

    d. Sets the name of the new object.

    e. Sets the artist of the new object.

    f. Returns the freshly initialized object, ready for use.

3. Now, edit the *main.m* file to match Example 3-10.

Example 3-10. Using the designated initializer

```
#import <Foundation/Foundation.h>
#import "Song.h"

int main (int argc, const char * argv[]) {
    NSAutoreleasePool * pool = [[NSAutoreleasePool alloc] init];

    Song * song1 = [[Song alloc] initWithName:@"We Have Explosive"
                                       artist:@"The Future Sound of London"];
    Song * song2 = [[Song alloc] initWithName:@"Loops of Fury"
                                       artist:@"The Chemical Brothers"];

    NSLog(@"Song 1: %@", song1);
    NSLog(@"Song 2: %@", song2);

    [pool release];
    return 0;
}
```

In this code, we've simply replaced the longer three lines with our new initializer.

4. Build and run the program. You should see the following familiar output:

```
2002-06-11 23:08:07.783 Songs[7195] Song 1: We Have Explosive
2002-06-11 23:08:07.784 Songs[7195] Song 2: Loops of Fury
```

As you can see in Example 3-10, a line of code is often too long to fit on one line. Project Builder has autoindentation functionality to make these constructs look good automatically, so you don't have to type in a bunch of spaces manually. Simply go into Project Builder's preferences, select the Indentation pane, and make sure that the "Syntax-aware indenting" checkbox is checked.

Object Deallocation

We have a flaw in our very simple program in the form of a memory leak. Of course, this leak is probably not going to hurt anybody—since the program exits so quickly, allowing the operating system to reclaim all the memory belonging to the process—but it doesn't pay to get into bad habits. As well, code has a tendency to be reused in ways that the original author did not expect. Therefore, you should always make a point of cleaning up after your code, no matter how simple it is.

When an object is no longer being used by the program, it must be deallocated. When an object is released, the dealloc method (provided by the NSObject class) is called, letting it release objects it has created, free allocated memory, and so on. Since our Song class has two instance variable objects, they need to be released when an instance of the class is released.

1. To do this, we need to add a dealloc method implementation to our Song class in the *Song.m* file, as shown in Example 3-11.

   Example 3-11. Adding a deallocation method

   ```
   #import "Song.h"

   @implementation Song

   - (id)init
   {
       return [self initWithName:nil artist:nil];
   }


   - (id)initWithName:(NSString *)newName artist:(NSString *)newArtist
   {
       [super init];
       [self setName:newName];
       [self setArtist:newArtist];
       return self;
   }

   - (void)dealloc                                              // a
   {
       NSLog(@"Deallocating %@", self);                         // b
   ```

Example 3-11. Adding a deallocation method (continued)

```
    [name release];                                          // c
    [artist release];                                        // d
    [super dealloc];                                         // e
}

- (NSString *)name
{
    return name;
}

- (void)setName:(NSString *)newName
{
    [newName retain];
    [name release];
    name = newName;
}

- (NSString *)artist
{
    return artist;
}

- (void)setArtist:(NSString *)newArtist
{
    [newArtist retain];
    [artist release];
    artist = newArtist;
}

- (NSString *)description
{
    return [self name];
}

@end
```

The code that we added in Example 3-11 performs the following tasks:

a. Declares the dealloc method. Note that since the dealloc method is defined by the NSObject class, we don't have to declare it in the *Song.h* header file.

b. Prints out a message saying that the object is being deallocated.

c. Releases the name instance variable.

d. Releases the artist instance variable.

e. Calls dealloc on the superclass, allowing the deallocation functionality of the NSObject class to operate. When you override the default dealloc functionality, you must always be sure to call dealloc in the superclass.

2. Edit the *main.m* source file with the changes shown in Example 3-12.

Example 3-12. Releasing the song objects created

```
#import <Foundation/Foundation.h>
#import "Song.h"

int main (int argc, const char * argv[]) {
    NSAutoreleasePool * pool = [[NSAutoreleasePool alloc] init];

    Song * song1 = [[Song alloc] initWithName:@"We Have Explosive"
                                       artist:@"The Future Sound of London"];
    Song * song2 = [[Song alloc] initWithName:@"Loops of Fury"
                                       artist:@"The Chemical Brothers"];

    NSLog(@"Song 1: %@", song1);
    NSLog(@"Song 2: %@", song2);

    [song1 release];
    [song2 release];

    [pool release];
    return 0;
}
```

The added code tells the system that we are no longer interested in the song1 and song2 variables. Because we are no longer interested, and there are no other objects interested in these variables, they will be deallocated immediately. This will plug up our memory leak, making it a good citizen.

3. Build and run the project. You should see the following output:

```
2002-06-11 23:12:07.783 songs[7200] Song 1: We Have Explosive
2002-06-11 23:12:07.784 songs[7200] Song 2: Loops of Fury
2002-06-11 23:12:07.783 songs[7200] Deallocating We Have Explosive
2002-06-11 23:12:07.784 songs[7200] Deallocating Loops of Fury
```

In Chapter 4, we present the finer details of memory management and explain why the act of releasing an object here calls the dealloc method of our Song objects.

Other Concepts

There are some other concepts in object-oriented programming and Objective-C that we haven't explored in depth in this chapter. Before you learn too much about these new concepts, you'll want to practice quite a bit with the concepts that you've already learned. We're telling you about these other concepts now so that when you come to them, you won't be surprised.

Categories

You can add methods to a class by declaring them in an interface file under a category name and defining them in an implementation file under the same name. The category name indicates that the methods are additions to a class declared elsewhere, not to a new class.

Protocols

Class and category interfaces declare methods that are associated with a particular class—methods that the class implements. Informal and formal protocols, on the other hand, declare methods that are not associated with a class, but which any class—and perhaps many classes—might implement. We'll talk more about protocols in Chapter 9.

Introspection

An object, even one typed as id, can reveal its class and divulge other characteristics at runtime. Several introspection methods, such as isMemberOfClass: and isKindOfClass:, allow you to ascertain the inheritance relationships of an object and the methods to which it responds.

Remember, you can find out much more information about Objective-C and object-oriented programming in the developer documentation installed on your hard drive along with the Developer Tools (*/Developer/Documentation/Cocoa/ObjectiveC*).

Exercises

1. Use the resources in Appendix C, and read the documentation for NSObject and NSString.

2. Read the documentation for the NSLog function.

3. Investigate the isa and self variables by having the designated initializer of the Song class print a description of the class.

CHAPTER 4

The Cocoa Foundation Kit

Now that we have filled your head with lots of theory about object-oriented programming, we'll look into some of the essential parts of Cocoa's Foundation framework. In this chapter we cover strings, collections, and memory management. Once you have a firm grasp on these topics, you'll be ready for the raison d'être of Cocoa: GUI programming.

The nature of these topics doesn't lend itself to a nifty, all-inclusive code example that shows everything in action at once. So, instead of contriving a single, awkward example, we're just going to work through a set of simple code samples to illustrate the concepts presented. We'll also augment the use of these samples with some usage of the debugger.

Strings

So far, we have worked with strings using the @"..." construct in various method and function calls. This construct is convenient when working with strings. When interpreted by the compiler, it is translated into an NSString object that is based on the 7-bit ASCII-encoded string (also known as a "C string") between the quotes. For example, the statement:

```
NSString * lush = @"Lush";
```

is functionally equivalent to:

```
NSString * lush = [[NSString alloc] initWithCString:"Lush"];
```

NSString objects are not limited to the ASCII character set; they can handle any character contained in the Unicode character set, allowing most of the world's living languages to be represented. Unicode is a 16-bit-wide character set, but can be represented in 8-bits using the UTF-8 encoding.

Basic String Operations

NSString provides several methods that are handy when working with strings. A few of these methods are as follows:

- (int)**length**

Returns the number of Unicode characters in the string object upon which it is called.

- (const char *)**cString**

Returns a representation of the string as a C string in the default encoding. This method is helpful when you need to operate with C-based functions, such as those found in traditional Unix system calls.

 It's important to note that since C strings are 7-bit, and the NSString class can handle the full Unicode character set, not all NSString objects can be represented as C strings.

- (const char *)**UTF8String**

Returns a representation of the string as a UTF-8 representation. UTF-8 allows the transmission of Unicode characters over channels that support 8-bit encodings. All of the lower levels of Mac OS X—including the HFS+ and UFS filesystems, as well as the BSD system routines—can handle char * arguments in the UTF-8 encoding.

- (NSString *)**stringByAppendingString:**(NSString *)aString

Returns a new string object by appending the given string to the string upon which the method is called.

To explore these methods, we'll create a simple program using the following steps:

1. In Project Builder, create a new Foundation Tool (File → New Project → Tool → Foundation Tool) named "strings", and save it in your ~/LearningCocoa folder.

 You may have noticed that sometimes our project names start with a lowercase letter and sometimes with an uppercase letter. The common practice in naming applications is that command-line applications should be lowercase and GUI applications should be initial capitalized. We'll use this practice through this book.

2. Open the *main.m* file, located in the "Source" group, and modify it to match the code shown in Example 4-1.

Example 4-1. Working with strings

```
int main (int argc, const char * argv[]) {
    NSAutoreleasePool * pool = [[NSAutoreleasePool alloc] init];

    NSString * artist = @"Underworld";                          // a
```

Example 4-1. Working with strings (continued)

```
NSLog(@"%@ has length: %d", artist, [artist length]);                    // b

[pool release];
return 0;
}
```

The code we added inExample 4-1 performs the following tasks:

a. Declares an object of type `NSString`, named `artist`, and sets it to the value `"Underworld"`

b. Obtains the `length` of the string and prints it using the `NSLog` function

3. Build and run (⌘-R) the application. You will be prompted to save the *main.m* file, and then Project Builder will compile and the run the code. You should see the following output in Project Builder's console:

```
2002-06-17 23:29:32.344 strings[1147] Underworld has length: 10
```

As we have seen before, the `NSLog` function prints the current date and time, the program name, and the process ID (PID) of the program, as well as the output that we told it to print. In the output, we see that the `artist` object was substituted for the `%@` token and that the return value from the `length` method was substituted for the `%d` token. Remember, you can use any of the standard `printf` substitution tokens in the format string, in addition to the `%@` token.

Setting breakpoints and debugging

Instead of adding code to the strings tool, we will use the debugger to explore the `UTF8String` and `stringByAppendingString` methods. This will give you some practice using the debugger, while you learn about these methods.

1. Set a breakpoint between the `NSLog` function and the `[pool release]` line of code in *main.m*. Remember to set a breakpoint, click in the column on the left side of the code editor. If you want to move the breakpoint, click and drag the breakpoint to its new location. In our code, this breakpoint is at line 8. An example of the breakpoint set is shown in Figure 4-1.

2. Build and debug the application (Build → Build and Debug, or ⌘-Y). Execution will start and then pause at the breakpoint we set, highlighting the line at which it stopped in a salmon colored bar.

3. Click on the Console tab above the variable viewer to open up the debugger console, as shown in Figure 4-2. You should see that the `NSLog` function outputs its string.

 The debugger console behaves similarly to working with the Terminal application. You enter a command, hit Return, and the result of the command is shown on the next line. Just like the default shell in the Terminal, the debugger maintains a history of commands that you can access by hitting the up and down arrows on your keyboard.

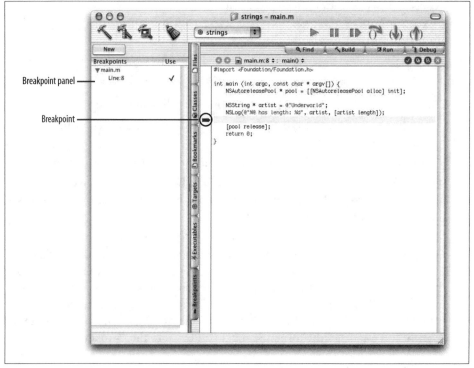

Figure 4-1. Setting a breakpoint in the main.m file

4. Type in print-object artist at the (gdb) prompt in the debugger console. You may have to click in the debugger console to give it focus, so that you can enter commands.

   (gdb) **print-object artist**

When you enter this command, the debugger outputs the following:

   Underworld

In addition to simply printing objects, we can print the result of any message that we can send to an object. This functionality is incredibly useful when trying to find the various states of an object while using the debugger.

5. Enter in the following into the debugger console:

   (gdb) **print-object [artist description]**

The following result, matching what we just saw in Step 4, will be printed:

   Underworld

6. Let's see the stringByAppendingString method in action. Enter the following into the debugger console:

   (gdb) **print-object [artist stringByAppendingString:@": Pearl's Girl"]**

The debugger outputs the following result of the method call:

   Underworld: Pearl's Girl

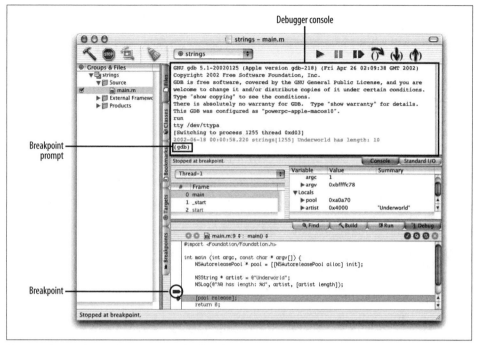

Figure 4-2. Program execution paused at breakpoint

7. You can also send messages to NSString objects created using the @"..." construct. Enter the following into the debugger console:

```
(gdb) print-object [@"The artist is: " stringByAppendingString:artist]
```

The debugger outputs:

```
The artist is: Underworld
```

The next debugger command we will learn is the print command. This command
prints out C types instead of objects. We will use the print command to evaluate the
return values of the length and UTF8String methods.

8. Enter the following into the debugger console:

```
(gdb) print (int) [artist length]
```

The debugger outputs:

```
$1 = 10
```

The $1 symbol is a temporary variable that holds the results of the message, and
the 10 denotes the number of characters (or length) in the artist object. Note
that we needed to cast the return type from the length message so that the print
command could operate. Try this again without the (int) cast.

9. To see the UTF8String method in action, enter the following:

```
(gdb) print (char *) [artist UTF8String]
```

The debugger outputs something similar to the following:

```
$2 = 0x9f738 "Underworld\000"...
```

This is the null-terminated char * string representation, in UTF-8 encoding, of our artist string.

To quit the debugger, you can either click the stop button or enter quit at the (gdb) prompt.

Debugger Command Cheat Sheet

There's a lot more that the debugger can do. Here are a few of our favorite debugger commands. Try them out to see what they do.

call [exp]
: Calls the given function on an object.

print [exp]
: Prints the primitive value of the expression given.

print-object [exp]
: Prints the value of the object returned by the expression.

set [variable] = [exp]
: Sets the variable to the value of the expression. For example, we can reset the artist variable to a new string by using the expression set artist = @"New Artist".

whatis [variable]
: Prints the kind, or type, of a variable.

help
: Prints out a list of the commands available while using the debugger.

Working with Portions of a String

When working with strings, it often is necessary to extract data from them. The NSString class provides the following methods for finding and obtaining substrings:

- (NSRange)**rangeOfString:**(NSString *)aString
    Returns an NSRange struct that contains the location and length of the first occurrence of the given string

- (NSString *)**substringFromIndex:**(unsigned)index
    Returns a string object that contains the characters of the receiver, from the index given to the end of the string

- (NSString *)**substringToIndex:**(unsigned)index
    Returns a string object that contains the characters of the receiver, from the beginning of the string to the index given

- (NSString *)**substringWithRange:**(NSRange)range

Returns a string object that contains the characters of the receiver, within the range specified

To explore these methods, we'll create a simple program (that works with just substrings) using the following steps:

1. In Project Builder, create a new Foundation Tool (File → New Project → Tool → Foundation Tool) named "substrings", and save it in your *~/LearningCocoa* folder.

2. Open the *main.m* file, located in the "Source" group, and modify it to match the code shown in Example 4-2.

Example 4-2. Working with substrings

```
int main (int argc, const char * argv[]) {
    NSAutoreleasePool * pool = [[NSAutoreleasePool alloc] init];

    NSString * song = @"Let Forever Be,The Chemical Brothers";      // a
    NSRange range = [song rangeOfString:@ ","];                     // b
    printf("comma location: %i\n", range.location);                 // c

    NSString * title = [song substringToIndex:range.location];      // d
    NSString * artist =
        [song substringFromIndex:range.location + range.length];    // e

    printf("title:  %s\n", [title UTF8String]);                     // f
    printf("artist: %s\n", [artist UTF8String]);                    // g

    [pool release];
    return 0;
}
```

The code we added in Example 4-2 performs the following tasks:

a. Declares a string object named song and sets it.

b. Obtains the range of the comma in the song string.

c. Prints the location of the comma. Notice that we are using the standard C printf function here. We will use printf instead of NSLog in many of the upcoming exercises, so the output from our programs won't be cluttered with timestamps and PIDs. Note that, unlike the NSLog function, we have to be sure to include the \n character to print out the new line.

d. Declares a string named title and sets it to the substring, from the start of the song string to the location of the comma.

e. Declares a string named artist and sets it to the substring, from the comma to the end of the song string. We use the range.location + range.length construction so that we find the index just after the comma value. If we just used the location of the comma, it would show up in our substring.

f. Prints the `title` to the console, using the UTF-8 representation of the string. Notice that we are using the `printf %s` token.

g. Prints the `artist` to the console, using the UTF-8 representation of the string.

3. Build and run (⌘-R) the application. You will be prompted to save your files, and then Project Builder will compile and run the code. You should see the following output in the console:

```
comma location: 14
title:  Let Forever Be
artist: The Chemical Brothers
```

Mutable Strings

Once created, instances of the `NSString` class cannot be changed; they are *immutable*. If you want to change the contents of an `NSString` object, you must create a new one, as we saw using the `stringByAppendingString` method. In programs that manipulate strings extensively, this would become cumbersome quickly. To let you modify the contents of a string, Cocoa provides the `NSMutableString` class.

 If you have programmed in Java, `NSMutableString` can be considered analogous to the `java.lang.StringBuffer` class.

Some of the methods that you frequently will use with mutable strings are the following:

- (void)**appendString:**(NSString *)aString
  Adds the characters of the given string to those already in the mutable string object upon which the method is called.

- (void)**deleteCharactersInRange:**(NSRange)range
  Deletes the characters in a given range.

- (void)**insertString:**(NSString *)aString **atIndex:**(unsigned index)
  Inserts the characters of the given string into the mutable string at the location specified by the index. All of the characters from the insertion point to the end of the mutable string are shifted to accommodate the new characters.

To explore these methods, we'll create yet another simple program, using the following steps:

1. In Project Builder, create a new Foundation Tool (File → New Project → Tool → Foundation Tool) named "mutablestrings", and save it in your *~/LearningCocoa* folder.

2. Open the *main.m* file, located in the "Source" group, and modify it to match the following code:

```
int main (int argc, const char * argv[]) {
    NSAutoreleasePool * pool = [[NSAutoreleasePool alloc] init];

    NSMutableString * song = [[NSMutableString alloc] init];          // a
    [song appendString:@"Deaf Leppard"];                             // b
    printf("%s\n", [song UTF8String]);                               // c

    NSRange range = [song rangeOfString:@"Deaf"];                    // d
    [song replaceCharactersInRange:range withString:@"Def"];         // e
    printf("%s\n", [song UTF8String]);                               // f

    [song insertString:@"Animal by " atIndex:0];                     // g
    printf("%s\n", [song UTF8String]);                               // h

    [song release];                                                  // i

    [pool release];
    return 0;
}
```

The code we added performs the following tasks:

  a. Creates a new empty mutable string named song.

  b. Appends the contents of the "Deaf Leppard" string to the song mutable string.

  c. Prints the song mutable string to the console.

  d. Gets the range of the "Deaf" substring.

  e. Replaces the "Deaf" substring with "Def" to correct the misspelling.

  f. Prints the song mutable string to the console.

  g. Inserts the string "Animal by" at the beginning the mutable string.

  h. Once again prints the song mutable string.

  i. Releases the song object. Because we created the Song object using the alloc method, we are responsible forr releasing it. We'll explain more about how this works later in this chapter.

3. Build and run (⌘-R) the application. You should see the following output in the console:

```
Deaf Leppard
Def Leppard
Animal by Def Leppard
```

Working with Files

A common use of strings is to work with paths to files in the filesystem. The NSString class provides several methods to manipulate strings as filesystem paths, extract a file name or an extension, resolve paths containing symbolic links, and even expand tilde expressions (such as ~duncan/Library) in paths. Some of the commonly used path manipulation methods are as follows:

Mutability Versus Immutability

Why does Cocoa provide both mutable and immutable versions of strings and the collection classes? The answer is that there are tradeoffs to both kinds of objects. An immutable object, once created, can't change. This means that a higher performing implementation can be used. Mutable objects, on the other hand, aren't nearly so amenable to performance tuning, as there is overhead involved in keeping them "editable."

In addition, immutable objects are inherently thread-safe and can be passed to code worked on by other programmers without fear that the contents of the object will be modified. When creating your own code, you should favor immutable objects unless you need the ability to change the contents of an object.

- (NSString *)**lastPathComponent**
   Returns the last path component of the receiver. For example, if you call this method on the string ~/LearningCocoa/substrings/main.m, it will return main.m.

- (NSString *)**pathExtension**
   Returns the extension, if any, of a file path. For example, if you call this method on the string main.m, it will return the value m.

- (NSString *)**stringByStandardizingPath**
   Returns a string with all extraneous path components removed or resolved. This method will resolve the initial tilde expression, as well as any .. or ./ symbols, to actual directories.

In addition to working with paths, you can also create string objects using the contents of a file and write string objects to files using the following methods:

- (NSString *)**stringWithContentsOfFile:**(NSString *)path
   Creates a new string by reading characters from the file specified by the path argument.

- (BOOL)**writeToFile:**(NSString *)path **atomically:**(BOOL)flag
   Writes the contents of the string to the given file. The atomically flag indicates whether the file should be written safely to an auxiliary file, then copied into place. Most of the time, this setting makes no difference. The only time it matters is if the system crashes when the file is being flushed to disk.

To see these methods in action, follow the following steps:

1. In Project Builder, create a new Foundation Tool (File → New Project → Tool → Foundation Tool) named "filestrings", and save it in your ~/LearningCocoa folder.

2. Open the *main.m* file, located in the "Source" group, and modify it to match the code shown in Example 4-3.

Example 4-3. Reading files into strings

```
int main (int argc, const char * argv[]) {
    NSAutoreleasePool * pool = [[NSAutoreleasePool alloc] init];

    NSString * filename = @"~/LearningCocoa/filestrings/main.m";      // a
    filename = [filename stringByStandardizingPath];                  // b
    printf("%s\n", [filename UTF8String]);                            // c

    NSString * source = [NSString stringWithContentsOfFile:filename]; // d
    printf("%s\n", [source UTF8String]);                             // e

    [pool release];
    return 0;
}
```

The code we added in Example 4-3 performs the following tasks:

a. Creates a string object, named `filename`, that contains the path to the
main.m source file of this project. Note that you must save your project in
your *~/LearningCocoa* folder for this example to work. If you are saving
your projects to some other location, you will need to edit the path appropriately.

b. Sets the `filename` variable to a standardized path. This will resolve the ~/
characters to your home directory.

c. Prints the resolved `filename` variable.

d. Creates a new string, named `source`, with the contents of the *main.m* source
file.

e. Prints the `source` string to the console.

3. Build and run (⌘-R) the application. You should see output similar to the following appear in the console:

```
/Users/duncan/LearningCocoa/filestrings/main.m
#import <Foundation/Foundation.h>

int main (int argc, const char * argv[]) {
    NSAutoreleasePool * pool = [[NSAutoreleasePool alloc] init];

    NSString * filename = @"~/LearningCocoa/filestrings/main.m";
    filename = [filename stringByStandardizingPath];
    printf("%s\n", [filename UTF8String]);

    NSString * source = [NSString stringWithContentsOfFile:filename];
    printf("%s\n", [source UTF8String]);

    [pool release];
    return 0;
}
```

We'll explore the `lastPathComponent` and `pathExtension` methods using the debugger.

4. Set a breakpoint between the last `printf` statement and the `[pool release];` line. If you typed the code exactly as shown in Example 4-3, the breakpoint will be on line 12.

5. Build and debug the application (⌘-Y). Execution will start and then pause at the breakpoint.

6. Click on the Console tab above the variable viewer to open up the debugger console.

7. Type in the following at the (gdb) prompt:

    (gdb) **print-object [filename lastPathComponent]**

    When you enter this command, the debugger should output the following:

    main.m

8. Type in the following at the (gdb) prompt:

    (gdb) **print-object [filename pathExtension]**

    When you enter this command, you should see the following:

    m

9. Quit the debugger; use the Stop button, or type in `quit` at the (gdb) prompt and hit return.

Now that we've covered quite a few things that you can do with strings, it's time to look at Cocoa's collection classes.

Collections

Cocoa provides several classes in the Foundation Kit whose purpose is to hold and organize instances of other classes. These are called the *collection classes*. There are three primary flavors of collections in Cocoa: *arrays*, *sets*, and *dictionaries*. These classes, shown in Figure 4-3, are extremely useful in Cocoa application development, and their influence can be found throughout the Cocoa class libraries.

Collection classes, like strings, come in two forms: *mutable* and *immutable*. Immutable classes allow you to add items when the collection is created, but no further changes are allowed. On the other hand, mutable classes allow you to add and remove objects programmatically after the collection is created.

Much of the power of collection classes comes from their ability to manipulate the objects they contain. Not every collection object can perform every function, but in general, collection objects can do the following:

- Derive their initial contents from files and URLs, as well as other collections of objects
- Add, remove, locate, and sort contents
- Compare their contents with other collection objects

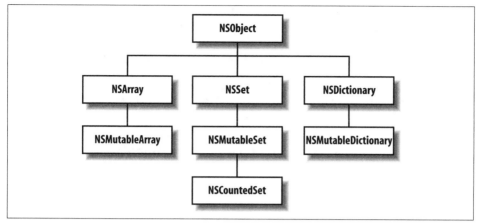

Figure 4-3. Cocoa collection classes

- Enumerate over their contents
- Send a message to the objects that they contain
- Archive their contents to a file on disk and retrieve it later*

Arrays

Arrays—instances of the NSArray class—are ordered collections of objects indexed by integers. Like C-based arrays, the first object in an array is located at index 0. Unlike C- and Java-based arrays whose size is set when they are created, Cocoa mutable array objects can grow as needed to accommodate inserted objects.

The NSArray class provides the following methods to work with the contents of an array:

- (unsigned)**count**
  Returns the number of objects currently in the array.

- (id)**objectAtIndex:**(unsigned)index
  Returns the object located in the array at the index given. Like C- and Java-based arrays, Cocoa array indexes start at 0.

- (BOOL)**containsObject:**(id)anObject
  Indicates whether a given object is present in the array.

To practice working with arrays do as follows:

1. In Project Builder, create a new Foundation Tool (File → New Project → Tool → Foundation Tool) named "arrays", and save it in your ~/*LearningCocoa* folder.

---

* Objects placed into an array must implement certain methods to support this functionality. All of the Foundation classes that you are likely to add to a collection are already prepared for this.

2. Open the *main.m* file, located in the "Source" group, and modify it to match the following code:

```
int main (int argc, const char * argv[]) {
    NSAutoreleasePool * pool = [[NSAutoreleasePool alloc] init];

    NSString * string = @"one two buckle my shoe";               // a
    NSArray * array = [string componentsSeparatedByString:@" "]; // b
    int count = [array count];                                   // c
    int i;
    for ( i = 0; i < count; i++ ) {
        printf("%i: %s\n", i, [[array objectAtIndex:i] UTF8String]); // d
    }

    [pool release];
    return 0;
}
```

The code we added performs the following tasks:

a. Declares a new string.

b. Creates an array of string objects using the componentsSeparatedByString: method of the NSString class. Note that in the first example of this chapter, where we looked for the range of the comma to split the spring, we could have used this method to get the two strings.

c. Obtains the count of the array to use in the for loop.

d. Prints each item of the array to the console.

3. Build and run (⌘-R) the application. You should see output similar to the following appear in the console:

```
0: one
1: two
2: buckle
3: my
4: shoe
```

Using the debugger to explore NSArray

We'll explore a few more NSArray methods using the debugger:

1. Set a breakpoint after the for loop. If you typed in the code exactly as noted previously, including the spaces and the comments that are part of the *main.m* file template, the breakpoint will be on line 15.

2. Build and debug (⌘-Y) the application. Execution will start and then pause at the breakpoint we set.

3. Click on the Console tab to open up the debugger console.

4. Type in the following at the (gdb) prompt:

```
(gdb) print-object [array objectAtIndex:4]
```

You should see the following output:

```
shoe
```

5. Type in the following:

```
(gdb) print (int) [array containsObject:@"buckle"];
```

You should see the following output:

```
$1 = 1
```

This indicates that the array did contain the string we specified. Try using a string that isn't in the array, and see what the return value is. You should see a return value of 0.

6. Quit the debugger, and close the project.

Mutable Arrays

The NSMutableArray class provides the functionality needed to manage a modifiable array of objects. This class extends the NSArray class by adding insertion and deletion operations. These operations include the following methods:

- (void)**addObject:**(id)anObject
  Inserts the given object to the end of the receiving array.

- (void)**insertObject:**(id)anObject **atIndex:**(unsigned index)
  Inserts the given object to the receiving array at the index specified. All objects beyond the index are shifted down one slot to make room.

- (void)**removeObjectAtIndex:**(unsigned index)
  Removes the object from the receiving array located at the index and shifts all of the objects beyond the index up one slot to fill the gap.

- (void)**removeObject:**(id)anObject
  Removes all occurrences of an object in the receiving array. The gaps left by the objects are removed by shifting the remaining objects.

The following steps will explore these methods:

1. In Project Builder, create a new Foundation Tool (File → New Project → Tool → Foundation Tool) named "mutablearrays", and save it in your *~/LearningCocoa* folder.

2. Open the *main.m* file, located in the "Source" group, and modify it to match the code shown in Example 4-4.

Example 4-4. Working with mutable arrays

```
int main (int argc, const char * argv[]) {
    NSAutoreleasePool * pool = [[NSAutoreleasePool alloc] init];

    NSMutableArray * array = [[NSMutableArray alloc] init];          // a
    [array addObject:@"sheryl crow"];                               // b
    [array addObject:@"just wants to have fun"];                    // c
    printf("%s\n", [[array description] UTF8String]);              // d

    [array release];                                                // e
```

Example 4-4. Working with mutable arrays (continued)

```
    [pool release];
    return 0;
}
```

The code we added in Example 4-4 performs the following tasks:

   a. Creates a new mutable array

   b. Adds an object to the array

   c. Adds another object to the array

   d. Prints the array

   e. Releases the array, since we created it using the alloc method

3. Build and run (⌘-R) the application. You should see the following output in the console:

```
("sheryl crow", "just wants to have fun")
```

Exploring NSMutableArray with the debugger

We'll further explore the NSMutableArray class using the debugger:

1. Set a breakpoint before the line of code that releases the array (line 10).

2. Build and debug (⌘-Y) the application. Execution will start and then pause at the breakpoint.

3. Click on the Console tab to open up the debugger console.

4. First, we insert an object into the array after the first object. Then we'll print it out to see the modified array. Type in the following:

```
(gdb) call (void) [array insertObject:@"santa monica" atIndex:1]
(gdb) print-object array
```

The following output should appear.

```
<NSCFArray 0x94be0>(
sheryl crow,
santa monica,
just wants to have fun
)
```

5. Now remove one of the objects:

```
(gdb) call (void) [array removeObject:@"just wants to have fun"]
(gdb) print-object array
```

The following will be output:

```
<NSCFArray 0x94be0>(
sheryl crow,
santa monica
)
```

6. Quit the debugger, and close the project.

Arrays and the Address Book

As a quick example of how to use arrays in a situation that isn't so contrived, we will use an API introduced in Mac OS X 10.2—the Address Book API. The Address Book serves as a central contact database that can be used by all applications on the system. The hope is that you won't need a separate contact database for your mailer, for your fax software, etc. Already, the applications that ship with Mac OS X, such as Mail and iChat, utilize the Address Book. The Address Book application is shown in Figure 4-4.

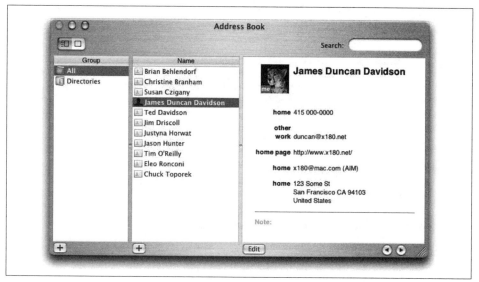

Figure 4-4. The Address Book

Use the following steps to guide you in this exploration:

1. Launch the Address Book application (it is installed in your Dock by default; you can find it in the */Applications* folder otherwise), and make sure that you have some contacts defined.

2. In Project Builder, create a new Foundation Tool (File → New Project → Tool → Foundation Tool) named "addresses", and save it to your *~/LearningCocoa* folder.

3. Add the Address Book framework to the project by selecting the Project → Add Frameworks menu item. A dialog box will open, asking you to select the framework to add. It should open up to the */System/Library/Frameworks* folder. If not, navigate to that folder, and select the *AddressBook.framework* folder to add to the project. After you click the Add button, a sheet will appear to control how the framework should be added. The settings shown will be fine, and all you need to do is click the Add button again.

This step ensures that Project Builder links against the AddressBook framework, as well as the Foundation framework, when it builds our application.

4. Open the *main.m* file, and modify it to match the following code:

```
#import <Foundation/Foundation.h>
#import <AddressBook/AddressBook.h>                              // a

int main (int argc, const char * argv[]) {
    NSAutoreleasePool * pool = [[NSAutoreleasePool alloc] init];

    ABAddressBook * book = [ABAddressBook sharedAddressBook];    // b
    NSArray * people = [book people];                            // c

    int count = [people count];
    int i;
    for (i = 0; i < count; i++) {
        ABPerson * person = [people objectAtIndex:i];            // d
        NSString * firstName = [person valueForProperty:@"First"]; // e
        NSString * lastName = [person valueForProperty:@"Last"];   // f
        printf("%s %s\n",
                [lastName UTF8String],
                [firstName UTF8String]);                         // g
    }

    [pool release];
    return 0;
}
```

The code we added performs the following tasks:

a. Imports the AddressBook API set. Without this line, the compiler cannot compile the *main.m* file, because it won't be able to find the definitions for the Address Book classes.

b. Obtains the Address Book for the logged-in user.

c. Obtains an array containing all of the people in the Address Book.

d. Loops through the people to obtain an ABPerson object. The ABPerson class provides the methods to work with the various attributes that a person record has in the Address Book database.

e. Gets the first name of the person.

f. Gets the last name of the person.

g. Prints the name of the person out to the console.

For more information about the various classes in the AddressBook framework, see the files in */Developer/Documentation/Additional-Technologies/AddressBook*.

5. Build and run (⌘-R) the application. You should see a list of your contacts output in the console. Here's a sample from our run of the application, using the contacts pictured in Figure 4-4:

```
Davidson James Duncan
Hunter Jason
Ronconi Eleo
Horwat Justyna
Driscoll Jim
Davidson Ted
Branham Christine
Behlendorf Brian
O'Reilly Tim
Toporek Chuck
Czigany Susan
```

We haven't gone into great detail on the use of the AddressBook, but just a little knowledge on arrays has already let you work with this important user data. By the time you're done with this book, just think how dangerous you will be! But no matter how dangerous you get, you should remember to use the Address Book API when you create an application that needs to keep track of contacts. Also, you'll be able to build some pretty neat apps using this data. For example, I'm considering building an application that automatically prints Christmas cards to send to all the contacts that I consider to be friends.

Sets

Sets—implemented by the NSSet and NSMutableSet classes—are an unordered collection of objects in which each object can appear only once. A set can be used instead of an array when the order of elements in the collection is not important, but when testing to see if an object is part of the set (usually referred to as "testing for membership"), speed is important. Testing to see if an object is a member of a set is faster than testing against an array.

Dictionaries

Dictionaries—implemented in the NSDictionary class—store and retrieve objects using *key-value* pairs. Each key-value pair in a dictionary is called an *entry*. The keys in a dictionary form a set; a key can be used only once in a dictionary. Although the key is usually a string (an NSString object), most objects can be used as keys.* To enable the retrieval of a value at a later time, the key of the key-value pair should be immutable or treated as immutable. If the key changes after being used to put a value

---

* The object used as a key must respond to the isEqual: message and conform to the NSCopying protocol. Since we have not covered protocols yet, the rule of thumb is that any Cocoa object provided in the Foundation framework can be used as a key. Other objects may not work.

in the dictionary, the value might not be retrievable. The NSDictionary class provides the following methods to work with the contents of an array:

- (unsigned)**count**

    Returns the number of objects currently in the dictionary

- (id)**objectForKey:**(id)aKey

    Returns the object that is indexed using the given key in the dictionary

- (NSArray *)**allKeys**

    Returns an array containing all of the keys in the dictionary

To practice working with dictionaries:

1. In Project Builder, create a new Foundation Tool (File → New Project → Tool → Foundation Tool) named "dictionaries", and save it in your ~/*LearningCocoa* folder.

2. Open the *main.m* file, located in the "Source" group, and modify it to match the code shown in Example 4-5.

Example 4-5. Working with dictionaries

```
int main (int argc, const char * argv[]) {
    NSAutoreleasePool * pool = [[NSAutoreleasePool alloc] init];

    NSArray * keys =
        [@"one two three four five" componentsSeparatedByString:@" "];        // a
    NSArray * values =
        [@"alpha bravo charlie delta echo" componentsSeparatedByString:@" "]; // b

    NSDictionary * dict = [[NSDictionary alloc] initWithObjects:values
                                              forKeys:keys];                  // c

    printf("%s\n", [[dict description] UTF8String]);                          // d

    [pool release];
    return 0;
}
```

The code we added in Example 4-5 performs the following tasks:

    a. Creates a new array based on a space-delimited string. This set of objects will serve as the keys for the dictionary.

    b. Creates a new array that will serve as the values of the dictionary.

    c. Creates a new dictionary with our keys and values.

    d. Prints the dictionary, so it can be examined.

3. Build and run (⌘-R) the application. You should see output similar to the following appear in the console:

```
{five = echo; four = delta; one = alpha; three = charlie; two = bravo; }
```

This is a representation of the structure of the dictionary. Note that the elements are not stored in any particular order. Remember that the keys form a set in which uniqueness, not order, is critical.

We'll explore this example further using the debugger.

4. Set a breakpoint after the `printf` statement. If you typed in the code exactly as listed earlier, the breakpoint will be on line 15.

5. Build and debug (⌘-Y) the application, open the debugger console, and type the following:

```
(gdb) print (int) [dict count]
```

The following will be output:

```
$1 = 5
```

This tells us that there are five elements in the collection.

6. Type the following:

```
(gdb) print-object [dict objectForKey:@"three"]
```

The following will be output:

```
charlie
```

7. Type the following:

```
(gdb) print-object [dict allKeys]
```

The following will be output:

```
<NSCFArray 0x97800>(
two,
four,
three,
one,
five
)
```

8. Quit the debugger, and close the project.

The strengths of the dictionary classes will become apparent when we discuss how they can hold and organize data that can be labeled, such as values extracted from text fields in a user interface. We'll show this in action in Chapter 9, when we show how you can work with dictionaries to drive tables in user interfaces.

Mutable Dictionaries

The `NSMutableDictionary` class provides the functionality needed to manage a modifiable dictionary. This class extends the `NSDictionary` class by adding insertion and deletion operations. These operations include the following methods:

- (void)**setObject:**(id)anObject **forKey:**(id)aKey
  Adds an entry to the dictionary, consisting of the given key-value pair. If the key already exists in the dictionary, the previous object associated with that key is removed from the dictionary and replaced with the new object.

- (void)removeObjectForKey:**(id)aKey**
    Removes the key and its associated value from the dictionary.

Working with Numbers

Collections can hold only objects; they cannot hold C-based primitive types such as int, float, and long. However, there will be many cases where you will want to store primitive types in your collections. To allow these types to be manipulated as objects, Cocoa provides the NSNumber class. This class can wrap any C numeric type and defines a group of methods to set and access the value. In addition, it defines a compare: method, allowing two numbers to be compared with each other.

Storing Collections as Files

One of the nicer things about Cocoa's collection classes is that they support the writing and reading of collection data to and from files called *property lists*, or *plist* files. This lets you store your data easily and read it later. In fact, Mac OS X uses property lists extensively to store all kinds of data, such as user preferences, application settings, and system-configuration data. In upcoming chapters, we'll be working with user preferences (also known as *defaults*) and we will see how Mac OS X uses plists in application bundles.

The methods to support this functionality are relatively simple. For the array and dictionary classes, these methods are as follows:

- (id)**initWithContentsOfFile:**(NSString *)aPath
    Initializes a newly allocated array or dictionary with the contents of the file specified by the path argument

- (BOOL)**writeToFile:**(NSString *)path **atomically:**(BOOL)flag
    Writes the contents of an array or dictionary to the file specified by the path argument

To practice working with collections and files do as follos:

1. In Project Builder, create a new Foundation Tool (File → New Project → Tool → Foundation Tool) named "collectionfiles", and save it in your *~/LearningCocoa* folder.

2. Open the *main.m* file, and modify it to match Example 4-6.

   Example 4-6. Working with property lists

   ```
   #import <Foundation/Foundation.h>

   int main (int argc, const char * argv[]) {
       NSAutoreleasePool * pool = [[NSAutoreleasePool alloc] init];
   ```

Example 4-6. Working with property lists (continued)

```
    NSMutableArray * array = [[NSMutableArray alloc] init];          // a
    [array addObject:@"San Francisco"];                             // b
    [array addObject:@"Houston"];
    [array addObject:@"Tulsa"];
    [array addObject:@"Juneau"];
    [array addObject:@"Pheonix"];

    [array writeToFile:@"cities.plist" atomically:YES];             // c

    NSString * plist =
        [NSString stringWithContentsOfFile:@"cities.plist"];       // d
    printf("%s\n", [plist UTF8String]);                            // e

    [array release];                                               // f

    [pool release];
    return 0;
}
```

The code we added inExample 4-6 does the following things:

a. Creates a new mutable array.

b. Adds a series of strings to the mutable array.

c. Writes the array to a file named *cities.plist*. Since this is not an absolute path, it will be written in the working directory of application. In our case, this file will be written in *~/LearningCocoa/collectionfiles/build/cities.plist*.

d. Creates a new string based on the contents of the file that we just wrote. Once again, we use a relative path.

e. Prints the contents of the file to the console.

f. Returns the array object that we created.

3. Build and run (⌘-R) the application. You should see output similar to the following appear in the console:

```
<?xml version="1.0" encoding="UTF-8"?>
<!DOCTYPE plist PUBLIC "-//Apple Computer//DTD PLIST 1.0//EN" "http://www.apple.
com/DTDs/PropertyList-1.0.dtd">
<plist version="1.0">
<array>
    <string>San Francisco</string>
    <string>Houston</string>
    <string>Tulsa</string>
    <string>Juneau</string>
    <string>Pheonix</string>
</array>
</plist>
```

This is an XML representation of the array. This data can be edited with a text editor, transmitted across the Internet, or turned back into a collection of strings in another Cocoa program.

Property Lists

Mac OS X uses *property lists*, frequently referred to as *plists*, to organize data into a form that is meaningfully structured, easily transportable, and storable. Property list files are saved in an XML format for easy editing and transportability.

You can see many examples of *plist* files in your *~/Library/Preferences* folder. Property lists organize data into named values and lists of values using several types directly represented as the following Cocoa objects: NSString, NSNumber, Boolean, NSDate, NSData, NSArray, and NSDictionary. They make it easy for applications to store preference data and, the case of the *Info.plist* file in an application bundle, communicate information about an application to the system. To take a look at how applications can use plists to store configuration information, look at the *plist* file for the menu bar clock.

1. Open the *~/Library/Preferences* folder, and locate the *com.apple. MenuBarClock.plist* file.

2. Double-click on the file to open it with the Property List Editor application (located in the */Developer/Applications* folder).

The Property List Editor application can be used to browse the tree of properties. You can also hit the Dump button to see the XML representation of the property list. Be careful not to save any edits you make, as you can severely confuse an application by making the wrong changes here.

Memory Management

Memory management is an important subject in programming. Quite a few of the problems encountered by novice application developers are caused by poor memory management. When an object is created and passed around among various "consumer" objects in an application, which object is responsible for disposing of it and when? If an object is not deallocated when it is no longer needed, memory leaks. If the object is deallocated too soon, problems may occur in other objects that assume its existence, and the application will most likely crash.

The Foundation framework defines a mechanism and a policy that ensures that objects are deallocated only when they are no longer needed. We have hinted at it before, but now it is time to explain things.

The policy is quite simple: you are responsible for disposing of all objects that you own. You own objects that you create, either by allocating or copying them. You also own (or share ownership in) objects that you retain. The flip side of this rule is that you should never release an object that you have not retained or created; doing so will free the object prematurely, resulting in bugs that are hard to track down, even though the fix is simple.

Object Initialization and Deallocation

As discussed in Chapter 3, an object is usually created using the alloc method and is initialized using the init method (or a variant of the init method). When an array's init method is invoked, the method initializes the array's instance variables to default values and completes other startup tasks. For example:

```
NSArray * array = [[NSArray alloc] init];
```

When done with an object that you created, you send the release message to the object. If no other objects have registered an interest in the object, it will be deallocated and removed from memory.

When an object is deallocated, the dealloc method is invoked, giving the object an opportunity to release objects it has created, free allocated memory, and so on. We saw this in action in Chapter 3, when we added the dealloc method to the Song class.

Reference Counting

To allow multiple objects to register interest in another object and yet have this object removed from memory when no other objects are interested in it, each object in Cocoa has an associated reference count. When you allocate or copy an object, its reference count is automatically set to 1. This indicates that the object is in use in one place. When you pass the object to other objects, wanting to make sure the object stays around for their use, they can use the retain method to increment the reference counter.

To visualize this, imagine that we have an object being held in three different arrays, as shown in Figure 4-5. Each array retains the object to make sure that it remains available for its use. Therefore, the object has a reference count of 3.

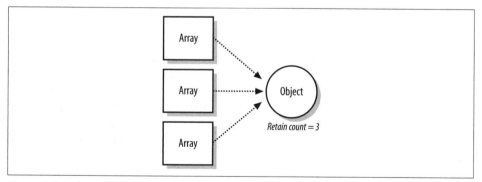

Figure 4-5. Reference counting

Whenever you are done with an object, you send a release message to decrement the reference count. When the reference count reaches 0, the release method will invoke the object's dealloc method that destroys the object. Figure 4-6 shows an object being removed progressively from a set of arrays. When it is no longer needed, its retain count is set to 0, and the object is deallocated.

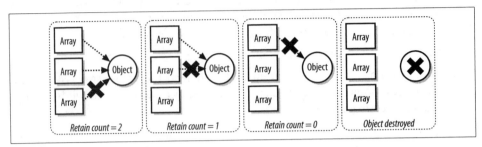

Figure 4-6. Releasing of an object

Autorelease Pools

According to the policy of disposing of all objects you create, if the owner of an object must release the object within its programmatic scope, how can the owner give that object to other objects? Or, said another way, how do you release an object you would like to return to the caller of a method? Once you return from a method, there's no way to go back and release the object.

The answer is provided by the autorelease method built into the NSObject class, in conjunction with the functionality of the NSAutoReleasePool class. The autorelease method marks the receiver for later release by an NSAutoreleasePool. This enables an object to live beyond the scope of the owning object so that other objects can use it. This mechanism explains why you have seen dozens of code examples that contain the following lines:

```
NSAutoreleasePool * pool = [[NSAutoreleasePool alloc] init];
...code...
[pool release];
```

Each application puts in place at least one autorelease pool (for each thread of control that is running in the application) and can have many more. You put an object in the pool by sending the object an autorelease message. In the case of an application's event cycle, when code finishes executing and control returns to the application object, the application object sends a release message to the autorelease pool, and the pool sends a release message to each object it contains. Any object that reaches a reference count of 0 automatically deallocates itself.

When an object is used solely within the scope of a method that creates it, you can deallocate it immediately by sending it a release message. Otherwise, use the autorelease message for all objects you create and hand off to other objects so that they can choose whether to retain them.

You shouldn't release objects that you receive from other objects, unless you have first retained them for some reason. Doing so will cause their reference count to reach 0 prematurely, and the system will destroy the object, thinking that no other object depends on it. When objects that do depend on the destroyed object try to access it, the application will most likely crash. These kinds of bugs can be hard to track down, even though their cause and fix are simple.

You can assume that a received object remains valid within the method in which it was received and will remain valid for the event loop that is handling it. If you want to keep it as an instance variable, you should send it a retain message and then autorelease it when you are done using it.

Retaining Objects in Accessor Methods

One of the primary places where you will need to be aware of memory management is in the accessor methods of your classes. At first glance, it is obvious that you will want to release an old object reference and retain the new one. However, because code that calls a class's setter method might call it multiple times with the same object as an argument, the order in which you release and retain the object references is important.

As a rule, you want to retain the new object before releasing the old one. This ensures that everything works as anticipated, even if the new and old objects are the same. If you reverse these steps, and if the new and old objects are actually the same, the object might be removed permanently from memory before being retained.

Here is the *retain, then release* rule expressed in code:

```
- (void)setProperty:(id)newProperty
{
    [newProperty retain];
    [property release];
    property = newProperty;
}
```

There are other ways to ensure connections in setter methods, many of which are valid and appropriate for certain situations. However, this is the simplest possible pattern we can give that will always work. We will use this pattern throughout the book.

Rules of Thumb

The important things to remember about memory management in Cocoa distill down to these rules of thumb:

1. Objects created by alloc or copy have a retain count of 1.

2. Assume that objects obtained by any other method have a retain count of 1 and reside in the autorelease pool. If you want to keep it beyond the current scope of execution, then you must retain it.

3. When you add an object to a collection, it is retained. When you remove an object from a collection, it is released. Releasing a collection object (such as an NSArray) releases all objects stored in it as well.

4. Make sure that there are as many `release` or `autorelease` messages sent to objects as there are `alloc`, `copy`, `mutableCopy`, or `retain` messages sent. In other words, make sure that the code you write is balanced.

5. Retain, then release objects in setter methods.

6. NSString objects created using the @"..." construct are effectively constants in the program. Sending retain or release messages to them has no effect. This explains why we haven't been releasing the strings created with the @"..." construct.

If you apply these rules of thumb consistently and keep the retain counts of your objects balanced, you can manage memory in your applications effectively.

Exercises

1. Investigate the `lowercase` and `uppercase` methods of NSString using the debugger.

2. Write a Foundation Tool command-line application that prints the contents of any filename given to it.

3. Read the documentation on your hard drive about the NSArray, NSSet, and NSDictionary classes.

4. Modify the arrays example application so that it saves the contents of the array to a file.

5. Write an example that saves a dictionary to disk. Don't just use string objects in the array, but use some other objects like dictionaries and numbers so that you can see how Cocoa saves different types out to XML property lists.

6. Examine the code we've written so far with an eye for how memory is managed. (A bug regarding memory management has been left in one of the examples.)

PART II

Single-Window Applications

This part of the book covers the basic building blocks of any Cocoa application that displays a single GUI window to the user. This section uses a series of examples to illustrate the concepts presented. The techniques and concepts you learn in each chapter will lay the foundation for the next chapter.

Chapters in this part of the book include:

Chapter 5, *Graphical User Interfaces*
Chapter 6, *Windows, Views, and Controls*
Chapter 7, *Custom Views*
Chapter 8, *Event Handling*
Chapter 9, *Models and Data Functionality*

Graphical User Interfaces

Now that we've covered the Foundation, we're going to take a step up and start working with the AppKit framework to create GUI-based applications. In this chapter, we'll build a single-window application from beginning to end, letting us introduce the various GUI subjects necessary to become proficient with Cocoa programming. For the first time, you'll see the complete workflow typical of Cocoa application development, composed of the following steps:

1. Design the application.
2. Create the project using Project Builder.
3. Create the interface using Interface Builder.
4. Define the classes using Interface Builder.
5. Connect the Model, View, and Controller objects using Interface Builder.
6. Implement the classes using Project Builder.
7. Build and run the project using Project Builder.

The application we'll build in this chapter is a currency converter—a simple utility that converts a dollar amount to an amount in some other currency. This example has been one of the mainstay examples of NeXTSTEP/OpenStep/Cocoa programming; it's been around almost long enough to reach "Hello World" status. Although it is a simple application, it consolidates quite a few of the concepts and techniques needed to get started with writing Cocoa GUI applications.

After working through this first complete GUI application, we'll spend the rest of this section of the book exploring in-depth the topics introduced in this chapter.

Graphical User Interfaces in Cocoa

Graphical user interfaces in Cocoa are built on the following four concepts:

- Windows
- Nib files

- Outlets
- Actions

Windows

A *window* in Cocoa looks similar to windows in other user environments, such as Microsoft Windows or earlier versions of the Mac OS. A window can be moved around the screen and stacked on top of other windows like pieces of paper. A typical Cocoa window, shown in Figure 5-1, has a titlebar, content area, and several control objects.

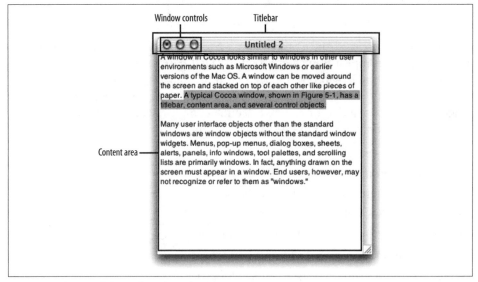

Figure 5-1. A typical Cocoa-based window

Many user-interface objects other than the standard windows are window objects without the standard window widgets. These include menus, pop-up menus, dialog boxes, sheets, alerts, panels, info windows, tool tips, tool palettes, and scrolling lists. In fact, anything drawn on the screen must appear in a window. End users, however, may not recognize or refer to them as "windows."

Nib Files

A *nib file* is an archive of object instances generated by Interface Builder. Unlike the product of many user interface–building systems, a nib file is not generated code. It is a set of true objects that have been encoded specially and stored on disk. The objects in the nib file are created and manipulated using Interface Builder's graphical tools.

Nib files typically package a group of related user-interface objects and supporting resources, along with information about how the objects are related—both to one another and to other objects in your application. Nib files hold all of the objects they describe by specially archiving, or freeze-drying, so that they can be reconstituted in a running application and then used again.

Every application with a graphical user interface has at least one nib file that is loaded automatically when the application is launched. The main nib file typically contains the application menu. Auxiliary nib files contain the application windows, as well as their associated user-interface objects. For example, an image-manipulation program such as Photoshop might have auxiliary nib files for the various palettes and controls that let you work with an image.

It can be useful to think of the objects that compose a user interface, and are contained within a nib file, as forming a hierarchy. Figure 5-2 shows the ownership hierarchy of nib-based objects for Figure 5-1. At the top of the nib file's hierarchy of archived objects is the *file's owner* object, a proxy object pointing to the actual object that owns, or controls, the nib file—typically the object that loaded the nib file from disk.

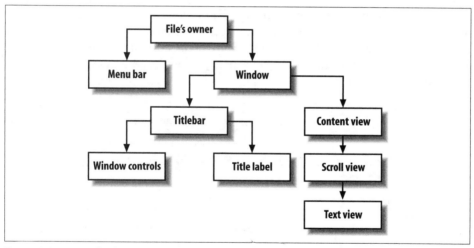

Figure 5-2. Ownership hierarchy of nib-based objects for Figure 5-1

Outlets

An *outlet* is a special-instance variable, marked with the IBOutlet keyword in a class's header, that contains a reference to another object, as shown in Figure 5-3. An object can communicate with other objects in an application by sending messages to them through outlets.

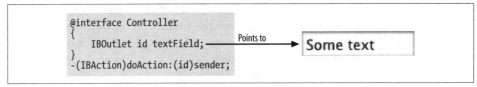

Figure 5-3. Object connected to a text field via an outlet

An outlet can reference any object in an application: user-interface objects, instances of custom classes, and even the application object itself. What distinguishes outlets from other instance variables is that Interface Builder recognizes the IBOutlet keyword and lets you manipulate the connections it defines. These connections, once defined, will be linked up for you when your application runs. Specifying these relationships between objects in Interface Builder saves you from having to write initialization code by hand. There are ways other than outlets to reference objects in an application, but outlets and Interface Builder's facility for initializing them are a great convenience.

Actions

Actions are special methods, indicated with the IBAction keyword, which are defined by a class and triggered by user-interface objects. Interface Builder recognizes action declarations in a header file, as it does with outlets. Similarly, Interface Builder allows you to connect actions that a user might take with an interface, such as pushing a button, to methods on an object. These connections are shown in Figure 5-4.

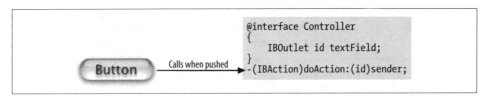

Figure 5-4. Targets and actions

An action refers both to a message sent to an object when the user clicks a button (or manipulates some other control), and to the invoked method.

Designing Applications Using MVC

Cocoa applications make use of a long-standing object-oriented paradigm called *Model-View-Controller* (MVC). As illustrated in Figure 5-5, MVC proposes three types of objects in an application—model, view, and controller:

Model
    Objects that hold data and define the logic that manipulates that data

---

View

Objects that represent something visible to the user, such as a window or a button

Controller

Objects that act as mediators between model and view objects

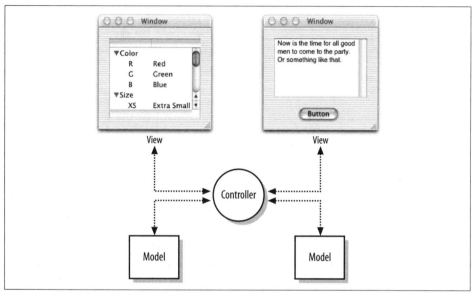

Figure 5-5. Model, view, and controller objects in an MVC design

The MVC paradigm works well for many applications, because the controller's central and mediating role frees the model objects from needing to know about the state and events of the user interface. Likewise, the view objects don't have to know about the programmatic interfaces of the model objects. Dividing the problem along these lines helps encapsulate the various objects in an application. This can also aid reuse, since the model could be used elsewhere, perhaps even on another platform.

MVC, strictly observed, is not advisable in all circumstances. Sometimes it can be advantageous to combine roles. For example, in an graphics-intensive application, such as an arcade game, you might have several view objects that merge the roles of view and model for performance reasons. In other applications, especially simple ones, you can combine the roles of controller and model; these objects join the special data structures and logic of model objects with the controller's hooks to the interface.

MVC in Currency Converter's Design

The Currency Converter application will consist of two custom objects: a Converter that will serve as our model and a Controller that will mediate between the user interface and the Converter object. We'll create the view of the application using a collection of AppKit objects, which we'll assemble using Interface Builder. The relationships between these objects are shown in Figure 5-6.

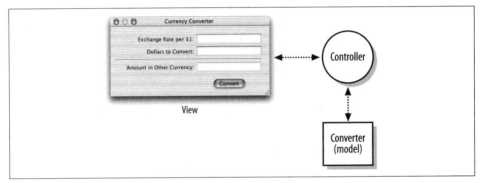

Figure 5-6. MVC in Currency Converter's design

The Controller object will assume the central role in the application. Like all controller objects, it communicates with the interface and model objects, and it handles tasks specific to the application. The Controller object gets the values that users enter into fields, passes these values to the Converter object, gets the result back from the Converter, and puts this result into a field in the interface. By insulating the Converter from the implementation-specific details of the user interface, the Converter object becomes a reusable component for other applications.

Create the Currency Converter Project

Now that we have designed the application, we can get to work on the implementation. In Project Builder, create a new Cocoa Application project (File → New Project → Application → Cocoa Application) as shown in Figure 5-7, then name the project "Currency Converter", and save it in your ~/LearningCocoa folder.

If you click on the disclosure triangle next to Other Sources in the left pane and click on main.m, you'll notice that the file looks a bit different from the Foundation projects we've worked with in the past. The main.m file contains the following code:

```
//
//  main.m
//  Currency Converter
//
//  Created by James Duncan Davidson on Fri Aug 30 2002.
//  Copyright (c) 2002 __MyCompanyName__. All rights reserved.
//

#import <Cocoa/Cocoa.h>
```

```
int main(int argc, const char *argv[])
{
    return NSApplicationMain(argc, argv);
}
```

Figure 5-7. Creating a new Cocoa Application

Notice that the import statement has changed to importing *Cocoa.h* instead of
Foundation.h. The *Cocoa.h* header contains the definitions for both the Foundation
and AppKit classes. Also notice that the main method makes a call to the
NSApplicationMain function. This function is defined by the AppKit and will start the
application, load the main nib file, and set up the event loop and autorelease pool for
that loop. Now that we have taken a look at this source file, we can let it be. You'll
very rarely, if ever, modify the *main.m* file of a Cocoa GUI application.

> Project Builder automatically generates the comments at the top of the
> source file from the Cocoa Application template. You'll probably want
> to change the __MyCompanyName__ text to the actual copyright holder
> and make sure that the copyright year is correct. See Chapter 17 for
> more details on how to finish and polish your applications.

Create the Interface

The Currency Converter's interface is actually quite simple to create. It consists of a
few text fields and a button. The process of creating it will give you an opportunity

to explore how Interface Builder works. Figure 5-8 shows a hand-drawn sketch of how we'd like the interface to look. This gives us something to go by when designing the interface in Interface Builder.

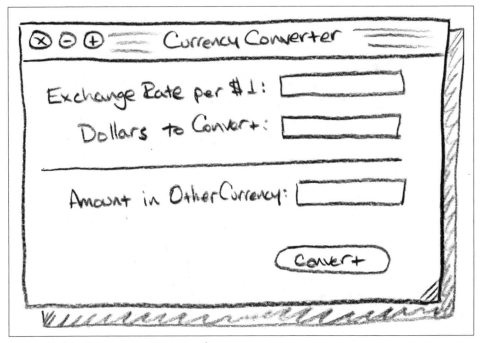

Figure 5-8. The Currency Converter interface

Open the Main Nib File

Begin by creating an application's user interface in Interface Builder.

1. In Project Builder's left pane, click on the disclosure triangle next to Resources to reveal the *MainMenu.nib* file.

2. Double-click on *MainMenu.nib* to open it in Interface Builder.

A default menu bar and window, titled Window, will appear when the nib file is opened.

Resize the Window

The window is a bit large for our purposes. You can change the size either by dragging the bottom-right corner of the window or by using the Info window, as shown in Figure 5-9. You can open this window by selecting Tools → Show Info from Interface Builder's menu (Shift-⌘-I).

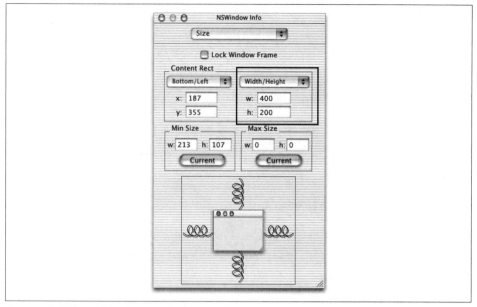

Figure 5-9. Info window showing the Size panel

When you have opened the Info window, use the following process to resize the window:

1. Select Size from the Info window's pop-up menu.

2. In the Content Rect area, select Width/Height from the right-hand pop-up menu.

3. In the text fields under the Width/Height menu, type 400 in the width (*w*) field and 200 in the height (*h*) field, as shown in Figure 5-9.

Set the Window's Title and Attributes

By default, our window has a title of Window. We want the application window to have a more meaningful title, as well as a few other attributes that we care about.

1. Select Attributes from the Info window's pop-up menu, and change the window's title to Currency Converter, as shown in Figure 5-10.

2. Verify that the Visible at launch time option is selected. This will ensure that this window is created on screen when the application is launched.

3. Deselect the Resize checkbox in the Controls area. This will prevent users from resizing the application.

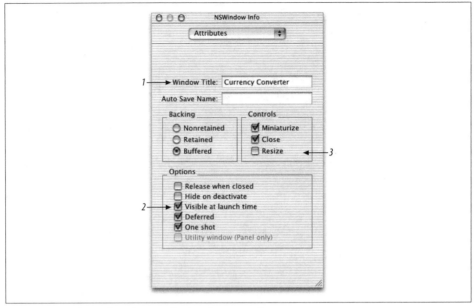

Figure 5-10. Info window showing the Attributes panel

Place the Text Fields

The Currency Converter will use text fields to accept user input and display converted values. To place a text field into the window:

1. Drag an NSTextField object from the Views palette (shown in Figure 5-11), and place it in the upper-right corner of the application window.

   When you drag the text field onto the window, Interface Builder helps you place objects according to the Aqua Human Interface Guidelines (HIG) by displaying guidelines when an object is dragged close to the proper distance from neighboring objects or the edge of the window.

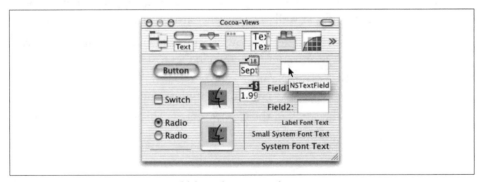

Figure 5-11. Dragging an NSTextField from the Views palette

2. Resize the text field by grabbing a handle and dragging it in the direction in which you want it to grow. In this case, drag the left handle to the left to enlarge the text field, as shown in Figure 5-12.

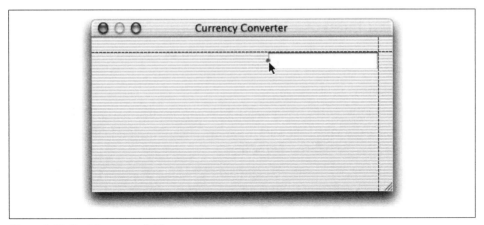

Figure 5-12. Resizing a text field

Just as you can specify the size of the application window, you can also specify exact sizes for other elements of your application. For example, if you want the text field to be 150 pixels wide, select the NSTextField object, and then select Size from the NSTextField Info window (Shift-⌘-I). In the width field (w), enter 150 as the value, and hit the Tab key to accept the value; the NSTextField object will conform to its newly defined dimensions.

Duplicating Objects

Currency Converter needs two more text fields, each the same size as the first. To place these fields, you have two options: you can drag another text field from the palette and make it the same size, or you can duplicate the first object. To create a new text field by duplication:

1. Select the text field, if it is not already selected.
2. Choose Edit → Duplicate (or use the keyboard shortcut, ⌘-D). The new text field appears slightly offset from the original field.

   Another way to duplicate a field is to click on the object, then hold down the Option and drag the object. A plus sign will appear next to the pointer to indicate that you're making a copy of the object, and the guidelines will help you move the newly duplicated object into place.

3. Reposition the new text field under the first text field. You'll notice that the guides will appear once again to help you move the second text field into place.

4. To make the third text field, make another duplicate. Notice that Interface Builder remembers the offset from the previous Duplicate command and automatically uses that offset to create and place the third text field.

Change the Attributes of a Text Field

Since the third text field will display the results of the computation, it should not be editable. To change its attributes:

1. Select the third text field.

2. Choose Attributes from the Info window's pop-up menu, as shown in Figure 5-13.

3. In the Options section of the Info window, uncheck the Editable attribute so users cannot alter the contents of the field.

4. Make sure that the Selectable attribute is on so that users can copy and paste the contents of this field to other applications.

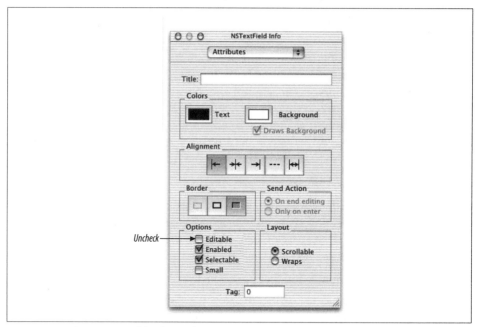

Figure 5-13. The NSTextField Info window

Add Text Labels

Next we need to add some labels to the text fields, so the user will know why the fields are there.

1. Using Figure 5-14 as a guide, drag a System Font Text object from the Views palette onto the Currency Converter window.

2. Right-align the text using the Info window.

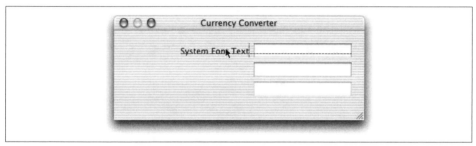

Figure 5-14. Aligning a text field with its label

3. Duplicate the text label twice, and then edit the text for all three labels, as shown in Figure 5-15. To edit a text label, double-click on the current label (System Font Text) to highlight it, then type in the new label. After entering the new label, hit the Tab key to accept the new label.

> Hitting the Return key will not accept the new label; instead, it will insert a carriage return.

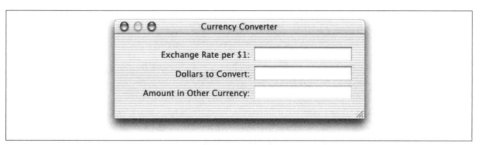

Figure 5-15. Currency Converter's text fields and labels

As you type in the new labels, you'll notice that the text fields aren't wide enough to hold the text shown in Figure 5-15. To correct this problem, resize the text fields by grabbing the middle-left field holder and dragging the edge of the text field to the left until all of the text appears.

Add a Button to the Interface

The last functional part of the user interface that we need to add is the Convert button. It needs to be set up so that it can be invoked either by clicking it or by pressing Return when the application has the user's focus.

1. Drag a button object from the Views palette, and place it in the lower-right portion of the window.

2. Double-click the title of the button to select its label, and change the title to Convert.

3. With the button selected, choose Attributes in the Info window, and then choose Return from the pop-up menu labeled Equiv, as shown in Figure 5-16. This allows the button to respond to the Return key, as well as to mouse clicks.

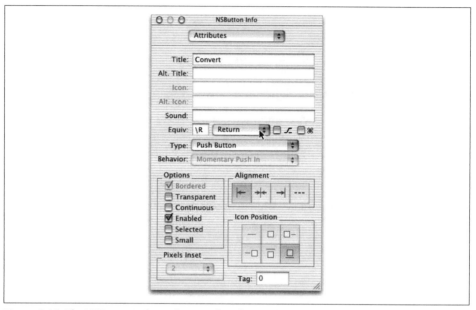

Figure 5-16. The NSButton Info window, used to change the Convert button's attributes, so it will respond to a mouse-click or to the Return key

4. Align the button under the text fields. To center the button under the text fields, you can pop up a set of measurement guides that tell you the distance from an object to any of its neighboring objects. With the button selected, hold down the Option key and point to an object whose distance from the button you want to see, as shown in Figure 5-17. With the Option key still down, use the arrow keys to nudge the button to the exact center of the text fields.

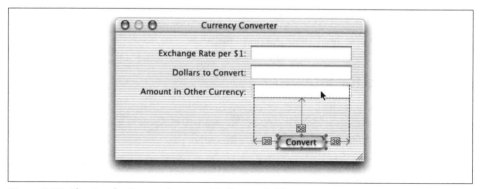

Figure 5-17. Aligning the Convert button with the text fields

Adding a Decorative Line

Lines can separate elements to help the user make sense of the objects in the user interface. We'll add a line between the editable fields and the result field.

1. Move the third text field and label down a bit in the user interface.

2. Drag a horizontal line from the Views palette onto the interface, and use the alignment guides to place it right under the dollars text field.

3. Use the selection handles on the line to extend it to each side of the interface.

4. Move the result text field and label back up into position using the guides, then move the Convert button up into place.

5. Resize the window using the guides to give you the proper distance from the text fields on the right and the Convert button on the bottom.

At this point, Currency Converter's application window should look like Figure 5-18.

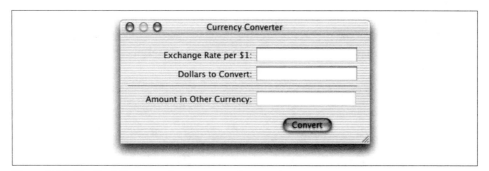

Figure 5-18. The final Currency Converter interface

Setting the Initial First Responder and Enabling Tabbing

The final step in composing Currency Converter's interface has little to do with appearance and everything to do with behavior. When users launch the application, they should immediately be able to enter information in the interface and tab between the text fields.

The first place a user's input should go when they launch the application is in the first text field. To ensure that this happens, specify the first text field as the application window's *initial first responder*—the object in the window that will be first in line to accept events from the keyboard. To do this:

1. In the Instances pane of nib file window, click on the Window instance and Control-drag a connection to the first text field in Currency Converter's window.

2. Select the `initialFirstResponder` outlet in the Info window, as shown in Figure 5-19, and click the Connect button.

Aqua Layout and Object Alignment

Aligning Aqua interface widgets could be difficult, because the objects have shadows, and UI guideline metrics don't typically take the shadows into account. To help alleviate this problem, Interface Builder uses visual guides and layout rectangles to aid with object alignment. Interface Builder provides the guides to indicate when your objects line up or are in the correct location.

In Cocoa, all drawing is done within the bounds of an object's frame. Because interface objects have shadows, they don't visually align correctly if you align the edges of the frames. For example, the Aqua UI guidelines say that a push button should be 20 pixels tall, but you actually need a frame height of 32 pixels for both the button and its shadow. The layout rectangle is what you must align, not the button itself.

You can view the layout rectangles of objects in Interface Builder by using Layout → Show Layout Rectangles (⌘-L). Also, Interface Builder's Size Inspector has a pop-up to toggle between the frame and layout rectangle, so you can set values by hand when appropriate.

Look in the Alignment and Guides submenus of the Layout menu for various alignment commands and tools. You can also use the alignment tool (Tools → Alignment) to provide a floating window with buttons that perform various types of alignment functions.

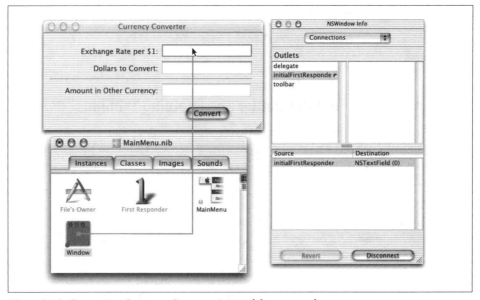

Figure 5-19. Connecting Currency Converter's initial first responder

Next, we want to ensure that when the user presses the Tab key, the focus moves to another text field. To do this:

1. Select the first text field, and Control-drag a connection line from it to the second text field, as shown in Figure 5-20.

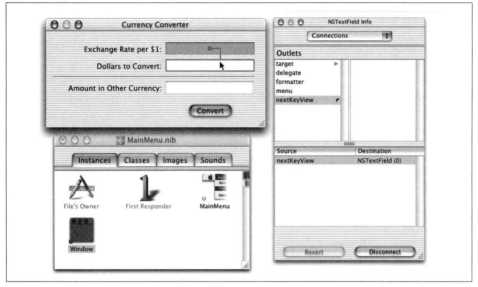

Figure 5-20. Connecting text fields for inter-field tabbing

2. Select the nextKeyView outlet in the Info window, and click the Connect button.
3. Repeat the previous two steps, but connect the second field to the first. This will make it so you can tab from the second field back up to the first text field.

Test the Interface

The Currency Converter interface is now complete. Interface Builder lets you test the interface without having to write any code.

1. Choose File → Save All to save your work.
2. Choose File → Test Interface (⌘-R) to launch the interface in a mode where you can test it.
3. Try various operations in the interface, such as tabbing, cutting, and pasting between text fields.
4. When finished, choose Quit New Application (⌘-Q) from the Interface Builder application menu to exit the text mode.

Notice that the screen position of the Currency Converter window in Interface Builder is used as the initial position for the window when the application is launched. Place the window near the top-left corner of the screen so that it will be a convenient (and traditional) initial location.

Define the Classes

We'll define the two classes needed for our application here in Interface Builder: a controller class and a model class. If you recall, the controller class controls the interaction between the model and view objects, while the model object holds data and defines the logic that manipulates that data.

Create the Controller Class

The controller class, Controller, doesn't need to inherit any special functionality from other classes, so it will be a subclass of NSObject. To define it:

1. Click the Classes tab of the *MainMenu.nib* window, as shown in Figure 5-21.

2. Select NSObject from the list of classes.

3. Press Return to create a new subclass of NSObject, and rename it Controller.

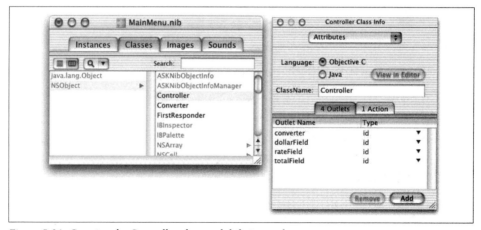

Figure 5-21. Creating the Controller class and defining outlets

Define outlets for the controller

The Controller object needs access to the text fields of the interface, so you must create *outlets* for them. Controller will also need to communicate with the Converter class (yet to be defined) and thus requires a fourth outlet for that purpose.

1. Select the Controller class in the Classes window, as shown in Figure 5-21.

2. Select the Attributes menu item in the Info window.

3. Add an outlet named `rateField` by clicking the Add button, entering the name, and pressing Return.

4. Create three more outlets, named `dollarField`, `totalField`, and `converter`, as detailed in step 3.

Define actions for the controller

The `Controller` class needs only one action method to respond to user-interface events. When the user clicks the Convert button (or uses the Return key, which we defined as an equivalent), we want a `convert:` message sent to an instance of the `Controller`.

1. Click on the Action tab in the Info window.

2. Add an action named "convert:". Interface Builder will add the ":" for you if you don't.

Define the Model Class

Like the `Controller` class, the `Converter` class—our model in MVC speak—doesn't need to inherit any special functionality, so you can make it a subclass of `NSObject`. Because instances of this class won't communicate directly with the interface, there's no need for outlets or actions.

1. In the Classes window, create the `Converter` object, and make it a subclass of NSObject by clicking on NSObject, hitting Return, and entering `Converter` as the subclass's name.

2. Save `MainMenu.nib`. As with any program, it's always a good idea to hit ⌘-S every now and then, so you won't lose your work.

Connect the Model, Controller, and View

The last task that remains in Interface Builder is to hook up the various parts of our application so that each part can talk to the others.

Generate an Instance of the Controller and Model

When the application is first launched and the nib file is loaded, we want to create an instance of both our controller and model classes. To do this:

1. Select `Controller` in the Classes tab of the nib file window.

2. Choose Instantiate from the Classes menu. The instance will appear in the Instances view of the MainMenu.nib window, as shown in Figure 5-22.

3. Repeat the process for the `Converter` class.

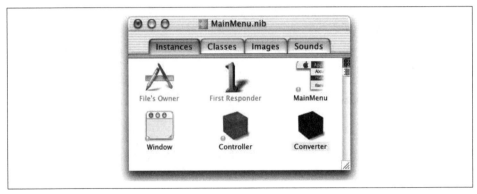

Figure 5-22. The Converter and Controller instances

Connect the Controller to the Interface

Now you can connect the Controller instance object to the user interface. By connecting it to specific objects in the interface, you initialize its outlets. Controller will use these outlets to get and set values in the interface.

1. In the Instances display of the nib file window, Control-drag a connection line from the Controller instance to the first text field, as shown in Figure 5-23.

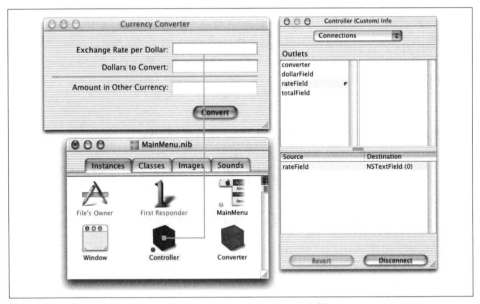

Figure 5-23. Connecting the Controller instance to the rate text field

2. Interface Builder will bring up the Connections display of the Info window. Select the action that corresponds to the first field, rateField.

3. Click the Connect button.

4. Following the same steps, connect the `Controller`'s `dollarField` and `totalField` outlets to the appropriate text fields.

To tell the controller that it is time to perform an action, we need to hook up the Convert button to the `Controller`.

1. Control-drag a connection from the Convert button to the `Controller` instance in the nib file window. Instead of dragging from the controller object to an interface object, we are dragging a connection from a user-interface object to the controller.

2. In the Connections Info window, make sure that the target is selected in the Outlets column, as shown in Figure 5-24.

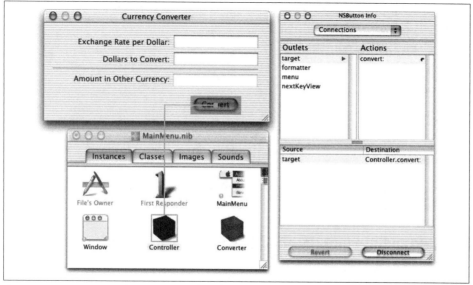

Figure 5-24. Connecting the Convert button to the Controller

3. Select convert: in the Actions column.

4. Click the Connect button.

Connect the Model to the Controller

The last connection is to hook up the instance of our `Converter` model class to the `Controller`.

1. In the Instances view of the nib file window, Control-drag the `Controller` instance to the `Converter` instance.

2. Connect the `Converter` instance to the converter outlet.

Implement the Classes

Now we come to the part of this exercise where we take all of that work done in Interface Builder, generate the source files for our classes, and finish the class implementations in Project Builder.

Generate the Source Files

To generate the source files, follow these steps:

1. Go to the Classes display of the nib file window.
2. Select the Controller class.
3. Choose Create Files from the Classes menu.
4. Verify that the checkboxes in the Create column next to the *.h* and *.m* files are selected.
5. Click the Choose button.
6. Repeat Steps 1–5 for the Converter class.
7. Save the nib file.

 You can also create the files for a class by Control-clicking (or right-clicking if you have a two-button mouse) on the class name in the Classes menu and selecting the "Create files for..." menu item.

Now, we leave Interface Builder for this application. You'll complete the application using Project Builder.

Examine an Interface (Header) File in Project Builder

When Interface Builder adds the header and source files to the Currency Converter project, it tries to put them in the same group folder as other source files in the same disk folder. Since the newly created files are class implementations, move them to the Classes group if Interface Builder did not do so automatically.

1. Click Project Builder's main window to activate it.
2. Select the Controller and Converter files in the Groups & Files list, and drag them into the Classes group, as shown in Figure 5-25.

Look at the *Controller.h* file that Interface Builder generated. Notice that in addition to being declared of type id, our variables have an IBOutlet declaration. This is a macro that, in the compiler, doesn't evaluate anything. It is used as a hint to Interface Builder's parser, telling it that the variable is an outlet. You will also notice that the convert: method has a return type of IBAction. This type is the same as void and

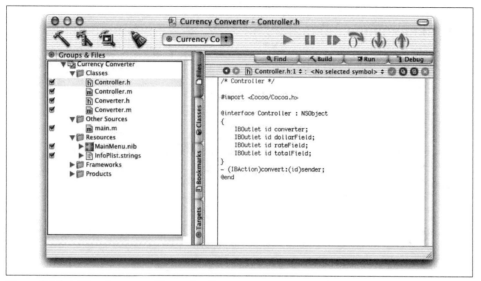

Figure 5-25. Adding the source files to the Classes group

also tells Interface Builder that the method serves as an action that can be hooked up to user-interface elements and other objects. These declarations allow you to add outlets and actions in the code and enable Interface Builder to parse them. We'll see this in action in later chapters.

Add the Conversion Method

We need to add a method to the Converter class that the controller object can invoke to perform our currency conversion.

1. Start by declaring the convertAmount:atRate: method in *Converter.h*, as shown in Example 5-1. This method declaration states that convertAmount:atRate: takes two arguments of type float and returns a float value.

Example 5-1. Converter.h header file

```
#import <Cocoa/Cocoa.h>
@interface Converter : NSObject
{
}
- (float)convertAmount:(float)amt atRate:(float)rate;
@end
```

2. Add the method implementation to the *Converter.m* file, as shown in Example 5-2. This method simply multiplies the two arguments and returns the result.

Example 5-2. Converter.m implementation file

```
#import "Converter.h"

@implementation Converter
- (float)convertAmount:(float)amt atRate:(float)rate
{
    return (amt * rate);
}
@end
```

3. Update the "empty" implementation of the convert: method in *Controller.m* that Interface Builder generated for you, as shown in Example 5-3.

Example 5-3. Controller.m implementation file

```
#import "Controller.h"
#import "Converter.h"                                             // a

@implementation Controller

- (IBAction)convert:(id)sender
{
    float rate = [rateField floatValue];                         // b
    float amt = [dollarField floatValue];                        // c
    float total = [converter convertAmount:amt atRate:rate];     // d
    [totalField setFloatValue:total];                            // e
}

@end
```

The lines we added do the following things:

a. Imports the Converter class interface.

b. Gets the value of the rateField outlet of the interface as a floating-point number. All text fields (and other classes that inherit from NSControl) can present the data that they contain in various forms, including doubles, floats, Strings, and integers.

c. Gets the value of the dollarField outlet of the interface as a floating-point number.

d. Calls the convertAmount:atRate: method of the Converter object instance.

e. Sets the value of the totalField outlet of the interface to the result obtained from the Converter object instance.

Build and Run

When you click the Build and Run button, the build process begins. When Project Builder finishes—and hopefully encounters no errors along the way—it displays Build succeeded on its status line and starts the application.

To exercise the application, enter some rates and dollar amounts, and click Convert. Of course, the more complex an application is, the more thoroughly you will need to test it. You might discover errors or shortcomings that necessitate a change in overall design, in the interface, in a custom class definition, or in the implementation of methods and functions.

Exercises

1. Change the font used by the text labels on the application to Helvetica.
2. Change the color of text displayed in the `totalField` to blue.

CHAPTER 6

Windows, Views, and Controls

All of the objects that you interact with on your computer screen are displayed within *windows*. This includes what we consider "normal" windows (those with title-bars and controls), as well as menu items, pop-up contextual menus, floating palettes, sheets, drawers, and the Dock.

Windows and the Window System

Two interacting systems create and manage Cocoa windows. On one hand, Mac OS X's window server creates a window and displays it on screen. The window server is a process that uses Quartz—the low-level drawing system—to draw, resize, hide, and move windows. As depicted in Figure 6-1, the window server also detects users events (such as mouse clicks or keyboard key presses) and forwards them to applications.

On the other hand, the window created by the window server is paired with an object supplied by the AppKit—an instance of the NSWindow class. Each physical window in a Cocoa program is managed by an instance of NSWindow or a subclass. As shown in Figure 6-2, when an NSWindow object is created, the window server creates the physical window being managed. The window server references the window by its window number and the NSWindow object instance by its own identifier.

Window, View, and Application

Three classes explicitly define the functionality at the core of a running application: NSWindow, NSView, and NSApplication. Each class plays a critical role in drawing the user interface of the application and directing user events to the various parts of a program. Each class inherits functionality from the NSResponder and NSObject classes, as shown in Figure 6-3. The structure of their interaction is sometimes called the "core program framework."

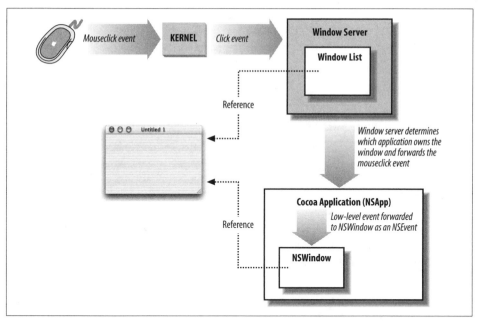

Figure 6-1. Cocoa and the window server

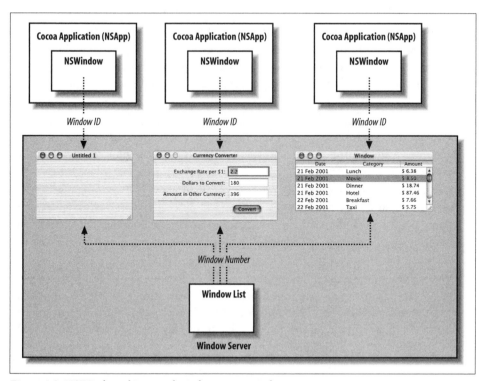

Figure 6-2. NSWindow objects and window server windows

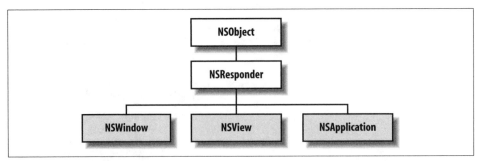

Figure 6-3. The core program framework

NSResponder

> NSResponder is an abstract class that enables event handling in all classes that inherit from it. It defines the set of messages invoked when different mouse and keyboard events occur. It also defines the mechanics of event processing among objects in an application. We'll cover events in more depth in Chapter 8.

NSWindow

> An NSWindow object manages each physical window on the screen. It draws the window's frame area and responds to user actions that close, move, resize, and otherwise manipulate the window. The main purpose of an NSWindow is to display an application's user interface, or at least a part of it, in its content area. The content area is that space below the titlebar and within the window frame.

> NSWindow allows you to assign a custom object as its delegate to participate in its activities. This allows you to add application-specific window functionality to your application without requiring knowledge of the NSWindow class internals.

NSView

> Any object you see in a widow's content area is an instance of a subclass of the NSView class. Each view owns a rectangular region associated with a particular window. A view produces the image content for that region and responds to events occurring within it.

> Graphically, a view can be regarded as a framed canvas. The *frame* locates the view in its superview, defines its size, and clips the drawing to its edges. The frame can be moved around resized, and rotated in the superview. Within the frame is the *bounds* of the view—the rectangle within which the view draws itself.

> Views draw themselves as an indirect result of receiving the display message or one if its variants. This message leads to the invocation of a view's drawRect: method and the drawRect: methods of all subviews of that view. The drawRect: method should contain all the code needed to redraw the view completely.

`NSApplication`

Every application has exactly one `NSApplication` object instance to supervise and coordinate the overall behavior of the application. This object dispatches events to the appropriate windows, which, in turn, distribute them onto their views. The application object manages its windows; it also detects and handles changes in their status, as well as its own active and inactive status. The application object is represented in each application by the global instance variable `NSApp`.

Key and Main Windows

Windows have numerous characteristics, the first of which being that they can be onscreen or offscreen. Onscreen windows are layered on the screen in tiers managed by the window server. Onscreen windows also can carry a status: *key* or *main*. Off-screen windows are hidden or minimized to the Dock and are not visible on the screen.

Key window

The *key window* responds to key presses for an application and is the primary recipient of messages from menus and dialog boxes. Usually a window is made key when the user clicks it. Each application can have only one key window at a time.

Main window

The *main window* is the principle focus of user actions for an application. Often user actions in a modal key window (typically a dialog box, such as the Font dialog or an Info window) have a direct effect on the main window. Main windows often have key status.

The Window Menu

Cocoa applications usually include a Window menu in the menu bar at the top of the screen. The Window menu automatically lists the windows that have a titlebar, are resizable, and can become the main window. When a window's title is changed, that new title is reflected in this menu. Figure 6-4 shows a Window menu in Project Builder, with two open windows.

 Not all applications have a Window menu, but it is automatically provided by Cocoa, and you should always use it. Also note that a list of an application's windows can be obtained by Control-clicking on the application's icon in the Dock.

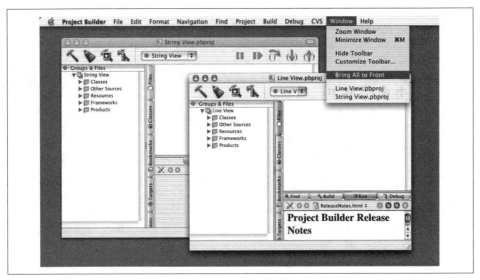

Figure 6-4. Window menu in Project Builder, with two open windows

Panels

A *panel* is a special kind of window that usually serves some auxiliary function in an application. For example, much of the functionality of Interface Builder, such as the view's palette and inspector, is implemented using panels. To support the roles they typically play, panels differ from windows in the following ways:

- To reduce screen clutter, an application's panels—except for attention panels—are displayed only when the application is active. For example, when you have more than one application running, only the panels for the active application are in the foreground.

- Panels can become the key window, but never the main window. For example, when working in Photoshop, you have a main window where you create and edit images. The other panels, such as the Layers panel, are open but not active (or key) until they are clicked; the focus then changes to that panel.

The user can close a panel that is the key window by pressing the Escape key (if the panel has a close button).

The View Hierarchy

Inside of each window—inside the area enclosed by the titlebar and the other three sides of the frame—lies the *content view*. The content view is the root, or top, view in a hierarchy of views that belongs to the window. Like a tree, one or more views may branch from the content view. For example, each button, text field, and label in the

Currency Converter application from Chapter 5 is a view located within the content view of the window, as illustrated in Figure 6-5. Enclosure determines the relationship between each view and its subviews.

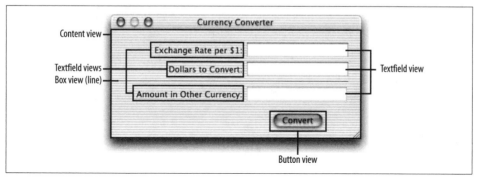

Figure 6-5. *Currency Converter views contained by the content view*

The core program framework provides several ways for your application to access the participating objects, so you need not define outlets or instance variables for every object in the hierarchy.

- By sending the appropriate message to the NSApp global variable, you can obtain the application's NSWindow objects.
- You can get the content view of a window by sending it the contentView message. From the returned NSView object, you can get all subviews of the view.
- You can obtain from an NSView instance most of the objects that it references. For example, you can discover its window, its superview, and its subviews.

The relationship between these parts of an application's view hierarchy is shown in Figure 6-6.

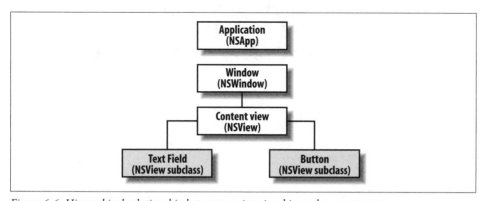

Figure 6-6. *Hierarchical relationship between major view hierarchy components*

Coordinate Systems

Positioning of windows and views, as well as the correct propagation of events within them, requires the use of a set of coordinate systems. These systems then help locate objects in relation to the various parts of the onscreen display. The following three types of coordinate systems are used by Cocoa:

- Screen coordinates
- Window coordinates
- View coordinates

Screen Coordinate System

The *screen coordinate system* is the basis for all other coordinate systems. Think of the entire screen as occupying the upper-right quadrant of a two-dimensional coordinate grid, as shown in Figure 6-7. The screen quadrant has its origin in the lower-left corner. The positive *x*-axis extends horizontally to the right, and the positive *y*-axis extends vertically upward. Each unit in the coordinate system represents an on-screen pixel.

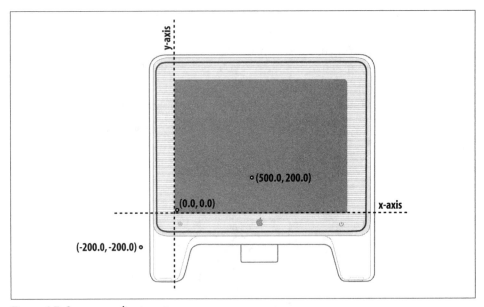

Figure 6-7. Screen coordinate system

 Although Figure 6-7 represents the coordinate system using a single display device, the screen coordinate system is really a logical rectangular union of all the screen rectangles of all physical frame buffers attached to the computer. The origin lies at the lower-left corner of that unioned rectangle.

The screen coordinate system has just one function: to position windows on the screen. When your application creates a new window, it must specify the window's initial size and location in screen coordinates.

Window Coordinate System

The *window coordinate system* defines the coordinates used within a single window on screen. It differs from the screen coordinate system in only two ways:

- It applies only to a particular window. Each window has its own coordinate system.
- Its origin is at the lower-left corner of the window. If the window moves, the origin and the entire coordinate system move with it.

View Coordinate System

For drawing, each view uses a coordinate system transformed from the window coordinate system, or from its superview in the case of a contained view. This coordinate system has its origin point in the lower-left corner of the view, as shown in Figure 6-8, making it convenient for drawing operations.

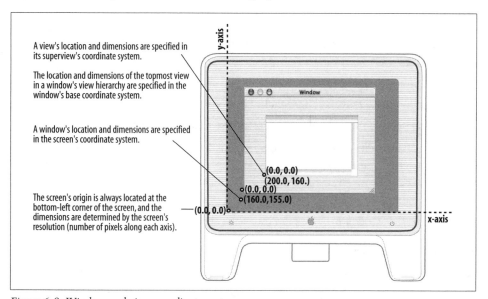

Figure 6-8. Window and view coordinate systems

This set of coordinate systems has several implications that are important in the layout and drawing of user-interface elements:

- Subviews are positioned in the coordinates of their superview.
- Each view's coordinate system is a transformation of its superview's system.

- When a view is moved or transformed, all subviews are moved or transformed in concert.
- Because a view has its own coordinate system for drawing, drawing instructions remain constant, regardless of any change in position of itself or its superview.

Controls, Cells, and Formatters

Controls are the user-interface objects that enable users to signal their intentions to an application and control what happens. Cells are rectangular areas embedded within a control. Each control can have one or more cells, allowing a single control to have multiple active areas. Figure 6-9 shows the relationship between controls and cells.

Figure 6-9. Controls and cells

Controls and cells lie behind the appearance and behavior of most user-interface objects in Cocoa, including buttons, text fields, sliders, and browsers. Although they are quite different types of objects, they interact closely. Controls are responsible for the following:

- Displaying the control to the user
- Accepting user events, such as clicking or typing
- Sending actions to other objects in response to a user event

A control usually delegates the first two responsibilities to cells. Cells, which are subclass instances of the NSCell class, let you display text or images in a view without the full overhead of an NSView subclass. This allows for greater flexibility when creating a control, such as a spreadsheet table, with many identical elements.

The controls that Cocoa provides fall into the categories listed in Table 6-1.

Table 6-1. Cocoa's NSView controls

Control	Description
Boxes	Group together other views, including controls, in an area that can have a border and title
Browsers	Display a list of data and allow the user to select items
Buttons	Send an action message to a target when clicked
Combo Boxes	Allow a user to enter a value either by entering it directly into a text field or choosing it from a pop-up list of preselected values
Forms	Group a related set of text fields

Table 6-1. Cocoa's NSView controls (continued)

Control	Description
Image Views	Display a single image in a frame and, optionally, allows a user to drag an image to it
Matrices	Group cells that work together in various ways, such as radio buttons
Outline Views	Display hierarchical data to let the user expand or collapse rows
Progress Indicators	Show that a lengthy task is underway and, optionally, can display how much of that task is complete
Sliders	Display a range of values and have an indicator, or knob, indicating the current setting
Steppers	Increment or decrement a value, such as a date or time, that is displayed next to them
Tab Views	Group views on multiple pages together into one user-interface element
Table Views	Display a set of related records, with rows representing individual records and columns representing the attributes of those records
Text Fields	Display text that a user can select or edit
Text Views	Allow the editing of text

Controls act as managers of their cells, telling them when and where to draw and notifying them when a user event occurs in their areas. This division of labor, given the relative "weight" of cells and controls, conserves memory and provides a great boost to application performance. For example, a matrix of buttons can be implemented as a single control with many cells instead of as a set of individual controls.

A control does not need a cell associated with it, but most user-interface objects available in Cocoa are cell-control combinations. Even a single button—from Interface Builder or programmatically created—is a control (an NSButton instance) with an associated cell (a NSButtonCell instance).

The cells in a control such as a matrix must be the same size, but they can be of different classes. More complex controls, such as table views and browsers, can incorporate various sizes and types of cells. Most controls that use a single cell, such as NSButton, provide convenience methods so you don't have to deal with the contained cell directly.

Cells and Formatters

When looking at the contents of cells, it is natural to consider only text (NSString) and images (NSImage). The content seems to be whatever is displayed. However, cells can hold other kinds of objects, such as dates (NSDate), numbers (NSNumber), and even application-supplied custom objects, which are shown in the user interface as strings.

One way to make your application's user interface more attractive is to format the contents of fields that display currencies and other numeric data. Fields can have fixed decimal digits, limit numbers to specific ranges, have currency symbols, and show negative values in a special color.

Formatters are objects that translate the values of certain objects to specific on-screen representations. Formatters can also convert a formatted string on a user interface into the represented object. For example, Figure 6-10 shows how a date formatter translates the contents of an NSDate object into a specific string for display.

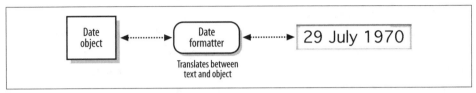

Figure 6-10. A date formatter

You can create, set, and modify formatter objects programmatically or with Interface Builder. Formatter objects handle the textual representation of the objects associated with the cells and translate what is typed into a cell to the underlying object. You can attach a formatter object to a cell in Interface Builder or use the setFormatter: method of NSCell to associate a formatter with a cell programmatically.

A Formatted Cell Example

To show formatters in action, we're going to create a simple application that shows the current date and time in a text field. In Project Builder, create a new Cocoa Application (File → New Project → Application → Cocoa Application) named "Simple Date", and save it in your ~/*LearningCocoa* folder.

Open the main nib file

Begin by opening the application's main nib file in Interface Builder:

1. In Project Builder's Groups & Files pane, click on the disclosure triangle next to Resources to reveal the *MainMenu.nib* file.
2. Double-click on the nib file to open it in Interface Builder.

A default menu bar and window will appear when the nib file is opened.

Create the user interface

Set the size and initial location of the application's main window by resizing and moving the window in Interface Builder

1. Move the window near the upper-left corner of the screen by dragging its titlebar.
2. Make the window smaller using the resize control at the bottom-right corner of the window, as shown in Figure 6-11.

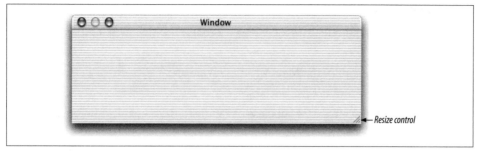

Figure 6-11. Cocoa window with resize control

Add a text field

Now, add a text field object to the application's window.

1. Select the Views palette by clicking the second button from the left in the tool-bar of the Cocoa Views window, as shown in Figure 6-12.

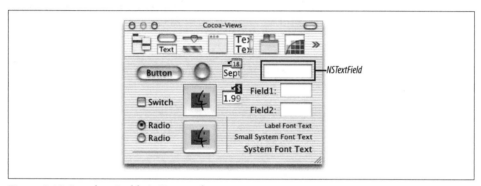

Figure 6-12. Interface Builder's Views palette

2. Drag a text field object onto the window.
3. Resize the text field to make it wider, using the handles on the text field, as shown in Figure 6-13.

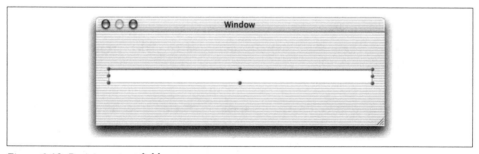

Figure 6-13. Resizing a text field

Create a controller

We'll create a very simple controller, MyController, which will be a subclass of NSObject. To define it:

1. Click the Classes tab of the *MainMenu.nib* window.

2. Select NSObject from the list of classes.

3. Press Return to create a new subclass of NSObject, and rename it MyController.

Define an outlet

Now the controller needs a way to send messages to the text field in the main window. Use Interface Builder to create an outlet for that purpose.

1. Select the MyController class in the Classes window.

2. Open the Show Info window (Tools → Show Info, or Shift-⌘-I), and select Attributes in the pull-down menu.

3. In the Outlets tab, click the Add button, and add an outlet named textField (as shown in Figure 6-14); enter the name, and press Return.

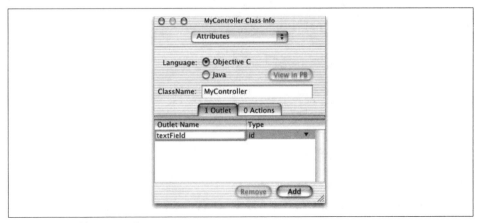

Figure 6-14. Adding an outlet

Generate a controller instance

As the final step of defining the controller in Interface Builder, create an instance of the MyController class.

1. Select MyController in the Classes pane of the *MainMenu.nib* window.

2. Choose instantiate from the Classes menu (Classes → Instantiate MyController, or Option-⌘-I).

When you instantiate a class (that is, create an instance of it), Interface Builder switches to the Instances pane and highlights the new instance, as shown in Figure 6-15. The instance is named after the class.

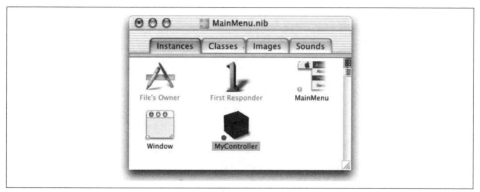

Figure 6-15. Instances pane showing a Controller object instance

 In fact, the instantiate command does not generate a true instance of MyController. It creates a proxy object used within Interface Builder for defining connections to other objects in the nib file. When the application is launched and the nib file's contents are loaded, the run-time system creates a true instance of MyController and uses the proxy object to establish connections to other objects.

Connect the controller to the interface

Now that you have created an instance of MyController, you can use it to declare a connection between it and the text field you created earlier.

1. In the Instances panel of the *MainMenu.nib* window, Control-drag a connection line from the MyController instance to the text field. When the text field is outlined, as shown in Figure 6-16, release the mouse button.

2. Interface Builder brings up the Connections pane of the Show Info window, as shown in Figure 6-17.

3. Select textField, and click the Connect button.

Generate the source files

Generate the source files so that we can add our controller code and run the application.

1. Go to the Classes tab of the *MainMenu.nib* file window.

2. Select the MyController class.

3. Choose Create Files from the Classes menu (Classes → Create Files for MyController, or Option-⌘-F).

Interface Builder displays the dialog box shown in Figure 6-18.

4. Verify that the checkboxes in the Create column next to the *.h* and *.m* files are selected.

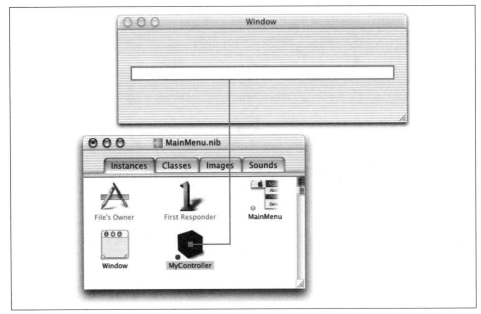

Figure 6-16. Connecting the instance to the text field

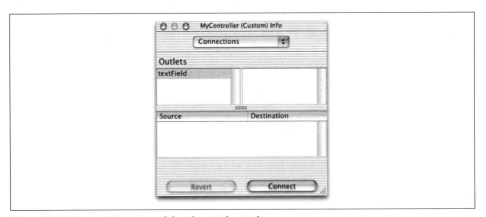

Figure 6-17. Connections pane of the Show Info window

5. Verify that the checkbox next to Simple Date is selected in the Insert into targets column.

6. Click on the Choose button.

7. Save the nib file (File → Save, or ⌘-S).

Now that we've built the basic interface, we can leave Interface Builder and switch to Project Builder to complete the application. Click on Project Builder's icon in the Dock to leave Interface Builder.

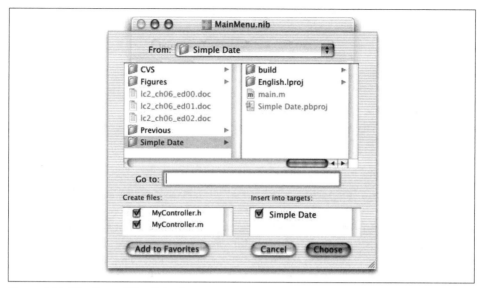

Figure 6-18. The Create Files dialog box

Statically type the outlet

By default, outlet declarations are dynamically typed using the id keyword. You can use id as the type for any object, meaning that the class of the object is determined at runtime. When you don't need a dynamically typed object, you can—and should—statically type it as a pointer to an object. It takes a little extra time, but it is good programming practice. Static typing also allows the compiler to perform type checking, potentially saving you debugging time later.

When you look at the source code for *MyController.h*, note that generic outlets are declared as follows:

```
IBOutlet id variableName;
```

There are two ways to type outlets. The first is to indicate the type in Interface Builder. Take another look at Figure 6-14, and notice the type pull-down as part of the textField outlet definition. You can use the pull-down to select which type of object the outlet should be typed as. The other way is to change the type in the header file. To do this, use the following steps:

1. In Project Builder, select *MyController.h* in the Other Sources folder in the left pane.

2. Change the declaration in *MyController.h* to match the code shown in Example 6-1. Don't forget to add the pointer star!

Example 6-1. MyController header file with a statically typed outlet

```
/* MyController */

#import <Cocoa/Cocoa.h>

@interface MyController : NSObject
{
    IBOutlet NSTextField * textField;
}
@end
```

Implement the awakeFromNib method

When an application is launched, the NSApplicationMain function loads the main nib file. After a nib file has been completely unpacked and its objects connected, the runtime system sends the awakeFromNib message to all objects derived from information in the nib file, signaling that the loading process is complete. All object's outlets are guaranteed to be initialized when awakeFromNib is called. This lets objects in the nib file do any extra setup required before the user or the rest of the application attempts to interact with them.

In this application, we'll use the awakeFromNib method to print the current time to the text field in the main window.

1. In the left pane, click on *MyController.m* in the Other Sources folder.
2. Edit the *MyController.m* file to match the code shown in Example 6-2.

   Example 6-2. Adding the awakeFromNib method

   ```
   #import "MyController.h"

   @implementation MyController

   - (void)awakeFromNib
   {
       [textField setObjectValue:[NSCalendarDate date]];
   }
   @end
   ```

3. Save the project (File → Save, or ⌘-S).
4. Build and run the application (⌘-R). You should see a window that resembles Figure 6-19.
5. Quit the application.

Add the formatter

Wait a minute … our date looks really nerdy. Instead of this representation for the date, we want to make a nicely formatted date. To do this, switch back to Interface Builder to perform the following steps:

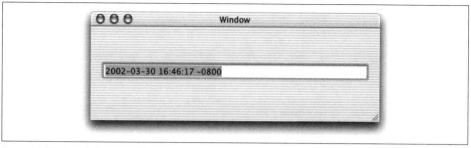

Figure 6-19. Simple Date application

1. Drag a date formatter from the Views palette to the text field, as shown in Figure 6-20.

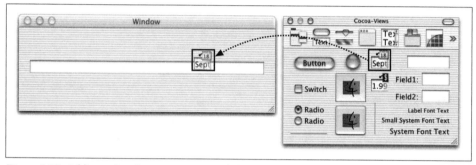

Figure 6-20. Adding a date formatter to a text field

2. While the text field is selected, bring up the Show Info window (Shift-⌘-I) if it isn't open already.

3. In the Formatter pane of the Show Info window, specify the %c date format, as shown in Figure 6-21.

4. Save the nib file (File → Save, or ⌘-S).

5. Return to Project Builder, and build and run (⌘-R) the project. You should see something like Figure 6-22.

6. Quit the application (Simple Date → Quit NewApplication, or ⌘-Q).

Targets and Actions

The target/action pattern is part of the mechanism by which user-interface controls respond to user actions, enabling users to communicate their intentions to an application. The target/action pattern specifies a one-to-one relationship between two objects: the control (more specifically, the control's cell) and its target. When a user clicks a user-interface control, it sends an action message to the target, as shown in Figure 6-23.

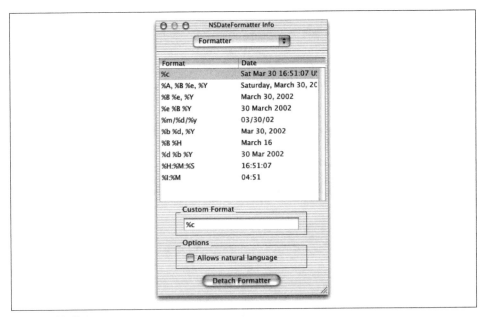

Figure 6-21. Formatter pane

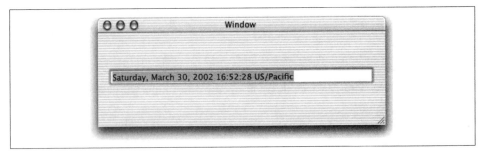

Figure 6-22. Simple Date application using a formatter

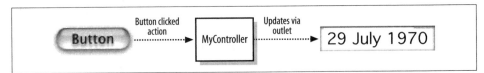

Figure 6-23. Target/action pattern

The target/action relationship is typically defined using Interface Builder, in which you select a target object for a control, along with a specific action message that will be sent to the target. Target/action relationships can also be set (or modified) while an application is running.

Target/Action Example

To show target/action pattern in practice, we are going to modify the Simple Date application we've already built.

Add a Refresh button

In Interface Builder, open the *MainMenu.nib* file, and add a button named "Refresh" to the main window, using the following steps:

1. In the Cocoa-Views window, grab an NSButton object, and drag it to the main window.

2. Change the name of the button by double-clicking on the "Button" name to highlight it, typing "Refresh", then hitting Return to accept the new name. The interface should now look similar to Figure 6-24.

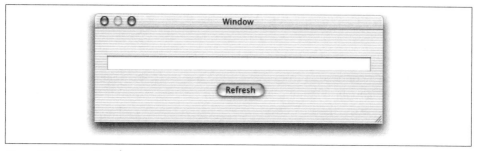

Figure 6-24. Target/action example interface

Define an action

When the user presses the Refresh button, we want the date to update itself. To do this, we need to define an action on our MyController object that the button will call. Define an action called refresh: using the following steps:

1. Select the MyController class in the Classes pane of the *MainMenu.nib* window.

2. In the Attributes pane of the Show Info window, click on the Actions tab and then on the Add button.

3. Change myAction: to refresh: and hit Return to add the action, as shown in Figure 6-25.

Connect the button to the action

For MyController to receive an action message from the button in the user interface, you must connect the button to the controller. The button object keeps a reference

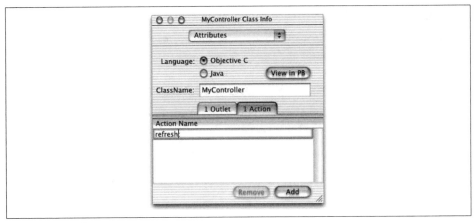

Figure 6-25. Defining an action

to its target using an outlet; not surprisingly, the outlet is named target. To make this connection:

1. Click on the Instances tab in the *MainMenu.nib* window.

2. Control-drag a connection from the Refresh button to the MyController instance in the *MainMenu.nib* window, as shown in Figure 6-26. When the instance is outlined, release the mouse button.

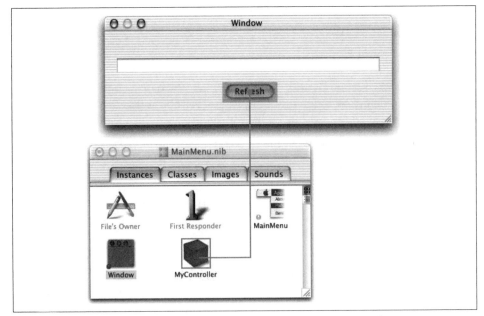

Figure 6-26. Creating a connection between the Refresh button and the controller

3. In the Connections pane of the Show Info window, make sure target is selected in the Outlets column.

4. Select refresh: in the right column, as shown in Figure 6-27.

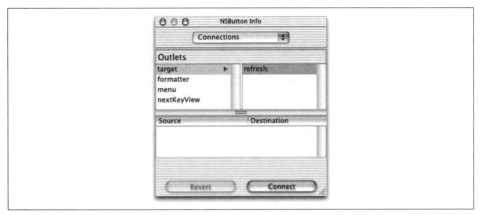

Figure 6-27. Connecting to the refresh: method

5. Click the Connect button.

6. Save the *MainMenu.nib* file (File → Save, or ⌘-S).

Update the source files

Since we made changes to the controller, the source files need to be updated so that we can add our controller code and run the application.

1. Go to the Classes tab of the *MainMenu.nib* file window.

2. Select the MyController class.

3. Choose Classes → Create Files for MyController (Option-⌘-F). Follow the dialog boxes to save the files into the project.

4. Interface Builder will warn you that the file *MyController.h* already exists. Click on the Merge button to bring up the FileMerge tool, as shown in Figure 6-28. If you don't see the window shown in Figure 6-28, look for the FileMerge icon on your Dock, and click it to bring the FileMerge window to the top.

5. The FileMerge tool consists of three panes. The left pane is the newly generated file from Interface Builder, the right pane is the file in your project, and the bottom pane is the result of the merge. We want to keep our edits that were statically typed for the textField outlet. To do this, we select the #1 arrow, then "Choose right" from the Actions pop-up at the bottom-right corner of the window.

6. Save the *MyController.h* file from FileMerge (File → Save Merge ,or ⌘-S) and then close the window.

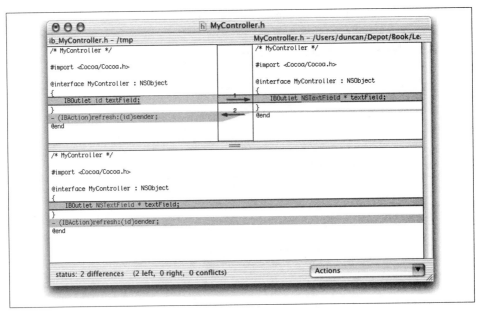

Figure 6-28. Merge tool in action

7. Return to Interface Builder. You will be prompted to merge the *MyController.m* file; do so.

8. Merge the Files (as shown in Figure 6-29) by selecting "Choose both (left first)" for the first block of code and "Choose right" for the second block of code. Unfortunately, at the time of writing this book, FileMerge isn't smart enough to handle this merge on its own. If you encounter this problem, you'll need to add the curly braces after the `refresh:` method yourself.

9. Save the resulting merged file (File → Save Merge, or ⌘-S), and quit the File-Merge tool (⌘-Q).

10. Save the nib file (File → Save, or ⌘-S).

There are other ways of adding outlets and actions to your source code and the nib files that don't involve using the FileMerge tool. We'll see some of these other ways in later chapters.

Implement the action method

Now switch back to Project Builder. Our next step is to edit the *MyController.m* file and insert the code for the `refresh:` method, as shown in Example 6-3.

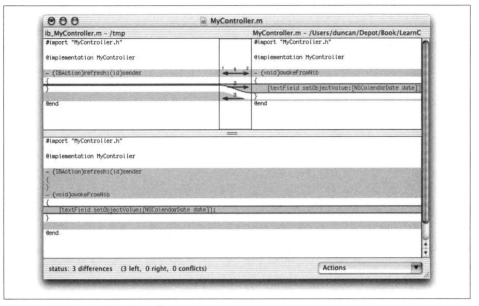

Figure 6-29. Merging MyController.m

Making Outlet and Action Connections

Developers new to Cocoa sometimes get confused when making action and outlet connections in Interface Builder. A general rule for determining which way to draw a connection line is to draw the connection in the direction that messages will flow:

- To make an action connection, draw a line from a control object in the user interface, such as a button or a text field, to the object instance that should receive the action message.
- To make an outlet connection, draw a line from the object instance to another object in the application.

Another way to clarify connections is to consider who needs to find whom. With outlets, the object needs to find some other object, so the connection is from the first object to the second object. With actions, the control object needs to find an object to send messages to, so the connection is from the control object to the target object.

Example 6-3. Implementing the refresh: method

```
#import "MyController.h"

@implementation MyController

- (void) awakeFromNib
```

Example 6-3. Implementing the refresh: method (continued)

```
{
    [textField setObjectValue:[NSCalendarDate date]];

}

- (IBAction)refresh:(id)sender
{
    [textField setObjectValue:[NSCalendarDate date]];
}

@end
```

1. Save the changes to the nib file (File → Save, or ⌘-S).
2. Build and run the application (⌘-R).

When the application launches, you can refresh the date display by pressing the Refresh button. Of course, the date won't change if you've selected to show only the date in the text field. If you've opted to also display the current time, hitting the Refresh button should update the time.

 As we progress through the chapters in this book, our examples will contain more and more methods. It doesn't matter to the compiler which order methods appear in your source files; they can be in any order you want.

Exercises

1. Read the online documentation for the NSWindow and NSView classes.
2. Give the window of our Simple Date application a title other than "Window".
3. Go back to the Currency Converter application in Chapter 5, and statically type the rateField, dollarField, and totalField outlets.

CHAPTER 7

Custom Views

Cocoa's default set of controls covers most common UI needs, but it can't cover everything. For example, you might want to create a drawing application and need a view that can have lines and other shapes drawn into it. Or, you might want to create a custom graph of stock data over time. Whenever you have these kind of needs, you will need to create a subclass of NSView: a *custom view*.

A custom view is responsible for drawing content into, and handling events that occur within, its *bounds*—the rectangular region given to it by its superview. You can use any of Cocoa's drawing tools to draw content into the view. In this chapter, we'll work through a couple of basic custom-view examples to show you how everything works. Then, in the next chapter, you'll build on what you learn in this chapter to create a custom view to respond to user events.

Custom View Creation Steps

When you make a custom subclass of NSView and want to perform custom drawing and handle events, the following procedure applies:

1. In Interface Builder, define a subclass of NSView, then generate header and implementation files.

2. Drag a Custom View object from the Views palette onto a window, and resize it.

3. With the Custom View object still selected, choose the Custom Class panel of the Info window, and select the custom class. Connect any outlets and actions.

4. If needed, override the designated initializer (initWithFrame:) to perform any custom initialization.

5. Implement the drawRect: method to draw.

We will walk you through the steps outlined here to show you how to create customized subclasses of NSView for your applications.

Create a Custom View

To start working with views, we will make a custom view. In Project Builder, create a new Cocoa Application project (File → New Project → Application → Cocoa Application) named "Red Square", and save it in your *~/LearningCocoa* folder.

Open the Main Nib File

Begin by opening the application's main nib file in Interface Builder.

1. In Project Builder's Groups & Files pane, click on the disclosure triangle next to Resources to reveal the *MainMenu.nib* file.

2. Double-click on the nib file to open it in Interface Builder.

A default menu bar and window will appear when the nib file is opened.

Define a Subclass of NSView

To define a class that will implement the custom functionality of our view, we need to define a subclass of the NSView class.

1. Click on the Classes tab of the *MainMenu.nib* window.

2. Find the NSView class in the hierarchy of available classes. (You may need to scroll through the browser to find it.) Its complete path in the hierarchy is NSObject → NSResponder → NSView.

3. Control-click on NSView, and select Subclass NSView from the pop-up menu to create a new subclass named MyView, as shown in Figure 7-1. (You can also hit Return with NSView selected to create a subclass automatically.)

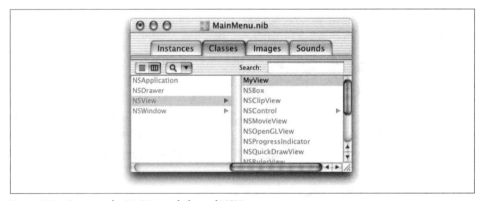

Figure 7-1. Creating the MyView subclass of NSView

4. Generate the source files for MyView from the Classes menu (Classes → Create Files for MyView). (You can also Control-click on MyView and select Create Files for MyView from the Context menu.)

5. Interface Builder then displays a dialog box.

6. Verify that the checkboxes next to *MyView.h* and *MyView.m* are selected in the Create column.

7. Verify that the checkbox next to Red Square is selected in the Target column.

8. Click the Choose button to create the files.

Add a Custom View to the Main Window

Next, we need to create a place for our custom view to draw.

1. Drag a CustomView object from the Cocoa-Containers window (as shown in Figure 7-2) into the main window, and resize it to occupy the entire window.

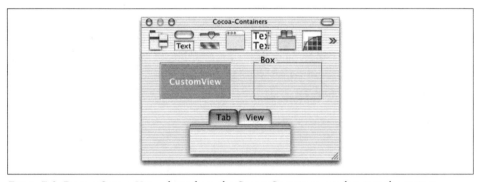

Figure 7-2. Drag a CustomView object from the Cocoa-Containers window into the project window

2. With the CustomView object still selected, choose the Custom Class pane of the Show Info window (Tools → Show Info, or Shift-⌘-I), and select the MyView custom class. The name of the view will change to MyView to confirm this change, as shown in Figure 7-3.

The nib now has enough information to create an instance of the MyView class and to assign it to an area of the window. Save the nib file (File → Save, or ⌘-S), and return to Project Builder by clicking on its icon in the Dock.

Implement the Drawing Method

To draw into the view, we only need to implement the drawRect: method of our MyView class. We're just going to fill the view with a red square.

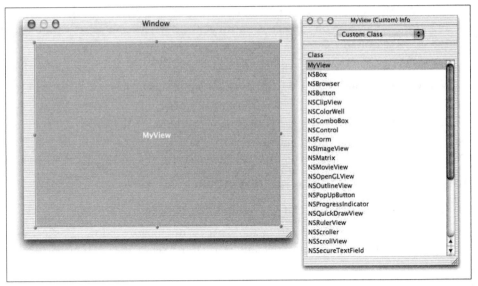

Figure 7-3. Setting the class for the custom view

1. Open the *MyView.m* implementation file in Project Builder by clicking on the filename in the Other Sources folder.

2. Edit it to match Example 7-1.

Example 7-1. Simple drawRect method

```
#import "MyView.h"

@implementation MyView

- (void)drawRect:(NSRect) rect                    // a
{
    [[NSColor redColor] set];                     // b
    NSRectFill([self bounds]);                    // c
}
@end
```

The code we added in Example 7-1 does the following things:

a. Adds a method declaration for the drawRect: method. This method is called by the display method of the NSView class and takes a single C structure (or *struct*), NSRect. This parameter is provided so that you can just draw the part of the view that needs it—critical when dealing with large, complex views that take time to redraw. In some cases—and this is one of them—redrawing the entire view won't really be a performance drag.

b. Sets the color that Cocoa uses for subsequent drawing operations. Here we use a convenience method of the NSColor class to get a red color.

c. Calls the NSRectFill function, defined by the AppKit framework, and tells it to fill the bounds of the view.

3. Save the project (File → Save, or ⌘-S).

4. Build and run the project (Build → Build and Run, or ⌘-R). You should see a window containing a red square, as shown in Figure 7-4.

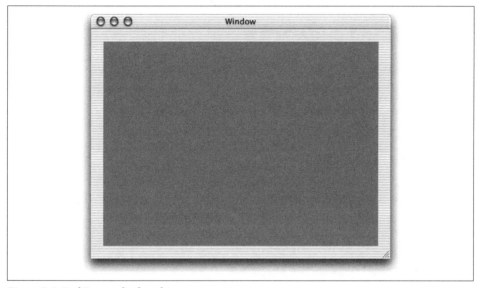

Figure 7-4. Red Square displayed

Our view looks like it works just fine. However, we have a slight problem. Resize the window and observe how the red square is anchored to the bottom-left corner of the window and moves down as the window is stretched and resized. Ideally, we'd like to have the square fill the window no matter how the user resizes it.

5. Quit the Red Square application (⌘-Q) before moving on to the next step.

> Why does the view stay anchored to the lower left-hand corner of the window? The answer lies in the fact that Cocoa's coordinate system starts at the lower-left corner. This behavior takes programmers who are used to a coordinate systembased on the upper-right corner (such as Carbon-based applications) a bit of time to adjust to.

Autosizing of Views

To ensure that our view occupies the whole window, no matter how it is resized:

1. Bring the *MainMenu.nib* file to the foreground in Interface Builder.

2. Select the MyView component in the interface.

3. Select Size from the pull-down menu of the Show Info window, and click once on the vertical and horizontal lines so that they appear to have springs in them, as shown in Figure 7-5.

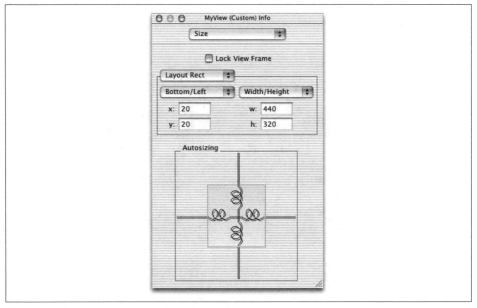

Figure 7-5. Setting the Autosizing behavior of a view

Setting the Autosizing to these settings means that the view will grow and shrink as necessary to keep the distance from the edges of its parent view (the content view of the window) constant. Think of the springs as making the inside of the view "springy" so that it can stretch in size, while the straight lines ensure that the distance between the view and the edge of its container remains constant. If you wanted the view to remain a constant size in the middle of the window's content view, you could turn the straight lines to springs and vice versa.

4. Save the nib file (⌘-S).

5. Switch back to Project Builder, and build and run (⌘-R) the project. Now when you run the program, you can resize the window to any size you want, and the red square expands or contracts as needed.

At this point, we're done with the Red Square application. Close the project in both Interface Builder and Project Builder before moving on to the next section.

Drawing into a View: Behind the Scenes

Before the NSView class's display method, or one of its variants, invokes a drawRect: method on a NSView subclass, there is a bit of work that is performed behind the

Drawing with Colors

In Red Square, we use the `set` method of the `NSColor` class to indicate that all subsequent drawing should be performed with the red color. However, this glosses over how colors work in Cocoa. An `NSColor` object represents a color composed of multiple components and sometimes *opacity* (otherwise known as *alpha* or *transparency*). These components can exist in multiple color spaces:

- Device RGB, where the primary components are red, green, and blue as generated by a device. Since monitors, printers, and other output devices operate differently, colors defined in this space will vary from device to device.

- Calibrated RGB, where the primary components are red, green, and blue in a consistent, abstract color space that can be translated to display with the same approximate colors on any output device. This is the recommended color space for most work.

- Calibrated HSB, where the primary components are hue, saturation, and brightness.

- CMYK, where the primary components are cyan, magenta, yellow, and key (or black). This color space is used by traditional four-color printing presses.

- Grayscale, where the primary component is white.

To get a color that is defined by one of these color spaces, the `NSColor` provides the following class methods:

```
+ colorWithDeviceRed:green:blue:alpha:
+ colorWithCalibratedRed:green:blue:alpha:
+ colorWithCalibratedHue:saturation:brightness:alpha:
+ colorWithDeviceCyan:magenta:yellow:black:alpha:
+ colorWithCalibratedWhite:alpha:
```

Each of these methods takes float values for the various components between 0.0 and 1.0. For example, to create a yellow color, you would use the following message on `NSColor`:

```
NSColor yellow = [NSColor colorWithCalibratedRed:1.0
                                           green:1.0
                                            blue:0.0
                                           alpha:1.0];
```

scenes. Core Graphics (CG) calls are needed to set up Quartz with information about the view, including the graphics context in which it draws, the coordinate system and clipping paths it uses, and other graphics state information. The `NSView` method that does this is `lockFocus`. There is a companion method that undoes the effects of `lockFocus`, called `unlockFocus`.

Focusing modifies the graphics state by doing the following:

- Making the view's window the current graphics context

- Creating a clipping path around the view's frame
- Making the CG coordinate system match the view's coordinate system

To produce proper results, all drawing code invoked by a view must be bracketed by invocations of these methods. The display method, and its variants, of the NSView class perform these duties automatically, so don't worry about locking focus in the drawRect method. However, if you define some methods that need to draw in a view without going through the display methods, you must first send a lockFocus message to the view in which you are drawing before performing any drawing; then you can send the unlockFocus message as soon as you are done.

Only one view at a time can have focus. If focus is already locked onto another view when the lockFocus method is invoked, the previous view's lock is put onto a stack, so focus can be restored to it when the lock of the current view is released with the unlockFocus message.

Draw Strings into a View

To continue working with drawing into views, we will create an application that renders a string into a custom NSView subclass. In Project Builder, create a new Cocoa Application project (File → New Project → Application → Cocoa Application) named "String View", and save it in your ~/LearningCocoa folder.

Create a Custom View

As in the Red Square application, a new custom view class needs to be created. Follow the same directions as before to accomplish the following tasks:

1. Open the *MainMenu.nib* file.
2. Define a subclass of NSView named MyView.
3. Generate the source files for MyView.
4. Add a CustomView to the main window.
5. Assign the MyView class to the CustomView from the Custom Class pull-down menu of the Info window.
6. Set the Autosizing attributes of the view so that the view fills the window when the window is resized.
7. Save the nib file, and return to Project Builder.

Implement the Drawing Method

Once again, we implement the drawRect: method of our MyView class.

1. Open the *MyView.m* implementation file in Project Builder, and edit it to match Example 7-2.

Example 7-2. Drawing a string into a view

```
#import "MyView.h"

@implementation MyView

- (void)drawRect:(NSRect)rect
{
    NSRect bounds = [self bounds];                          // a
    NSString * hello = @"Hello World!";                     // b
    NSMutableDictionary * attribs = [NSMutableDictionary dictionary];  // c

    [[NSColor whiteColor] set];                             // d
    NSRectFill(bounds);                                     // e

    [hello drawAtPoint:NSMakePoint((bounds.size.width/2),   // f
                            (bounds.size.height/2))
        withAttributes:attribs];
}

@end
```

The code we added implements the same drawRect: method that was overridden in the Red Square application (Example 7-1) and does the following things:

a. Gets an NSRect structure containing the bounds of the view.

b. Initializes an NSString containing the string that we want to draw into the view.

c. Creates an empty dictionary object (a Cocoa collection object like those we covered in Chapter 4) that will be needed for the drawAtPoint: withAttributes: method in line f.

d. Sets the active drawing color to white.

e. Calls the NSRectFill function to fill the view. This will paint the entire view white.

f. Calls the drawAtPoint:withAttributes: method on the hello string. This draws the string at a point that is half the width and half the height of the view. We give this method an empty attributes argument to tell the system not do anything special when the string is drawn.

2. Save the project (⌘-S).

3. Build and run the project (⌘-R). You should see the string drawn in the window, as shown in Figure 7-6.

Note that the string isn't perfectly centered in the view. This is because the drawing point that the string uses to draw itself onto the view is at the lower-left hand corner of the bounding box of the string. This follows the same logic as the screen, window, and view coordinate systems.

4. Quit the String View application (⌘-Q).

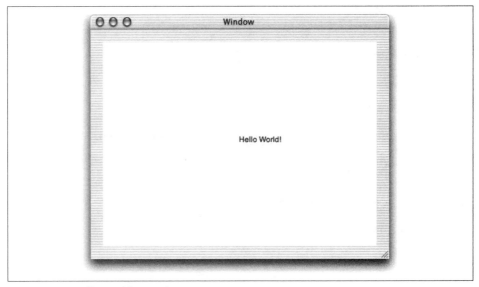

Figure 7-6. A Hello World string drawn into a view

Drawing Strings with Attributes

You'll notice that when we drew our "Hello World!" string, it was drawn with a small Helvetica font. You'll often want to draw strings in other fonts and sizes. Do this by setting attributes that will be used when drawing a string. We'll talk much more about string attributes in Chapter 11. For now, we just use the attributes needed to set the font and color of our string.

1. Modify the drawRect: method in *MyView.m* to match Example 7-3:

   Example 7-3. Setting font attributes

   ```
   - (void)drawRect:(NSRect)rect
   {
       NSRect bounds = [self bounds];
       NSString * hello = @"Hello World!";
       NSMutableDictionary * attribs = [NSMutableDictionary dictionary];

       [attribs setObject:[NSFont fontWithName:@"Times" size:24]          // a
               forKey:NSFontAttributeName];
       [attribs setObject:[NSColor redColor]                              // b
               forKey:NSForegroundColorAttributeName];

       [[NSColor whiteColor] set];
       NSRectFill(bounds);
       [hello drawAtPoint:NSMakePoint((bounds.size.width/2),
                                      (bounds.size.height/2))
           withAttributes:attribs];
   }
   ```

The code we added in Example 7-3 does the following things:

a. Obtains a font object for the Times font with a size of 24 points and sets it into the attribs dictionary.

b. Obtains a red color object and sets it into the attribs dictionary.

2. Build and run (⌘-R) the application. You should see the string drawn into the window with our attributes, as seen in Figure 7-7.

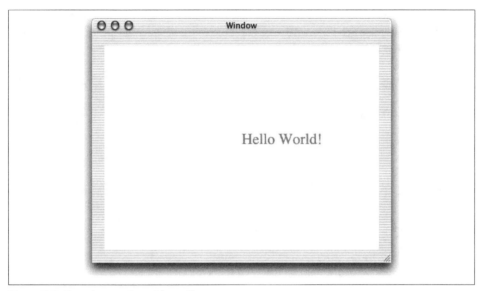

Figure 7-7. Drawing a string with attributes

We're now done with the String View application. Close the project in both Project Builder and Interface Builder before moving on.

Draw Paths into a View

Next in our exploration of drawing into views, we are going draw some lines into a custom NSView subclass. In Project Builder, create a new Cocoa Application project (File → New Project → Application → Cocoa Application) named "Line View", and save it in your *~/LearningCocoa* folder.

Create a Custom View

As before, a new custom view class needs to be created. Perform the following tasks:

1. Open the *MainMenu.nib* file.

2. Define a subclass of NSView named MyView.

3. Generate the source files for MyView.

4. Add a custom view to the main window.

5. Assign the MyView class to the CustomView.

6. Set the Autosizing attributes of the view so that the view fills the window when the window is resized.

7. Save the nib file, and return to Project Builder.

Implement the Drawing Method

Once again, we will implement the drawRect: method of our MyView class. This time we will use the NSPoint structure to keep track of the various points of the view between which we want to draw lines.

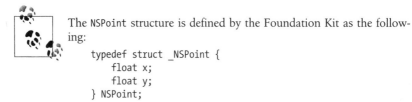

The NSPoint structure is defined by the Foundation Kit as the following:

```
typedef struct _NSPoint {
    float x;
    float y;
} NSPoint;
```

1. Open the *MyView.m* implementation file in Project Builder, and edit it to match Example 7-4.

Example 7-4. Drawing a string into a view

```
#import "MyView.h"

@implementation MyView

- (void)drawRect:(NSRect)rect
{
    NSRect bounds = [self bounds];

    NSPoint bottom = NSMakePoint((bounds.size.width/2.0), 0);                  // a
    NSPoint top = NSMakePoint((bounds.size.width/2.0), bounds.size.height);    // b
    NSPoint left = NSMakePoint(0, (bounds.size.height/2.0));                    // c
    NSPoint right = NSMakePoint(bounds.size.width, (bounds.size.height/2.0));  // d

    [[NSColor whiteColor] set];
    [NSBezierPath fillRect:bounds];                                            // e

    [[NSColor blackColor] set];
    [NSBezierPath strokeRect:bounds];                                          // f
    [NSBezierPath strokeLineFromPoint:top toPoint:bottom];                     // g
    [NSBezierPath strokeLineFromPoint:right toPoint:left];                     // h
}
@end
```

The code we added in Example 7-4 does the following things:

    a. Creates an NSPoint halfway along the bottom of the view

    b. Creates an NSPoint halfway along the top of the view

c. Creates an NSPoint halfway up the left side of the view

d. Creates an NSPoint halfway up the right side of the view

e. Draws a path that encompasses the entire view and fills that path with the current drawing color (white)

f. Draws a path that encompasses the entire view and draws a line along that path in the current drawing color (black)

g. Draws a path from the NSPoint along the top of the view to the NSPoint along the bottom of the view

h. Draws a path from the NSPoint along the right side of the view to the NSPoint along the left side of the view

2. Save the project (⌘-S).

3. Build and run the application (⌘-R). You should see the lines drawn in the view as shown in Figure 7-8.

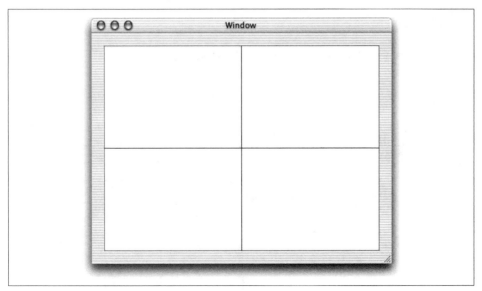

Figure 7-8. The Line View application in action

Now quit the Line View application (⌘-Q) before going on to the next example.

Draw an Oval Path

To finish the chapter, we're going to modify the *MyView.m* used in the Line View application and draw an oval path in the view. To accomplish this task, you need to add one line to the *MyView.m* file, as shown in Example 7-5.

Example 7-5. Drawing an oval path

```
#import "MyView.h"

@implementation MyView

- (void)drawRect:(NSRect)rect
{
    NSRect bounds = [self bounds];
    NSPoint bottom = NSMakePoint((bounds.size.width/2.0), 0);
    NSPoint top = NSMakePoint((bounds.size.width/2.0), bounds.size.height);
    NSPoint left = NSMakePoint(0, (bounds.size.height/2.0));
    NSPoint right = NSMakePoint(bounds.size.width, (bounds.size.height/2.0));

    [[NSColor whiteColor] set];
    [NSBezierPath fillRect:bounds];

    [[NSColor blackColor] set];
    [NSBezierPath strokeRect:bounds];

    [NSBezierPath strokeLineFromPoint:top toPoint:bottom];
    [NSBezierPath strokeLineFromPoint:right toPoint:left];

    [[NSBezierPath bezierPathWithOvalInRect:bounds] stroke];
}
@end
```

The single line of code creates a oval path the size of the bounds of the view, then draws it using the stroke method. Save the project (⌘-S), then build and run the application (⌘-R). You should see something that looks like Figure 7-9.

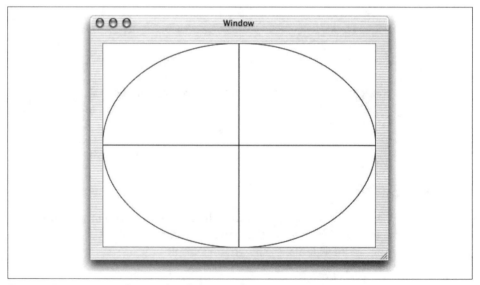

Figure 7-9. Line View with an oval path drawn

Exercises

1. Define the red color in Red Square by using the `colorWithCalibratedRed:green:blue:alpha:` method.

2. Draw the string from String View into the Line View project, noticing where the string is drawn.

3. Vary the width of the lines drawn by using the `setDefaultLineWidth:` method of `NSBezierPath`.

4. Use Project Builder's "Find" feature to look up occurrences of `NSBezierPath` in your project; then use it to find the occurrences of `NSBezierPath` in the AppKit headers.

CHAPTER 8
Event Handling

Graphical interfaces are driven by user events—mouse clicks and keystrokes. Most of an application's time is spent waiting for the user to tell the application what to do next. However, a running application can also receive events not originating from the user interface, such as packets arriving over a network interface or timers firing periodically. In Cocoa, both types of events result in a message sent to an object in your application, as depicted in Figure 8-1.

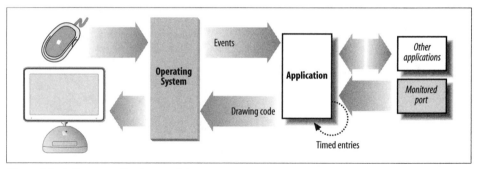

Figure 8-1. A Cocoa application receiving events

This chapter focuses on events—both user- and program-generated—and how you intercept, handle, and coordinate them in Cocoa.

Events

Events in Cocoa are represented by instances of the NSEvent class. An event object can be queried to discover its window, the location of the event within the window, and the time the event occurred (relative to system startup). You can also find out which, if any, modified keys (such as Command, Shift, Option, and Control) were pressed. An event also contains the type of event it represents. There are many event types, falling primarily into the following categories:

Keyboard events

Generated when a key is pressed or released or when a modified key changes. Of these event types, key-down events are the most useful. When you handle a key-down event, you can determine the character or characters associated with the event by calling the `characters` method on the event object.

Mouse events

Generated by changes in the state of the mouse button (down and up) and during mouse dragging. Optionally, mouse events can also be generated when the mouse moves without any button depressed.

Tracking-rectangle events

Generated by the window server when the mouse enters or exits a programmatically set area (a *tracking rectangle*) in a window. This lets an application change either the cursor or the content that the mouse is currently over. For example, when you move the mouse over the window control buttons, you generate events triggered by the mouse entering and exiting a rectangular region around the control. This lets the control highlight itself. Also, an application usually changes the cursor to an I-beam when the mouse is moved over editable text.

Periodic events

Generated by timers to notify an application that a certain time interval has elapsed. An application can request that periodic events be placed in its event queue at a certain event frequency. This is useful for applications that want to perform some task at regular intervals, such as updating the frames of an animation or checking email every few minutes.

The Event Cycle

Every application has a central object named NSApp, which is an instance of the NSApplication class. At the core of its responsibilities is the management of the *run loop*. A run loop monitors the various sources of events and decides which object is responsible for handling each event. It then sends a message, passing to the object an NSEvent object instance to describe the particulars of the event. The event message passes from NSApp to the appropriate window, to a view (commonly a control) within the window, and eventually to the target object.

This is how a button "knows" that it has been clicked. The application forwards mouse click events to it. The button object can then either process the event directly or, more commonly, pass it on to a custom object that you define through the target/action pattern or delegation. When the handling objects are finished responding to the message, control unwinds and returns to NSApp, where the run loop processes the next event.

This cycle, also known as the *event cycle*, usually starts at launch time when the application sends a stream of Quartz commands to the window server for it to draw the application interface. The application then begins its main run loop and begins accepting input from the user. When users click or drag the mouse or type on the keyboard, the window server detects and processes these actions, passing them to the application as events.

Events sent to the application by the window server are placed on a queue in the order they are received. On each cycle of the run loop, NSApp processes the topmost event in the queue, as shown in Figure 8-2. When NSApp finishes processing the event, it gets the next event from the queue and repeats the process again and again until the application terminates.

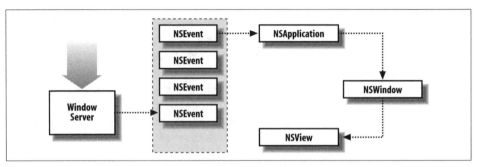

Figure 8-2. The event queue

Responders

Recall that when we introduced the core program framework of NSWindow, NSView, and NSApplication in Chapter 6, we mentioned that each of these classes inherits functionality from the NSResponder class, as shown in Figure 8-3.

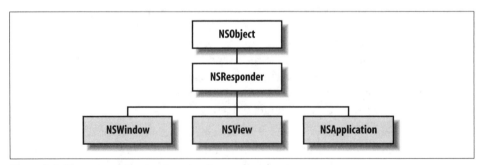

Figure 8-3. The core application framework

The NSResponder class defines the default message-handling behavior of all event-handling objects in an application. The responder model is built around the following three concepts:

Event messages
> Messages that correspond directly to an input event, such as a mouse click or a key press.

Action messages
> Messages describing a higher-level command to be performed, such as cut: or paste:.

Responder chain
> A series of responder objects to which an event or action message is applied. When a given responder object doesn't handle a message, that message is passed to the next object in the chain.

Responder chains allow responder objects to delegate responsibility to other objects in the system. The series in a responder chain is determined by the interrelationships between the application's view, window, and its NSApp object. For a view, the next responder is usually its superview. The next responder of a window's content view is the window itself. From there, the event is passed to the NSApp object.

For action messages, the responder chain is longer. Messages are first passed up the responder chain to the window. Then, if the previous sequence occurred in the key window, the same path is followed for the main window. After that, the message is passed to the NSApp object.

First Responder

Each window in an application keeps track of the object in its view hierarchy with *first responder* status, which is the view that first responds to keyboard events for that window. For example, in TextEdit, the new document window is the first responder, as it is the first to receive events from the keyboard. By default, a window is its own first responder, but any view within the window can become the first responder when the user clicks it with the mouse. If the view cannot handle the event, the event is passed on to the next object in the responder chain.

In a desktop environment where multiple windows can be open at any given time, a user selects a window with the mouse to make it active. When this happens, that window becomes key, and the window's first responder becomes the target of any events generated by the user. If a different window is selected, it becomes key, and its first responder becomes current. If no object has been selected, or if the window has no controls, the window is its own first responder.

Using Interface Builder, or programmatically, you can configure an initialFirstResponder so that when a window appears, the first logical control capable of using keystrokes is brought into focus as the first responder. Recall that in Chapter 5's Currency Converter application, we set the first text field to be the initial first responder.

Views and controls can reject first responder status. For example, a view displaying a static image probably shouldn't accept first responder status. A responder can indicate that it doesn't want to accept first responder status by implementing the `acceptFirstResponder` method and returning NO.

Event Routing

An event is routed based on its type. The NSApp object sends most event messages to the window in which the user action occurred. A mouse event is then forwarded to the view in the window's view hierarchy within which the mouse was clicked. Key events are routed to the first responder. If the view can respond to the event—that is, if it can accept first responder status and define an NSResponder method corresponding to the event message—it handles the event. If the view cannot handle an event, the event is forwarded to the next responder in the responder chain.

The NSWindow class handles some events itself, such as window-moved, window-resized, and window-exposed events, and doesn't forward them to a view. NSApp also processes a few events, such as application-activate and application-deactivate events.

Dot View Application

To illustrate event handling, we'll build an application using a custom NSView subclass that responds to a mouse click by drawing a colored dot. Working through this example will let you see how custom event handling works, while reinforcing the work we did with NSBezierPath in the last chapter. In addition, we'll use the Slider and Color Well controls for the first time.

In Project Builder, create a new Cocoa Application project (File → New Project → Application → Cocoa Application) named "Dot View", and save it in your ~/*LearningCocoa* folder. Then open the *MainMenu.nib* file in Interface Builder.

Create the DotView Class

Creating the functionality of this application will utilize many of the same skills presented in previous chapters. We will start shortening the descriptions of how to perform tasks that we've performed before so that we can provide more details on new topics as they are introduced. If you can't remember how to do something, you should use the procedures presented in previous chapters to help you out. Create the DotView class using the following steps:

1. Create a subclass of NSView called DotView.
2. Open the Show Info window (Tools → Show Info).

3. Add an outlet named `colorWell` to `DotView` using the Info window, and set its type to `NSColorWell` using the drop-down box in the Type column of the Outlet display, as shown in Figure 8-4.

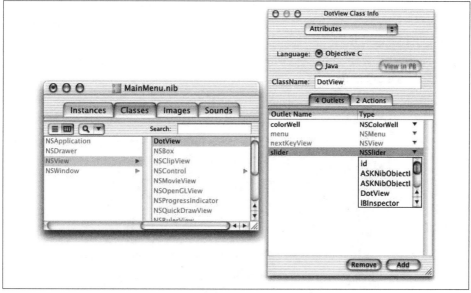

Figure 8-4. Adding the colorWell and slider outlets to DotView

4. Add an outlet named `slider` to `DotView`, and set its type to `NSSlider`.

5. Add an action named `setRadius:` to `DotView`.

6. Add an action named `setColor:` to `DotView`.

7. Click on the `DotView` subclass in the Classes tab, and generate its source files (Classes → Create Files for Dot View).

8. Save the project (File → Save, or ⌘-S).

Create the Interface

To create our interface, perform the following steps:

1. Change the title of the main window to "Dot View". To do this:

   a. Click on the main window, and the title of the Show Info window should change to "NSWindow Info".

   b. Select Attributes from the pull-down menu.

   c. In the Window Title field, change "Window" to "Dot View".

2. Drag a CustomView view from the Containers Palette onto the Dot View window.

3. Assign the DotView class to the CustomView.

   a. Click on the CustomView view.

   b. In the Info window, scroll up and select DotView from the Class list; the name of the view will change from CustomView to DotView.

4. Drag a Slider from the Other Palette onto the Dot View window, and place it as shown in Figure 8-5.

5. Drag a Color Well from the Other Palette onto the Dot View window, and place it as shown in Figure 8-5.

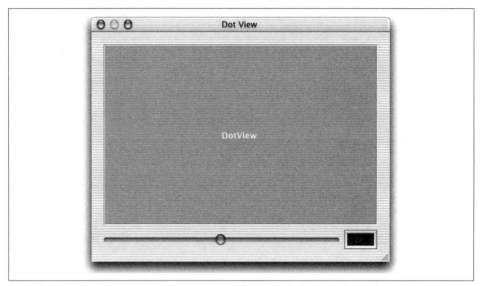

Figure 8-5. The Dot View user interface

Connect the Controls to DotView

Create the following connections using Interface Builder.

1. Control-drag a connection from the slider to the DotView. Make the target/action connection to the setRadius: method in the Connections pane of the Info window.

2. Control-drag a connection from the color well to the DotView. Make the target/action connection to the setColor: method.

3. Control-drag a connection from the DotView to the slider. Make the outlet connection to the slider outlet.

4. Control-drag a connection from the DotView to the color well. Make the outlet connection to the colorWell outlet.

Save (⌘-S) the nib file, and return to Project Builder, where we will finish the application.

Define the DotView Header

Our next step is to finish defining the *DotView.h* header file. Edit the source to match that of Example 8-1. The code that you need to add to the Interface Builder code is shown in boldface.

Example 8-1. DotView.h

```
/* DotView */

#import <Cocoa/Cocoa.h>

@interface DotView : NSView
{
    IBOutlet NSColorWell * colorWell;
    IBOutlet NSSlider * slider;

    NSPoint center;                                            // 1
    NSColor * color;                                           // 2
    float radius;                                              // 3
}
- (IBAction)setColor:(id)sender;
- (IBAction)setRadius:(id)sender;

@end
```

This code defines the following functionality:

1. Defines an NSPoint structure that we'll use to store the center of the dot that will be drawn

2. Defines the color of the dot

3. Defines the radius for the dot

Define the DotView Class

Now that we have defined the header, it's time to add the code for the implementation of the DotView class. The code for this class is too long to fit nicely on one page, so we're going to approach this in two steps. First, Example 8-2 shows the skeleton of our class, with all the methods to implement shown in boldface. As you can see, you will be asked to insert code from later examples as we build the Dot View application. The sections that follow will provide the necessary code, along with explanations of what that code will do.

First, enter the **boldface** text from Example 8-2 into your *DotView.m* file, and insert the appropriate code from Example 8-3 through Example 8-10 as you work through the following sections. A complete version of how your *DotView.m* file should look is shown in Example 8-11.

Example 8-2. Skeleton code for DotView.m

```
#import "DotView.h"

@implementation DotView

- (id)initWithFrame:(NSRect)frame
{
// Insert code from Example 8-3
}

- (void)awakeFromNib
{
// Insert code from Example 8-4
}

- (void)dealloc
{
// Insert code from Example 8-5
}

- (void)drawRect:(NSRect)rect
{
// Insert code from Example 8-6
}

- (BOOL)isOpaque
{
// Insert code from Example 8-7
}

- (void)mouseDown:(NSEvent *)event
{
// Insert code from Example 8-8
}

- (IBAction)setColor:(id)sender
{
// Insert code from Example 8-9
}

- (IBAction)setRadius:(id)sender
{
// Insert code from Example 8-10
}

@end
```

Implement the initWithFrame: method

The initWithFrame: method is the designated initializer for NSView and its subclasses (see the "Designated Initializers" section in Chapter 3 for a refresher of what this means). Add the initWithFrame: method, as shown in Example 8-3.

Example 8-3. The designated initializer method

```
- (id)initWithFrame:(NSRect)frame
{
    self = [super initWithFrame:frame];                     // 1
    center.x = 50.0;                                        // 2
    center.y = 50.0;                                        // 3
    radius = 20.0;                                          // 4
    color = [[NSColor redColor] retain];                   // 5
    return self;                                            // 6
}
```

This code performs the following tasks:

1. Starts the initialization process by calling the designated initializer of the NSView class.

2. Sets the *x*-coordinate of the center of the dot to 50.0.

3. Sets the *y*-coordinate of the center of the dot to 50.0.

4. Sets the radius of the dot to 20.0.

5. Sets the initial color in which the dot will be drawn to red. This line also retains the color so that it will be able for use later. Refer back to the memory management "Rules of Thumb" section in Chapter 4 if necessary.

6. Returns self, the newly initialized view object.

Implement the awakeFromNib: method

As introduced in Chapter 6, the awakeFromNib: method is called when the interface has been fully unpacked from the nib file and all connections have been made. At this point, we want to set the initial state of the slider and color well controls. Add the awakeFromNib: method as shown in Example 8-4.

Example 8-4. Finish setting up the view

```
- (void)awakeFromNib
{
    [colorWell setColor:color];                            // 1
    [slider setFloatValue:radius];                         // 2
}
```

This code performs the following tasks:

1. Sets the color of the color well to the color set up in the initializer. In this case, the default color will be set to red. (For reference, see line 5 in Example 8-3.)

2. Sets the initial value of the slider to the radius we defined in the initializer (line 4 from Example 8-3).

When this method completes, the application will be displayed to the user.

Implement the dealloc method

The dealloc method is called when the view is disposed of, giving it a chance to clean up its memory usage. Add the dealloc method as shown in Example 8-5.

Example 8-5. DotView deallocation method

```
- (void)dealloc
{                                              // 1
    [color release];                           // 2
    [super dealloc];
}
```

This code performs the following tasks:

1. Releases the NSColor object that we've retained in the object instance
2. Calls the dealloc method of the parent NSView class so that any cleanup performed by the super class can be performed

Implement the drawRect: method

The drawRect: method is where the view draws itself to the screen. Add the drawRect: method as shown in Example 8-6.

Example 8-6. Drawing the interface

```
- (void)drawRect:(NSRect)rect
{                                              // 1
    NSRect dotRect;

    // Draw the background                     // 2
    [[NSColor whiteColor] set];
    NSRectFill([self bounds]);

    // Set the location of the dot             // 3
    dotRect.origin.x = center.x - radius;
    dotRect.origin.y = center.y - radius;

    // Define the size the dot                 // 4
    dotRect.size.width = 2 * radius;
    dotRect.size.height = 2 * radius;

    // Set the default color                   // 5
    [color set];

    // Draw the dot                            // 6
    [[NSBezierPath bezierPathWithOvalInRect:dotRect] fill];

}
```

The code performs the following tasks:

1. Declares an NSRect structure that defines the rectangle into which our dot will be drawn.

2. Sets the current drawing color to white (whiteColor) and draws the background of the view.

3. Determines the origin of the rectangle into which our dot will be drawn. Because we have to determine the rectangle of the dot by specifying its origin rather than its center, and we want the center of the dot to be the location of our center NSPoint, we have to offset the origin appropriately. This code finds a point offset towards the origin of the view's coordinate system that will place the dot's center exactly where the user clicked.

4. Defines the size of the rectangle into which our dot will be drawn. Since the code in step 3 determined the lower-left corner of the rectangle, we simply need to size the rectangle to be the diameter (2 * radius) of the dot.

5. Sets the current color of DotView to the active drawing color, based on the color we defined in line 5 of Example 8-3.

6. Creates an oval Bezier path inside the dotRect rectangle and fills it with the default color.

Implement the isOpaque method

The Quartz graphics engine is designed to draw multiple layers of content quickly with various levels of transparency. However, no matter how much performance the engineers at Apple manage to squeeze out of the code, the Quartz engine can operate faster if it knows that a view doesn't need to be composited with its background. The isOpaque method of NSView lets this optimization be performed. Add the isOpaque method as shown in Example 8-7.

Example 8-7. Telling Cocoa that our view is opaque

```
- (BOOL)isOpaque
{
    return YES;
}
```

If we return NO to this method, Quartz will composite anything drawn by our view with the contents of views behind it. Since we return YES, Quartz doesn't need to perform this operation and can save a bit of time.

Implement the mouseDown: method

Overriding NSResponder methods in a view is the best way to handle events for the view. One such method is mouseDown:, which is invoked when the user presses the mouse button. All of the NSResponder event-handling methods receive an NSEvent object instance as an argument. This event contains the mouse location where the click occurred in the coordinate system of the window.

Add an implementation of this method to match, as shown in Example 8-8.

Example 8-8. Handling mouse-down events

```
- (void)mouseDown:(NSEvent *)event
{
    NSPoint eventLocation = [event locationInWindow];         // 1
    center = [self convertPoint:eventLocation fromView:nil];  // 2
    [self setNeedsDisplay:YES];                               // 3
}
```

This code performs the following tasks:

1. Gets the location of the mouse click from the event. The location of a mouse click is expressed in terms of the coordinate system of the window in which the click occurred.

2. Converts the location of the event from the window coordinate system to the coordinate system of the view. When called with a nil view parameter, it translates the point from the window coordinate system to which the view belongs. If you call this method with a view object, the coordinates will be converted into the coordinate system of that view. In this case, we need the coordinates converted from the coordinate system of the window.

3. Sets a flag indicating that the view needs to be redrawn. The redraw will be done automatically by the NSApp object after the event is handled and the run loop has exited our code.

Implement the setColor: action method

This method is called by the color well whenever the user changes the color of the dot. This method assumes that the sender is a control capable of returning a color. Edit the setColor: method as shown in Example 8-9.

Example 8-9. Changing the color with which we draw

```
- (IBAction)setColor:(id)sender
{
    NSColor * newColor = [sender color];   // 1
    [newColor retain];                     // 2
    [color release];                       // 3
    color = newColor;                      // 4
    [self setNeedsDisplay:YES];            // 5
}
```

This code performs the following tasks:

1. Sets the newColor variable to the color obtained from the sender of the event.

2. Retains the newColor object.

3. Releases the old color object. Remember, as presented in Chapter 4, that we release the old object after retaining the new one so that there will be no problems if the two objects are actually the same.

4. Sets the color variable to the newColor object.

5. Sets a flag indicating that the view needs to be redrawn to display the new color defined by the user. The redraw will be done automatically by the AppKit after the event is handled.

Implement the setRadius: action method

This method is called by the slider whenever the user moves the slider left or right to change the size of the dot. This method assumes that the send is a control capable of returning a floating-point number. Edit the setRadius: method as shown in Example 8-10.

Example 8-10. Changing the size of our dot

```
- (IBAction)setRadius:(id)sender
{
    radius = [sender floatValue];                            // 1
    [self setNeedsDisplay:YES];                              // 2
}
```

This code performs the following tasks:

1. Sets the radius variable to a float value (floatValue) obtained from the slider.

2. Sets a flag indicating that the view needs to be redrawn to display the newly resized dot, based on the movement of the slider. The redraw will be done automatically by the AppKit after the event is handled.

When you've completed entering all of the code from Example 8-2 through Example 8-10, your *DotView.m* file should look like the code shown in Example 8-11.

Example 8-11. The complete DotView.m file

```
#import "DotView.h"

@implementation DotView

- (id)initWithFrame:(NSRect)frame
{
    self = [super initWithFrame:frame];
    center.x = 50.0;
    center.y = 50.0;
    radius = 20.0;
    color = [[NSColor redColor] retain];
    return self;
}
```

Example 8-11. The complete DotView.m file (continued)

```objc
- (void)awakeFromNib
{
    [colorWell setColor:color];
    [slider setFloatValue:radius];
}

- (void)dealloc
{
    [color release];
    [super dealloc];
}

- (void)drawRect:(NSRect)rect
{
    NSRect dotRect;

    [[NSColor whiteColor] set];
    NSRectFill([self bounds]);

    dotRect.origin.x = center.x - radius;
    dotRect.origin.y = center.y - radius;

    dotRect.size.width = 2 * radius;
    dotRect.size.height = 2 * radius;

    [color set];

    [[NSBezierPath bezierPathWithOvalInRect:dotRect] fill];
}

- (BOOL)isOpaque
{
    return YES;
}

- (void)mouseDown:(NSEvent *)event
{
    NSPoint eventLocation = [event locationInWindow];
    center = [self convertPoint:eventLocation fromView:nil];
    [self setNeedsDisplay:YES];
}

- (IBAction)setColor:(id)sender
{
    NSColor * newColor = [sender color];
    [newColor retain];
    [color release];
    color = newColor;
    [self setNeedsDisplay:YES];
}
```

Example 8-11. The complete DotView.m file (continued)

```
- (IBAction)setRadius:(id)sender
{
    radius = [sender floatValue];
    [self setNeedsDisplay:YES];
}

@end
```

Once your *DotView.m* file is complete, save the project (File → Save, or ⌘-S), and then build and run the Dot View application (Build → Build and Run, or ⌘-R). You should see something that looks like Figure 8-6.

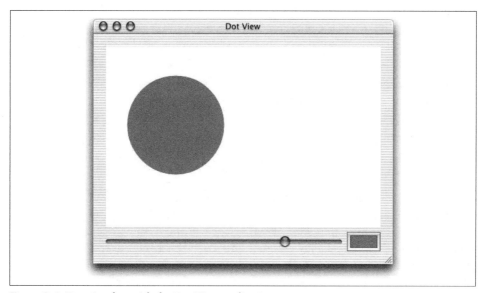

Figure 8-6. Drawing dots with the Dot View application

Perform the following actions on the application to see if the code that we added works:

- Click anywhere in the view, and you'll see the dot move to the point that you clicked. Each time you click the mouse, a mouseDown event is sent to the view, resulting in the mouseDown: method being called.

- Move the slider left and right, and watch the size of the dot get smaller or bigger, respectively. Notice that the slider issues events to the application as it moves, allowing you to see the results of the action dynamically.

- Click on the color well, and pick a new color for the dot from the palette that appears. Just like the slider, the color well responds dynamically.

Note that when you resize the application, the view doesn't autosize as we'd probably like. Exercise 6 at the end of this chapter adds this functionality.

Event Delegation

In an object-oriented application, an object often must know what's going on with other objects in the system. One of the patterns used extensively in Cocoa is *delegation*. Think of delegation as a means by which an object's behavior can be modified without needing to create a custom subclass.

A *delegate* is a helper object that receives messages from another object when specific events occur. An object sends requests to its delegate, allowing the delegate to influence its behavior and aid in decision-making.

For an object to delegate responsibility, it must declare a delegate outlet, along with a set of delegate messages that will be sent to it when "interesting" things happen. To become a delegate, an object must implement one or more of the delegate methods. There are several types of delegation messages, depending on the expected role of the delegate:

- Some messages are purely informational, occurring after an event has happened. These allow a delegate to coordinate its actions with the delegating object.

- Some messages are sent before an action will occur, allowing the delegate to veto or permit the action.

- Other delegation messages assign a specific task to a delegate, such as filling a browser with cells.

As an example, take a child who is told by a friend to act silly. Depending on the circumstances, he may or may not do as his friend suggests. If his parents are around, the child might ask his parents (or at least glance at one of the parents to see if they are looking) if he should act silly before doing so. In this case, the child is delegating the decision of whether to act silly in front of his parents. The parent then has the opportunity to approve or deny the request to act silly. Figure 8-7 shows this relationship, albeit abstractly.

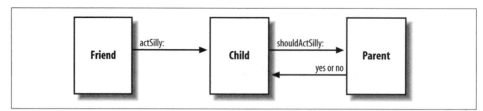

Figure 8-7. Delegation in action

You can set a custom object as the delegate of a Cocoa framework object by making a connection in Interface Builder, or you can set it programmatically by using the setDelegate: method. Your custom classes can also define their own delegate variables and delegation protocols for client objects. Just remember that delegates are not retained by the objects that delegate messages to them.

To show delegation in action, we will modify our Dot View application to respond to a request to close the application's window. We will create and add a delegate that, when a window sends a `windowShouldClose` message to it, will create an alert box asking the user if it is okay to close. To create the alert box, Cocoa provides the `NSRunAlertPanel` function. This function has the following signature:

```
int NSRunAlertPanel (NSString * title,
                     NSString * message,
                     NSString * defaultButtonLabel,
                     NSString * alternateButtonLabel,
                     NSString * otherButtonLabel,
                     ...)                        // printf style args for message
```

Table 8-1 provides a brief summary of the parameters for this function.

Table 8-1. NSRunAlertPanel parameters

Parameter	Description
`title`	The title of the sheet, displayed near the top of the sheet in a bold font.
`Msg`	An optional message string that appears near the bottom of the sheet. The string can contain `printf`-style arguments such as %@, %s, and %i.
`defaultButton`	The label for the sheet's default button, typically "OK".
`alternateButton`	The label for the sheet's alternate button, typically "Cancel".
`otherButton`	The label for a third button. If you pass `nil`, only two buttons will appear on the sheet.

Create a Delegate

Open the Dot View project in Project Builder, if you don't already have it open, and open the *MainMenu.nib* file in Interface Builder. Perform the following steps to create a delegate class and to assign an instance of it as a delegate to the window:

1. Create a new subclass of `NSObject` called `MyDelegate`.
2. Instantiate `MyDelegate` (Classes → Instantiate MyDelegate).
3. In the Instances pane of the *MainMenu.nib* window, Control-drag a connection from the Window icon to the `MyDelegate` object icon, as shown in Figure 8-8.
4. Make the connection to the delegate outlet of the window by clicking on the Connect button in the Info window.
5. Save the nib file (⌘-S).
6. Create the files for the `MyDelegate` class, and add them to the project.
   a. Click on the Classes tab in the *MainMenu.nib* window.
   b. Select MyDelegate.
   c. Select Classes → Create Files for MyDelegate from the menu bar.

Return to Project Builder, and edit *MyDelegate.m* to match the code in Example 8-12.

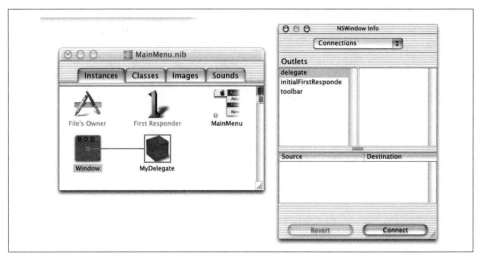

Figure 8-8. Control-dragging from Window to MyDelegate

Example 8-12. MyDelegate.m

```
#import "MyDelegate.h"

@implementation MyDelegate

- (BOOL)windowShouldClose:(NSWindow *)sender                        // 1
{
    int answer = NSRunAlertPanel(@"Close", @"Are you certain?",    // 2
                                 @"Close", @"Cancel", nil);
    switch (answer) {                                              // 3
        case NSAlertDefaultReturn:
            return YES;
        default:
            return NO;
    }
}

@end
```

The code we added performs the following tasks:

1. Implements the windowShouldClose: method. When a window has a delegate that implements this method, it asks the delegate if it should close before doing so.

2. Calls the NSRunAlertPanel function, which will open an alert dialog box that asks the user's permission to close the window.

3. Returns YES or NO depending on the result from the alert dialog box. If the alert dialog box returns a value that matches the constant NSAlertDefaultReturn, then the window will be closed.

Now save the project (⌘-S), and build and run the application (⌘-R). When you try to close the application window, you will see something that looks like Figure 8-9. Notice what happens when you hit the Cancel button on the alert box. Notice that the alert only comes up when you close the window. If you quit the application, the alert panel will not appear. A different delegate method, the `applicationShouldTerminate:` method of the `NSApplication` class, is needed to enable this functionality. Exercise 4 at the end of the chapter will do so.

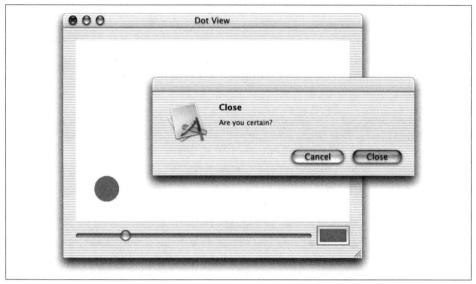

Figure 8-9. Dot View asking permission to close

Delegation Using Sheets

Another example of delegation appears in the implementation of Aqua's *sheets*—a new type of dialog box that is attached to a document window's titlebar. Sheets slide out from the window title, making their relationship to a document clear. Sheets are modal only for the window to which they are attached, so you can proceed to other tasks in an application before dismissing them.

Adding support for sheets is more complicated than using a standard dialog box, because the function that displays an alert sheet—`NSBeginAlertSheet`—is asynchronous. In other words, it does not wait for the user to dismiss the sheet before returning control to the caller. Instead, it returns control immediately after presenting the sheet. To discover the result of the user's interaction with the sheet, you must pass a reference to a delegate object, along with a method selector to invoke as a callback when the sheet is dismissed. When the sheet finished, the callback method will be invoked and passed a result code, indicating which button the user pressed.

The NSBeginAlertSheet function has the following signature:

```
void NSBeginAlertSheet(NSString * title,
                       NSString * defaultButtonLabel,
                       NSString * alternateButtonLabel,
                       NSString * otherButtonLabel,
                       NSWindow * docWindow,
                       id modalDelegate,
                       SEL didEndSelector,
                       SEL didDismissSelector,
                       void * contextInfo,
                       NSString * message,
                       ...)                      // printf args for message
```

This looks a bit daunting at first, but it's really not as difficult to use as it might look. Table 8-2 provides a brief parameter summary for NSBeginAlertSheet.

Table 8-2. NSBeginAlertSheet parameters

Parameter	Description
title	The title of the sheet, displayed near the top of the sheet in a bold font.
defaultButton	The label for the sheet's default button, typically "OK".
alternateButton	The label for the sheet's alternate button, typically "Cancel".
otherButton	The label for a third button. If you pass nil, only two buttons will appear on the sheet.
docWindow	A reference to the window to which the sheet will be attached.
modalDelegate	A reference to the object that will respond when the user dismisses the sheet.
didEndSelector	A selector for a method implemented by the modalDelegate. The method will be invoked when the modal session is ended, but before the sheet is dismissed.
didDismissSelector	A selector for a method implemented by the modalDelegate. The method will be called after the sheet is dismissed. It is useful for any extra cleanup that might be necessary. Pass NULL if you don't need this functionality.
contextInfo	Additional data to pass to the modalDelegate as a parameter of the didEnd and didDismiss methods.
msg	An optional message string that appears near the bottom of the sheet. The string can contain printf-style arguments such as %@, %s, and %i.

Edit the *MyDelegate.m* code, replacing the windowShouldClose: method and adding the sheetClosed: method, as shown in Example 8-13.

Example 8-13. Changing MyDelegate.m to use sheets

```
#import "MyDelegate.h"

@implementation MyDelegate

- (BOOL)windowShouldClose:(NSWindow *)sender
{
    NSString * msg = @"Should this window close?";          // 1
    SEL sel = @selector(sheetClosed:returnCode:contextInfo:);  // 2
```

Example 8-13. Changing MyDelegate.m to use sheets (continued)

```
    NSBeginAlertSheet(@"Close",       // title                            // 3
                      @"OK",          // default label
                      @"Cancel",      // alternate button label
                      nil,            // other button label
                      sender,         // document window
                      self,           // modal delegate
                      sel,            // selector to method
                      NULL,           // dismiss selector
                      sender,         // context info
                      msg,            // message
                      nil);           // params for msg string
    return NO;                                                            // 4

}

- (void)sheetClosed:(NSWindow *)sheet
         returnCode:(int)returnCode
         contextInfo:(void *)contextInfo
{
    if (returnCode == NSAlertDefaultReturn) {                             // 5
        [(NSWindow *)contextInfo close];
    }
}

@end
```

This code performs the following tasks:

1. Creates a string that will be displayed in the sheet.

2. Obtains a selector to the method that calls the sheet back when finished. In this case, we want the `sheetClosed:returnCode:contextInfo:` method (which we define in step 5) called.

3. Calls the `NSBeginAlertSheet` function with a whole set of arguments describing what the sheet should display and what object and methods it should call when it is done.

4. Returns `NO` so that the application's run loop can continue. The window will remain open, but a sheet will be attached to it.

5. Checks the value returned using the equality (`==`) operator from the sheet—which checks to see if two values are equal to each other—and closes the window or not, depending on its value.

Too often, newcomers to C (and many not-so-newcomers) make the error of using the assignment operator (`=`) when they mean to use the equality (`==`) operator. Using the assignment operator in a check like this will usually result in an expression that is legal, but will not work as expected. Such errors can be subtle and hard to catch.

Save the project (⌘-S), and then build and run the application (⌘-R). Now when you try to close the window (⌘-W), you should see something like Figure 8-10.

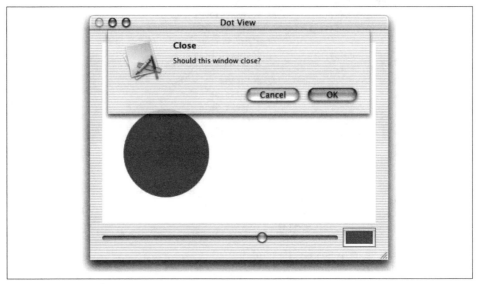

Figure 8-10. Aqua sheets in action

Notifications

Another way to communicate events between objects in Cocoa is via a *notification*. A notification is a message broadcast to all objects in an application that are interested in the event that the notification represents.

Notifications can also pass along relevant data about the event. Notifications differ from delegation in that notification happens after the object has performed the action instead of before. The object receiving a notification doesn't get a chance to say whether or not an action will be taken. Also, an object can have many notification observers, but only one delegate.

Using our child/friend/parent example again, once the child has acted silly, there might be a set of friends who will want to know about it. Through notification, our child can tell his friends that he acted silly, as shown in Figure 8-11.

It would be impractical for everyone who wanted to know that the child had acted silly to register her interest directly with the child. The child would have to implement the functionality needed to keep track of all the interested friends and send notifications to them in turn. Luckily, Cocoa has provided a set of classes to help us with this. Here's the way the notification process, shown in Figure 8-12, works in Cocoa:

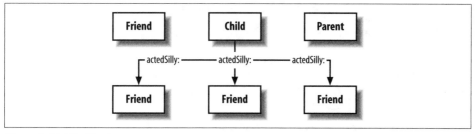

Figure 8-11. Notification

1. Objects interested in an event that happens elsewhere in an application—say, the addition of a record to a database—register themselves with a notification center (an instance of the NSNotificationCenter class) as observers of that event. During the registration process, the observer specifies that a method should be invoked by the notification center when the event occurs.

2. The object that adds the record to the database (or some such event) posts a notification (an instance of the NSNotification class) to the notification center. The notification object contains a tag that identifies the notification, the ID of the object posting the notification, and, optionally, a dictionary of supplemental data.

3. The notification center then sends a message to each registered observer, invoking the method specified by each observer and passing the notification.

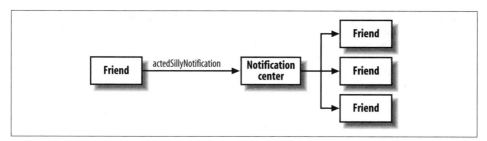

Figure 8-12. Notifications

How Notifications Work

A class that posts notifications defines the names of those notifications in its header file as static NSString objects. For example, the NSWindow class defines a set of 16 notifications in its header file that allow other objects to monitor changes in the window's status:

```
APPKIT_EXTERN NSString * NSWindowDidBecomeKeyNotification;
APPKIT_EXTERN NSString * NSWindowDidBecomeMainNotification;
APPKIT_EXTERN NSString * NSWindowDidChangeScreenNotification;
APPKIT_EXTERN NSString * NSWindowDidDeminiaturizeNotification;
APPKIT_EXTERN NSString * NSWindowDidExposeNotification;
```

```
APPKIT_EXTERN NSString * NSWindowDidMiniaturizeNotification;
APPKIT_EXTERN NSString * NSWindowDidMoveNotification;
APPKIT_EXTERN NSString * NSWindowDidResignKeyNotification;
APPKIT_EXTERN NSString * NSWindowDidResignMainNotification;
APPKIT_EXTERN NSString * NSWindowDidResizeNotification;
APPKIT_EXTERN NSString * NSWindowDidUpdateNotification;
APPKIT_EXTERN NSString * NSWindowWillCloseNotification;
APPKIT_EXTERN NSString * NSWindowWillMiniaturizeNotification;
APPKIT_EXTERN NSString * NSWindowWillMoveNotification;
APPKIT_EXTERN NSString * NSWindowWillBeginSheetNotification;
APPKIT_EXTERN NSString * NSWindowDidEndSheetNotification;
```

An object that wants to receive one of these notifications must use the notification name when registering with the notification center.

Notifications in Action

To show how to work with notifications, we will add some functionality to our Dot View application delegate to listen to notifications that NSWindow generates when sheets are used. Edit the *MyDelegate.m* file, adding the code shown in Example 8-14. The order of methods in a source-code file doesn't matter; however, you usually see init methods towards the top of a class implementation.

Example 8-14. Adding a notification handler to Dot View

```
- (id)init
{
    NSNotificationCenter * center = [NSNotificationCenter defaultCenter];    // 1
    [center addObserver:self                                                 // 2
                selector:@selector(sheetDidBegin:)
                    name:NSWindowWillBeginSheetNotification
                  object:nil];
    return self;
}

- (void)sheetDidBegin:(NSNotification *)notification
{
    NSLog(@"Notification: %@", [notification name]);                         // 3
}
```

The code that we added performs the following functionality:

1. Obtains the default notification center for the application. All applications have a default notification center available to them.

2. Adds the MyDelegate instance object as an observer requesting that the sheetDidBegin: method be called whenever an NSWindowWillBeginSheetNotification is received by the notification center. Passing nil as the object parameter indicates that our object is interested in notifications from any window. If we want to limit the notifications to just a particular window, we can pass a reference to that window here.

---

3. Logs a message whenever the `sheetDidBegin:` method is called.

Save the project (⌘-S), and then build and run the application (⌘-R). When you run Dot View and try to close the window, the sheet will appear with the following message in the console pane of Project Builder:

```
2002-04-01 12:07:47.837 Dot View[800] Notification:
NSWindowWillBeginSheetNotification
```

Obviously, you wouldn't display notifications like this to users of your applications. Rather, you would use them inside your application to coordinate various activities.

Memory-Management Considerations

Notification centers do not retain observer objects, so you should be careful to remove any observers before they are deallocated. This is to prevent the notification center from sending a message to an object that no longer exists. MyDelegate registers itself as an observer in its init method, so the object should remove itself in its dealloc method. Add the dealloc method implementation to *MyDelegate.m*, as shown in Example 8-15.

Example 8-15. Removing an object from the Notification Center

```
- (void)dealloc
{
    [[NSNotificationCenter defaultCenter] removeObserver:self];
    [super dealloc];
}
```

If an object registers another object with the notification center without releasing it after removing it from the notification center, the application will leak memory. Therefore, any object that registers itself, or another object, with the notification center should remove itself or the registered object from the notification center before it is deallocated.

Exercises

1. Allow the dot in the Dot View application to follow a mouse drag so that the user can interactively place the dot. Hint: use the `mouseDragged:` method defined in the NSResponder class.

2. Set the initial position of the dot in the Dot View application to the center of the view instead of the coordinates (50.0,50.0).

3. Optimize the `setRadius:` method so that `setNeedsDisplay` is only called if the original value and the new value for `radius` variable are not the same.

4. Implement the NSApplication delegate method of applicationShouldTerminate: to display a confirmation dialog box when the user tries to quit the application.

5. Change the initial color of the dot from red to some other color.

6. Change the Dot View Application so the size of the view changes if the user resizes (or maximizes) the window. What happens to the slider and color well when the window is resized?

CHAPTER 9

Models and Data Functionality

In the previous four chapters, we covered the front end of Cocoa applications, windows and views, and how you can use controllers behind them. Now we turn our attention to the back end—the model—and how the data functionality of an application works.

To take full advantage of Cocoa's data-handling mechanisms, we must first explain two concepts that we didn't cover when we first introduced Objective-C and the Foundation Kit (see Chapter 4): protocols and key-value coding. After covering these topics, we deal with how to connect a user interface to an underlying data model and how that model can be saved and opened.

Protocols

Many pieces of Cocoa functionality make use of an Objective-C language feature called a *protocol*. A protocol is simply a list of method declarations. A class is said to *conform* to a protocol when it provides implementations of the methods that a protocol defines.

To help explain the concept of a protocol, think of the similarities between a waiter at a restaurant and a vending machine.* Even though the waiter and the vending machine are nowhere close to being similar objects from an inheritance standpoint, they can both implement methods related to serving food and taking money. Roughly, we could describe a protocol implemented by these two objects as the following methods:

```
takeOrder
serveFood
takeMoney
returnChange
complainTo
```

---

* Duncan waited tables for many years while in college and is thankful that nobody tried to tip him over in order to get more food or money out of him.

Of course, a vending machine doesn't usually serve very tasty or nutritious food and doesn't respond very well, if at all, to complaints. Additionally, you usually have to give vending machines money before they will take your order. But let's not get caught up too much in the details of our analogy. At a very basic level, the vending machine and waiter aren't all that different from each other—at least from the point of view of the person getting food. And note that it is easy to take this protocol and find other food-service situations in which it applies, such as getting a donut from the local convenience store.

In object-oriented programming, protocols are useful in the following situations:

- To declare methods that other classes are expected to implement. This lets programs define methods that they will call on objects but that other developers will actually implement, and this is crucial to loading bundles and plug-ins.

- To declare the public interface to an object while concealing its class. This lets more than one implementation of an object "hide" behind a protocol and prevents users from using unadvertised methods.

- To capture similarities among classes that are not hierarchically related. Classes that are unrelated in most respects might need to implement similar methods for use by similar outside components. Protocols help formalize these relationships while preserving encapsulation.

Objective-C defines two kinds of protocols: informal and formal. An *informal protocol* uses *categories* to list a group of methods but doesn't associate them with any particular class or implementation.

Categories

Categories are Objective-C constructs that allow you to add methods to existing classes. This lets you add functionality to undefined classes in a way that is different than inheritance. For example, the drawAtPoint: method that we used on NSString in Chapter 7 is not defined in the Foundation Kit. Instead, the AppKit defines it as a category that adds methods to the NSString class so you can draw strings into views.

A detailed discussion of categories is beyond the scope of this book. For more information on categories, see the *Object-Oriented Programming and the Objective-C Language* book installed with the Developer Tools in the */Developer/Documentation/Cocoa /ObjectiveC* folder.

A *formal protocol*, on the other hand, binds the list methods to a type definition that allows typing of objects by protocol name. Additionally, when a class declares that it implements a formal protocol, all of the methods of the protocol must be implemented.

Key-Value Coding

Key-value coding is a kind of shorthand. It is defined by an informal protocol used for accessing instance variables (also known as *properties*) indirectly by using string names (known as *keys*), rather than directly through the invocation of an accessor method* or as instance variables. The key-value coding informal protocol (more accurately, the NSKeyValueCoding protocol) is available for use by any object that inherits from NSObject. Several Cocoa components, as well as its scripting support, take advantage of key-value coding.

The two basic methods for manipulating objects using the key-value coding protocol are as follows:

valueForKey:

Returns the value for the property identified by the key. The default implementation searches for a public accessor method based on the key name given. For example, if the key name given is *price*, a method named price or getPrice will be invoked. If neither method is found, the implementation will look for an instance variable named price and access it directly.

takeValue:forKey:

Sets the value for the property identified by the key to the value given. For our example of *price*, the default implementation will search for a public accessor method named setPrice. If the method is not found, it will attempt to access the price instance variable directly.

Key-Value Coding and Primitive Types

The methods in the NSKeyValueCoding protocol work only with objects. Therefore, if you have properties that deal in numbers, you need to use the NSNumber class instead of primitive types such as int, float, and double.

A Key-Value Coding Example

To show key-value coding in action, we will create a simple example based on a FoodItem class. By now, you should be familiar with what you'll see in this example, except for how we use key-value coding. Perform the following steps:

1. Create a new Foundation Tool in Project Builder (File → New Project → Tool → Foundation Tool) named "keyvaluecoding", and save it in your ~/*LearningCocoa* folder.

---

* Accessor methods, along with properties, were introduced in Chapter 3.

2. Create a new Objective-C class named FoodItem (File → New File → Cocoa → Objective-C Class), as shown in Figure 9-1. Be sure to create both the *.h* and *.m* files.

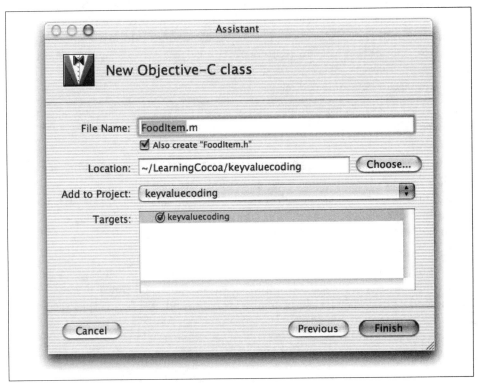

Figure 9-1. Creating the FoodItem class

3. Edit the *FoodItem.h* file as follows:

```objc
#import <Foundation/Foundation.h>

@interface FoodItem : NSObject {
    NSString * name;                          // a
    NSNumber * price;                         // b
}

- (NSString *)name;                           // c
- (void)setName:(NSString *)aName;            // d

- (NSNumber *)price;                          // e
- (void)setPrice:(NSNumber *)aPrice;          // f

@end
```

This code adds the following things:

a. The name instance variable of type NSString. This variable will store the name of the food item.

b. The price instance variable of type NSNumber. This variable will store the price of the food item.

c. Accessor method that returns the name of the food item.

d. Accessor method that allows the name of the food item to be set.

e. Accessor method that returns the price of the food item.

f. Accessor method that allows the price of the foot item to be set.

4. Edit the *FoodItem.m* file as follows:

```objc
#import "FoodItem.h"

@implementation FoodItem

- (id)init                                              // a
{
    [super init];
    [self setName:@"New Item"];
    [self setPrice:[NSNumber numberWithFloat:0.0]];
    return self;
}

- (NSString *)name                                      // b
{
    return name;
}

- (void)setName:(NSString *)newName                     // c
{
    [newName retain];
    [name release]
    name = newName;
}

- (NSNumber *)price                                     // d
{
    return price;
}

- (void)setPrice:(NSNumber *)newPrice                   // e
{
    [newPrice retain];
    [price release];
    price = newPrice;
}

@end
```

The code we added performs the following tasks:

    a. Initializes the object with some default values.

    b. Implements the `name` accessor method.

    c. Implements the `setName:` accessor method. Notice that we retain the new object, release the old one, then set the `name` variable to the new object, in accordance with the rules we discussed in Chapter 4.

    d. Implements the `price` accessor method.

    e. Implements the `setPrice:` accessor method.

5. Edit the *main.m* file (located in the *Sources* folder in Project Builder's left pane) as follows:

```
#import <Foundation/Foundation.h>
#import "FoodItem.h"

int main (int argc, const char * argv[]) {
    NSAutoreleasePool * pool = [[NSAutoreleasePool alloc] init];

    FoodItem * candyBar = [[FoodItem alloc] init];

    [candyBar takeValue:@"Aero" forKey:@"name"];                     // a
    [candyBar takeValue:[NSNumber numberWithFloat:1.25] forKey:@"price"]; // b

    NSLog(@"item name: %@", [candyBar valueForKey:@"name"]);        // c
    NSLog(@"    price: %@", [candyBar valueForKey:@"price"]);       // d
    [candyBar release];                                             // e

    [pool release];
    return 0;
}
```

The code that we added performs the following tasks:

    a. Instructs the `candyBar` object to set the name instance variable to Aero.[*]

    b. Instructs the `candyBar` object to set the price instance variable to 1.25. We use the `NSNumber` class to wrap primitive types for use as objects in collections and in key-value coding.

    c. Instructs the `candyBar` object to return the object assigned to the name variable and prints it using the `NSLog` function.

    d. Instructs the `candyBar` object to return the object assigned to the price variable and prints it out using the `NSLog` function.

    e. Releases the `candyBar` object.

6. Save the project (⌘-S), and then build and run the application (Build → Build and Run, or ⌘-R).

---

[*] Aero is a very tasty chocolate bar made in Europe by Nestlé. You can occasionally find them in the U.S. at specialty stores.

The following output appears in Project Builder's console:

```
2002-04-10 15:31:57.584 Key Value Coding[1382] item name: Aero
2002-04-10 15:31:57.585 Key Value Coding[1382]     price: 1.25

Key Value Coding has exited with status 0.
```

Obviously, for a real program of this length, using key-value coding is overkill compared to setting and retrieving the instance variables directly through accessor methods. Where key-value coding comes into its own is for hooking up model objects—those that implement logic and/or store data—to the generic view objects that Cocoa provides.

Some of Cocoa's view components let you define an *identifier* attribute. When the identifier attribute is set to a property key name for a model object, the component can automatically get, display, and set the value of the property without having to know anything about its implementation. We're going to see how this works with table views in the next section.

We're now done with this example application. Close the project in Project Builder before moving on.

Table Views

Table views are objects that display data as rows and columns. In a table view, a row typically maps to one object in your data model, while a column maps to an attribute of the object for that row. Figure 9-2 shows a table view and its component parts.

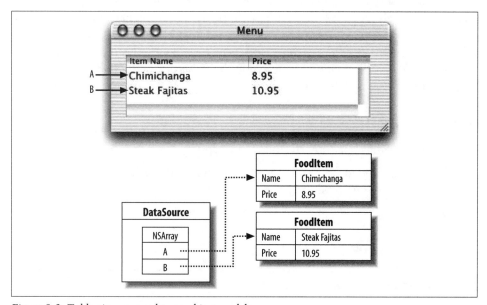

Figure 9-2. Table view mapped to an object model

In Model-Viewer-Controller (MVC) terms, a data source is a controller object that communicates with a model object (typically an array) and the view object. This relationship is shown in Figure 9-3.

Figure 9-3. A data source as a controller between a model and a view

To have their data displayed properly, model objects must implement a couple of methods from the NSTableDataSource informal protocol:

```
- (int)numberOfRowsInTableView:(NSTableView *)tableView;
```

```
- (id)tableView:(NSTableView *)tableView
        objectValueForTableColumn:(NSTableColumn *)tableColumn row:(int)row;
```

The first method allows the table view to ask its data source how many rows of data are in the data model. The second method is used by the table view to retrieve an object value from the data model by row and column.

Table View Example

To show how table views and models go together, we'll build a simple application to keep track of food items in a form that might be used to generate a menu. In Project Builder, create a new Cocoa Application project (File → New Project → Application → Cocoa Application) named "Menu", and save it in your *~/LearningCocoa* folder. Then open the *MainMenu.nib* file (located in the *Resources* folder of Project Builder's left pane) in Interface Builder.

Create the Interface

To create the interface, perform the following steps:

1. Title the main window "Menu" in the Window Title field of the Info window (Tools → Show Info, or Shift-⌘-I).

2. Drag a table view object (NSTableView) from the Cocoa-Data views palette, as shown in Figure 9-4.

3. Resize the table view to fill the window.

4. Change the Autosizing attributes so that the table view will always occupy the entire window, as shown in Figure 9-5.

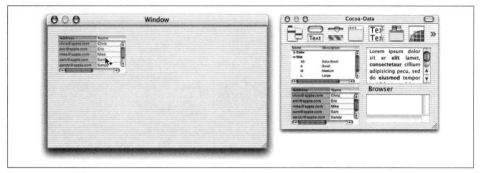

Figure 9-4. Adding a table view object to the interface

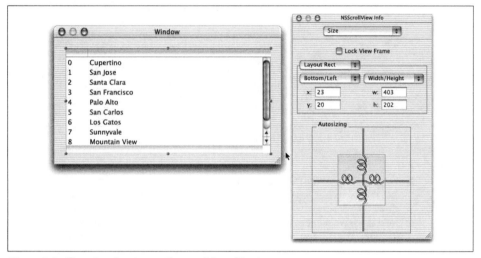

Figure 9-5. Changing the size attributes of the table view

Configure the Table Columns

The next step is to configure the columns by adjusting their width, giving them titles, and, most importantly, assigning identifiers to the columns so Cocoa's key-value coding can operate.

1. Make the width of the columns equal. Select the leftmost column (you may have to double-click), hold the cursor over the right edge of the column so that it turns into a pair of horizontally opposed arrows, then drag the column edge so the column view is divided in half.

2. Double-click on the header bar for the left column and type *Item Name*, then press Tab to move to the header bar for the right column.

3. Type *Price* as the header for the right column, then press Tab to select the left column.

4. Edit the Identifier field for the left column in the Attributes pane of the Info panel so it reads *name*, as shown in Figure 9-6.

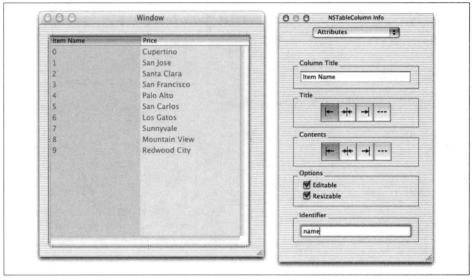

Figure 9-6. Editing the identifier attribute of a table column

 Don't confuse the Column Title field, located at the top of the Attributes panel, with the Identifier field at the bottom of the window. These serve two entirely different purposes. The Column Title field is for the benefit of your users and should contain the title you've assigned to that column in steps 2 and 3. The Identifier is an internal programmatic name that refers to the name of the property that should be displayed in the column.

5. Repeat for the right column, assigning it an Identifier of *price*.

Declare the Data Source Class

A data source can be any object in your application that supplies the table view with data.

1. Create a subclass of NSObject, and name it MyDataSource.
2. Instantiate the MyDataSource class (Classes → Instantiate MyDataSource).
3. Draw a connection from the table view object to the MyDataSource object in the Instances window. Make sure that you have selected the table view, not its surrounding scroll view before you draw the connection. The table view will turn a darker shade of gray when selected.

4. Select the dataSource outlet in the Connections pane of the Info window, as shown in Figure 9-7, and click the Connect button.

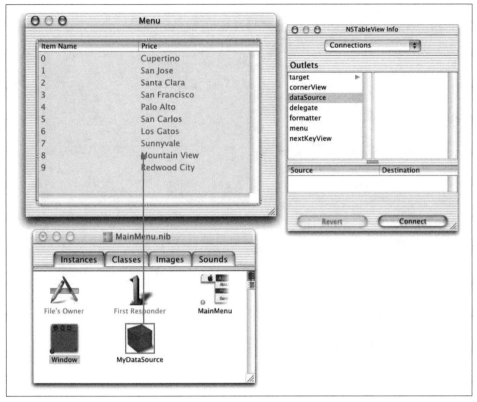

Figure 9-7. Connecting the table view to MyDataSource

5. Click on MyDataSource in the Classes tab of the *MainMenu.nib* window, and create the interface files (Classes → Create Files for MyDataSource).

6. Save (⌘-S) the nib, and return to Project Builder.

Create the Data Source

The back end of our table will consist of two classes: the MyDataSource class that we defined in Interface Builder and the same FoodItem class that we created earlier in this chapter.

1. Add the files for the FoodItem class to the project. Using the Finder, locate the *FoodItem.h* and *FoodItem.m* files (in the *~/LearningCocoa/Key View Coding* directory), and drag them into the Other Sources folder of the Groups & Files panel in Project Builder. When the sheet appears to confirm your copy, ensure

that the "Copy items" checkbox is selected, and then click the Add button, as shown in Figure 9-8.

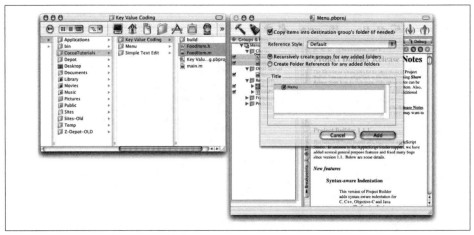

Figure 9-8. Adding our FoodItem class files to the Menu Project

2. Open the *MyDataSource.h* file, and edit it to match the following code:

```
#import <Cocoa/Cocoa.h>

@interface MyDataSource : NSObject
{
    NSMutableArray * items;
}

@end
```

The code we added in the header file simply declares a single array, named items, as an instance variable. We will hold the many items to be displayed in the user interface of our application in this array.

3. Open the *MyDataSource.m* file, and edit it to match the following code:

```
#import "MyDataSource.h"
#import "FoodItem.h"

@implementation MyDataSource

- (id)init
{
    [super init];

    // Some initial data for our interface
    FoodItem * chimi = [[FoodItem alloc] init];              // a
    FoodItem * fajitas = [[FoodItem alloc] init];

    [chimi setName:@"Chimichanga"];
    [chimi setPrice:[NSNumber numberWithFloat:8.95]];
    [fajitas setName:@"Steak Fajitas"];
```

```
    [fajitas setPrice:[NSNumber numberWithFloat:10.95]];

    items = [[NSMutableArray alloc] init];
    [items addObject:chimi];
    [items addObject:fajitas];
    [chimi release];
    [fajitas release];                                      // b
    return self;
}

- (int)numberOfRowsInTableView:(NSTableView *)tableView
{
    return [items count];                                   // c
}

- (id)tableView:(NSTableView *)tableView
objectValueForTableColumn:(NSTableColumn *)tableColumn
          row:(int)row
{
    NSString * identifier = [tableColumn identifier];       // d
    FoodItem * item = [items objectAtIndex:row];            // e
    return [item valueForKey:identifier];                   // f
}

@end
```

The code that we added performs the following tasks:

a. Creates a couple of sample menu items and puts them into an NSMutableArray instance.

b. Releases the food items, now that they are stored safely in the array.

c. Returns the number of items in the food items array. This lets the table view know how many rows contain data.

d. Gets the identifier of the column for which the table view wants data.

e. Obtains the food item that is at the specified index in the array.

f. Returns the value of the food item object that matches the property name of the identifier obtained from the table column.

4. Save the project (File → Save, or ⌘-S), and then build and run the application (Build → Build and Run, or ⌘-R). You should see something like Figure 9-9.

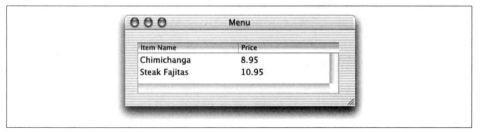

Figure 9-9. The Menu application in action

Play with the application a little bit: resize the window; resize the individual table columns; reorder the table columns by dragging around the column headers. Quit the application (⌘-Q) when you are done.

Allow Modification of Table Entries

When playing with our Menu application so far, you could select the items in the table, and you could even edit them. But when you try to complete editing an item name or a price by hitting Return or exiting the table cell, the edit doesn't take. To let the user edit the fields, a third method must be implemented to save changes back to the data source:

```
- (void)tableView:(NSTableView *)tableView
    setObjectValue:(id)object
    forTableColumn:(NSTableColumn *)tableColumn
            row:(int)row;
```

Add the following method to our *MyDataSource.m* file after the tableView: objectValueForTableColumn:row: method:

```
- (void)tableView:(NSTableView *)tableView
    setObjectValue:(id)object
    forTableColumn:(NSTableColumn *)tableColumn
            row:(int)row
{
    NSString * identifer = [tableColumn identifier];            // 1
    FoodItem * item = [items objectAtIndex:row];               // 2
    [item takeValue:object forKey:identifer];                  // 3
}
```

The code that we added does the following things:

1. Gets the `identifier` of the column for which the table view wants to set data.

2. Obtains the food `item` that is at the specified index in the array.

3. Sets the property of the food item that matches the `identifier` that we obtained in step 1.

Now save the project (File → Save, or ⌘-S). Before you can build and run the application to test the editing features, you first need to ensure that you have quit out of any running Menu application. Build and run the app again (Build → Build and Run, or ⌘-R) from within Project Builder. You should now be able to edit the fields in the table and have those changes made in the underlying data model.

Adding Entries to the Model

With an application like Menu, adding entries to the model can be useful. The following steps guide you through the process of adding this functionality to the application:

1. We're going to add a button to the interface. To enable a new row to be added when this button is pushed, we'll need to add an action `newButtonPressed:` and an outlet `table` to `MyDataSource`. An easy way to do this is to add the declarations yourself in the code. In Project Builder, edit the *MyDataSource.h* file to match the following code. The code you need to add is shown in **boldface**.

    ```
    #import <Cocoa/Cocoa.h>

    @interface MyDataSource : NSObject
    {
        NSMutableArray * items;
        IBOutlet NSTableView * table;
    }

    - (IBAction)newButtonPressed:(id)sender;

    @end
    ```

2. Save the header file (File → Save, or ⌘-S).

3. In Interface Builder's Classes pane, select `MyDataSource`, and reload the source file (Classes → Read MyDataSource.h). This causes Interface Builder to reparse the header file and pick up the new outlet and action.

4. Resize the table view to make room for a button.

5. Drag a button from the Cocoa-Views panel onto the interface, and change its name to New Item.

6. Select the table view, and reset its Autosizing attributes as shown in Figure 9-10.

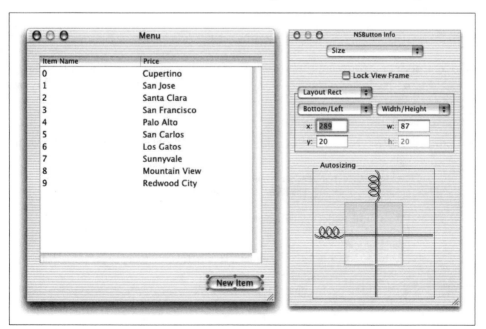

Figure 9-10. Adding a button to Menu

7. Control-drag a connection between the MyDataSource object in the Instances tab of the *MainMenu.nib* window and the table view. Connect it to the table outlet, as shown in Figure 9-11.

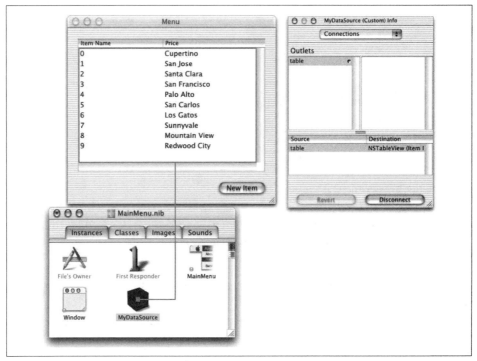

Figure 9-11. Connecting the table view to the table outlet

8. Control-drag a connection between the New Item button and the MyDataSource object in the Instances tab. Connect it to the newActionPressed: button, as shown in Figure 9-12.

9. Save the nib file (File → Save, or ⌘-S), and return to Project Builder.

10. Edit the *MyDataSource.m* file, adding the newButtonPressed: method shown in the following code:

```
- (IBAction)newButtonPressed:(NSEvent *)event {
    FoodItem * item = [[FoodItem alloc] init];          // a

    [items insertObject:item atIndex:0];                // b
    [item release];
    [table reloadData];                                 // c
    [table selectRow:0 byExtendingSelection:NO];        // d
}
```

The code we added performs the following tasks:

a. Creates a new item object.

b. Inserts the new item object into our data model array.

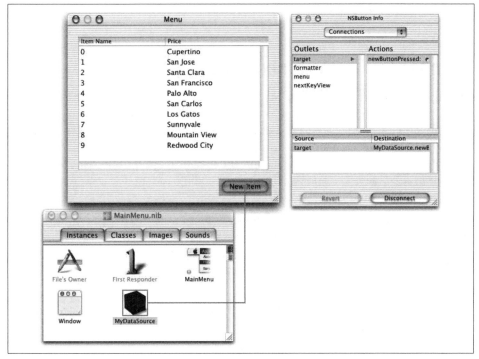

Figure 9-12. Connecting the button to the data source

  c. Instructs the table view to reload its data. This will cause the table view to call the numberOfRowsInTableView: method again and load all the rows from the model.

  d. Selects the row we just added into the table. This highlights the new row, so the user of the application can edit it.

11. Save the project files (File → Save, or ⌘-S), and then build and run the application (Build → Build and Run, or ⌘-R). When you press the New Item button, a new row should be created, as shown in Figure 9-13.

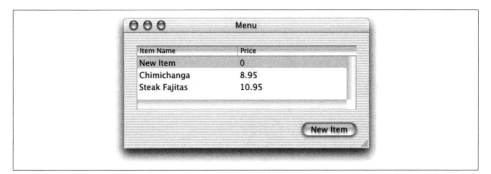

Figure 9-13. Adding a new entry to our application

To edit the new fields, simply click in either column, and enter a new food item and price.

Saving Data: Coding and Archiving

Virtually all applications need to make some of their objects persistent. In user-speak, this means that all applications need a way to *save* their data. For example, the Menu application doesn't save the state of the data model, so all changes are lost as soon as you quit the application. Cocoa applications typically use *coding* and *archiving* to store document contents and other critical application data to disk for later retrieval. Some applications may also use coding and archiving to send objects over a network to another application.

Coding, as implemented by the NSCoder class, takes a connected group of objects, such as the array of food items in our sample application (an *object graph*), and serializes that data. During serialization, the state, structure, relationships, and class memberships are captured. To be serialized, an object must conform to the NSCoding protocol (consisting of the encodeWithCoder: and initWithCoder: methods).

Archiving, as implemented by the NSArchiver class (which extends NSCoder), extends this behavior by storing the serialized data in a file.

Adding Coding and Archiving to the Menu Application

To show how to archive objects, we will modify our Menu application to save and load files that contain the list of food items. To do this, we need to hook up the File → Open and File → Save menu items, add the save and open sheet functionality, and make sure that the FoodItem class can be archived.

1. In Project Builder, open *FoodItem.h* and modify the @interface declaration as follows. Adding <NSCoding> declares that the Song class conforms to the coding protocol.

   ```
   #import <Foundation/Foundation.h>

   @interface FoodItem : NSObject <NSCoding> {
       NSString * name;
       NSNumber * price;
   }

   .
   .
   .
   ```

   NSCoding appears in brackets to signify that the FoodItem interface implements the coding protocol. If you were to read this declaration aloud, it would sound like: "FoodItem extends from the NSObject class and implements the NSCoding protocol."

2. Open the *FoodItem.m* file, and add the NSCoding methods after the init method as follows:

```
- (id)initWithCoder:(NSCoder *)coder
{
    [super init];
    [self setName:[coder decodeObject]];                    // a
    [self setPrice:[coder decodeObject]];                   // b
    return self;
}

- (void)encodeWithCoder:(NSCoder *)coder
{
    [coder encodeObject:[self name]];                       // c
    [coder encodeObject:[self price]];                      // d
}
```

The code we added performs the following tasks:

  a. Decodes the next object from the coder's data stream and sets the name instance variable.

  b. Decodes the next object from the coder's data stream and sets the price instance variable.

  c. Encodes the name instance variable to the coder's data stream.

  d. Encodes the price instance variable to the coder's data stream.

3. Open *MyDataSource.h*, and add the following two action methods:

```
#import <Cocoa/Cocoa.h>

@interface MyDataSource : NSObject
{
    NSMutableArray * items;
    IBOutlet NSTableView * table;
}

- (IBAction)newButtonPressed:(id)sender;
- (IBAction)save:(id)sender;
- (IBAction)open:(id)sender;

@end
```

4. Save the source files, and then open the *MainMenu.nib* file in Interface Builder.

5. Reparse the *MyDataSource.h* file in Interface Builder. To do this, click on the MyDataSource object in the Classes tab, and then select the Classes → Read File MyDataSource.h menu option.

6. Click on the File menu of the MainMenu.nib – MainMenu window to reveal the menu options.

7. Control-drag a connection from the File → Open... menu item to the MyDataSource instance in the Instances tab, as shown in Figure 9-14. Connect it to the open: target.

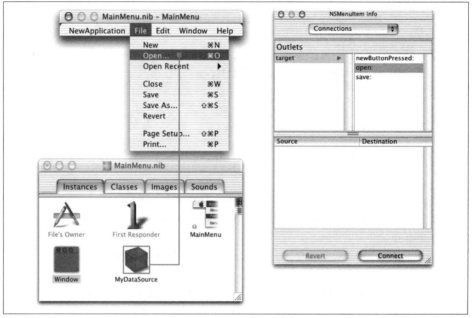

Figure 9-14. Connecting the Open... menu item to MyDataSource

8. Control-drag a connection from the File → Save menu item to the MyDataSource instance. Connect it to the save: target.

9. Save the nib file (File → Save, or ⌘-S), and return to Project Builder.

10. Add the save: and open: methods to *MyDataSource.m*, as well as two helper methods, as shown here:

```
#import "MyDataSource.h"
#import "FoodItem.h"

@implementation MyDataSource



.
.
.


- (IBAction)save:(id)sender
{
    NSSavePanel * savePanel = [NSSavePanel savePanel];                        // a
    SEL sel = @selector(savePanelDidEnd:returnCode:contextInfo:);            // b
    [savePanel beginSheetForDirectory:@"~/Documents"                         // c
                                 file:@"menu.items"
```

```
                        modalForWindow:[table window]
                         modalDelegate:self
                        didEndSelector:sel
                           contextInfo:nil];
    }

    - (void)savePanelDidEnd:(NSSavePanel *)sheet
                 returnCode:(int)returnCode
                contextInfo:(void *)context
    {
        if (returnCode == NSOKButton) {                                    // d
            [NSArchiver archiveRootObject:items toFile:[sheet filename]];
        }
    }

    - (IBAction)open:(id)sender
    {
        NSOpenPanel * openPanel = [NSOpenPanel openPanel];                 // e
        SEL sel = @selector(openPanelDidEnd:returnCode:contextInfo:);
        [openPanel beginSheetForDirectory:@"~/Documents"
                                     file:nil
                                    types:nil
                           modalForWindow:[table window]
                            modalDelegate:self
                           didEndSelector:sel
                              contextInfo:nil];
    }

    - (void)openPanelDidEnd:(NSOpenPanel *)sheet
                 returnCode:(int)returnCode
                contextInfo:(void *)contextInfo
    {
        if (returnCode == NSOKButton) {
            NSMutableArray * array;                                        // f
            array = [NSUnarchiver unarchiveObjectWithFile:[sheet filename]];
            [array retain];
            [items release];
            items = array;
            [table reloadData];
        }
    }

    @end
```

The code that we added does the following things:

a. Creates a new Save panel—Cocoa's standard user-interface widget for selecting where a file should be saved. The way we use the Save panel uses delegation in a manner similar to the sheet we added to the Dot View application (Chapter 8).

b. Obtains the selector for the callback method that the Save panel should use when the user has selected the file to which data will be saved.

c. Instructs the Save panel to display itself as a sheet attached to the current window. MyDataSource doesn't have a direct reference to the window to which the sheet should be attached, but since it does have a reference to the table, we can simply ask the table for the window object.

d. Archives the items array to the given file if the callback method gets a status code indicating that the user selected the file to which to save.

e. Creates a new Open panel—Cocoa's standard user-interface widget for selecting files to open. Open panels work very much like save panels.

f. Unarchives an array object from the file selected by the user; this releases the old array assigned to the items variable and assigns a retained instance of the new items.

11. Now save the project (File → Save, or ⌘-S), and then build and run the application (Build → Build and Run, or ⌘-R).

Add a few items to your list of food items, then save (⌘-S), and you should see the save dialog sheet slide out from the titlebar of the application window, as shown in Figure 9-15.

Figure 9-15. Saving our menu list

Quit the application, restart it (⌘-R), and then open (⌘-O) the data file you just saved. All the changes you made should show up. Make sure to quit (⌘-Q) the application when you are done.

Using Formatters

The next task for the Menu application is to add a formatter to the Price column so that the amounts of our food items are shown using a currency format.

1. Open *MainMenu.nib* in Interface Builder.

2. Drag a currency formatter (NSNumberFormatter) from the Cocoa-Views palette to the price column, as shown in Figure 9-16.

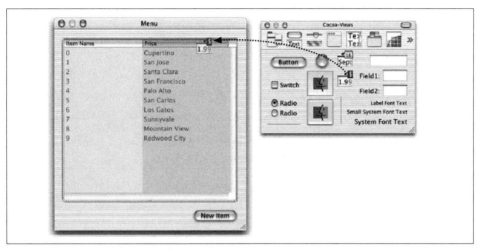

Figure 9-16. Adding a number formatter to the Menu application

3. In the number-formatter inspector, set up the format to use the currency settings shown in Figure 9-17.

4. Save the nib file.

Return to Project Builder, and build and run the application (Build → Build and Run, or ⌘-R). The menu interface should look like Figure 9-18.

Sorting Tables

The last thing we will add to our Menu application is the ability for the contents of the table to be sorted when a table column header is clicked. To do this, we will rely upon the ability of Cocoa collections to be sorted using comparators. We will add comparison methods to the FoodItem class so that an instance object can say that it should be sorted either before or after another instance.

1. In Interface Builder, set the data view as the delegate of the table view by Control-dragging a connection between the table view and the MyDataSource instance object and connecting it to the delegate outlet, as shown in Figure 9-19.

2. Save the nib file (File → Save or ⌘-S), and return to Project Builder.

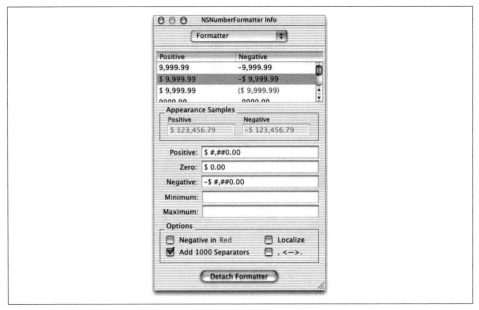

Figure 9-17. The number formatter inspector

Figure 9-18. Menu with the prices nicely formatted

Open the *FoodItem.m* file, and add the following two methods to the file after the other methods:

```
- (NSComparisonResult)compareName:(FoodItem *) item                    // a
{
    return [name compare:[item name]];
}

- (NSComparisonResult)comparePrice:(FoodItem *) item                   // b
{
    return [price compare:[item price]];
}
```

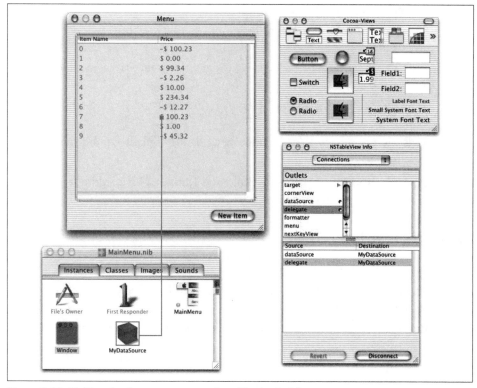

Figure 9-19. Making the data source act as the table view's delegate

These methods perform the following actions:

a. This method returns a comparison result by using the compare: method of the NSString class to compare the name of the given object with the name of the current instance.

b. This method returns a comparison result by using the compare: method of the NSNumber class to compare the price of the given object with the price of the current instance.

3. Open the *MyDataSource.m* file, and add the following method:

```
- (void)tableView:(NSTableView *)tableView
    didClickTableColumn:(NSTableColumn *)tableColumn
{
    NSString * identifier = [tableColumn identifier];          // a
    if ([identifier isEqualToString:@"name"]) {
        [items sortUsingSelector:@selector(compareName:)];     // b
    } else {
        [items sortUsingSelector:@selector(comparePrice:)];    // c
    }
    [table reloadData];                                        // d
}
```

This method does the following things:

   a. Obtains the `identifier` from the column so that we know with which property to sort.

   b. Tells the `items` array to sort itself using the `compareName:` method of each item in the array.

   c. Tells the `items` array to sort itself using the `comparePrice:` method of each item in the array.

   d. Tells the `table` view that the underlying data has changed and that it needs to reload itself.

Build and run the application (Build → Build and Run, or ⌘-R). Add a few items to the Menu, and then sort by name, then price, and see the results.

Exercises

1. Change the title of the left column from Item Name to Food Item.

2. Add the code necessary to display a confirmation dialog box when the user tries to quit the application.

3. Examine the code in the Menu application for memory management problems.

PART III

Document-Based Applications

Many applications today, such as word processors and web browsers, are built around the concept of a document. Creating an application that can handle multiple documents is tedious at best. Luckily, Cocoa allows an application to handle multiple documents with ease. This part of the book uses an extended tutorial that covers use of Cocoa's built-in multiple-document architecture, as well as its text-handling abilities.

Chapters in this part of the book include:

CHAPTER 10

Multiple Document Architecture

So far, our examples have centered on applications that have a single GUI. However, in reality many of the applications we use day-in and day-out—such as word processors and web browsers—are based around the idea of a document. They provide a framework for viewing or generating identically-contained, but uniquely-composed, sets of data that can be stored in files.

A document-based application must perform the following tasks:

- Create new documents
- Open existing documents stored in files
- Save documents to user-designated files and locations
- Revert to previously saved documents
- Close documents, usually after prompting the user to save changes
- Print documents and allow the page layout to be modified
- Monitor and set the document's edited status, as well as reflect that status to the user
- Manage document windows, including setting window titles

Cocoa provides a multiple-document architecture, helping you take care of these tasks easily. Using this architecture drastically simplifies the work developers must do to implement a multidocument application. Once you understand how this architecture works, you can have a multidocument application up and running in minutes.

This chapter begins with an overview of Cocoa's multiple-document architecture and then presents an in-depth look at the classes that make up this architecture. The final part of the chapter guides you through the process of creating a simple multiple-document text-editing application.

Architectural Overview

From a user's perspective, a *document* is a unique body of information contained in its own window. The window gives the user an area in which to edit the document. Users can create an unlimited number of documents and save each to a separate file.

From a Cocoa programming perspective, a document is managed by an instance of the NSDocument class, which, along with NSDocumentController and NSWindowController, provides the functionality for a document-based application. Objects of these classes divide and orchestrate the work of creating, saving, opening, and managing the documents that an application creates. They are tiered in a one-to-many relationship, as depicted in Figure 10-1.

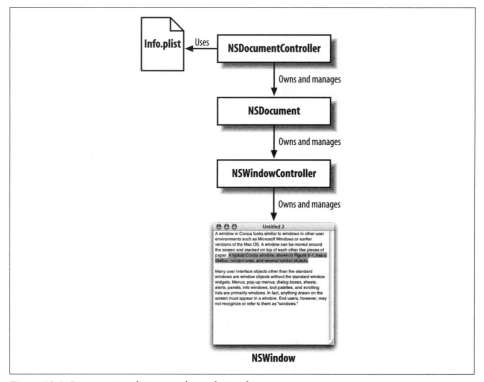

Figure 10-1. Document architecture class relationships

Document-based applications have one instance of the NSDocumentController class, which creates and manages many potential NSDocument objects (one for each new or open document). In turn, an NSDocument object creates and manages one or more NSWindowController objects, one for each of the windows displayed for a document.

In addition to these three AppKit classes, the multiple-document architecture uses information in the application's info property list (saved as *Contents/Info.plist* in the application's bundle—we'll discuss bundles more in Chapter 13) to determine the types of data with which the application can work. The information is stored in the property list as an array of document types. Each document-type entry in the array includes the following information:

- The name of the document type.
- An array of filename extensions, such as *.rtf* and *.txt*, which correspond to a document's data type.
- An array of Mac OS-style type identifiers, such as TEXT and PICT, which also correspond to a document's data type.
- A string that determines the role of the application when interacting with data. An application can be an Editor or a View for a given type.
- The class name of the NSDocument subclass that handles the data type in your application.

Project Builder provides a simple user interface for creating and editing entries in an application's document type array. Even though there's usually no need to modify the property list directly, the document controller uses the information from the info property list to do the following things:

- Filter out inappropriate file types automatically, allowing users to select only files that the application can handle when an open dialog box is presented
- Instantiate the appropriate NSDocument subclass for a document's data type when a document is opened

The Document Object

The primary job of a document object—an instance of an NSDocument subclass that you provide as part of your application—is to represent, manipulate, store, and load the data associated with a document. Based on the document types it claims to understand (as specified in the application's info property list), a document object must be prepared to do the following things:

- Provide other objects in the application that the data displayed in its window(s). The document object must provide the data in any of the formats supported by the application.
- Load data into internal data structures and display it in windows. The document object must accept the data in any format supported by the application.
- Store document data in a file at a specified location in the filesystem.
- Read document data stored in a file.

With the assistance of its window controllers, a document-object instance manages the display and capture of the data in its windows. The document-object instance associated with the key window is made the first responder to action messages indicating that a user wants to save, print, revert, or close a document. A fully implemented document object knows how to track its edited status, print document data, and perform undo and redo operations. As you'll see in the examples in this and later chapters, these behaviors aren't provided completely by default, but the NSDocument class goes a long way to assist you in implementing each.

For edited-status tracking, the NSDocument class provides an API for updating a document change counter. For undo/redo operations, NSDocument creates an NSUndoManager when one is requested, which responds appropriately to the Edit → Undo and Edit → Redo menu commands, updating the change counter when undo and redo operations are invoked.

Every application that takes advantage of the AppKit's document-based application architecture must create at least one subclass of NSDocument. The architecture requires that you override some methods of the NSDocument class. These methods must be implemented:

- (NSString *)windowNibName;
  Called by the document controller to determine the name of the nib file that contains the user interface to view and edit the document.

- (void)windowControllerDidLoadNib:(NSWindowController *)aController;
  Called once the window controller has loaded the nib file and all of the user interface connections have been made. This provides an opportunity for any initialization that needs to be performed.

- (NSData *)dataRepresentationOfType:(NSString *)aType;
  Must be implemented to create and return document data of a supported type, usually in preparation for writing that data to a file as an NSData object.

- (BOOL)loadDataRepresentation:(NSData *)data:(NSString *)aType;
  Must be implemented to convert an NSData object (that contains the document data of a particular type) into the document's internal data structures so that the document is ready to display its contents. The NSData object usually results from the document reading a document file.

 A common mistake made by novice Cocoa programmers is to treat the document object as a model, though it's really a controller object that adapts between the view of the document itself and whatever model is being used to hold the representation.

The NSData Class

NSData and NSMutableData provide object-oriented wrappers for byte buffers. They let simple allocated buffers take on the behavior of first-class Cocoa objects. They are typically used for data storage and are also useful in applications that rely on Distributed Objects. For more information, see *Overview of Programming Topic: Binary Data*, in */Developer/Documentation/Cocoa/TasksAndConcepts/ProgrammingTopics/BinaryData*.

The Document Controller

The primary job of an application's document-controller object (NSDocumentController) is to create and open documents, as well as to track and manage these documents. The document controller maintains a list of document objects and tracks the current document (the document whose window is currently key). It is hardwired to respond appropriately to certain application events, such as when the application starts up, when it terminates, when the system powers off, and when documents are opened or printed from the Finder. For example, when a user chooses New from the File menu, the document controller does the following things:

1. Allocates an instance of the NSDocument subclass specified in the first entry of the application's document type array
2. Initializes the instance by invoking the subclass's init method

When the user chooses Open from the File menu, the document controller does the following things:

1. Displays the Open panel, filtering the file list using the data type(s) from the application's info property list, and gets the user's selection
2. Uses the type information from the file and data to allocate an instance of the appropriate NSDocument subclass
3. Initializes the object by invoking its initWithContentsOfFile:ofType: method, which loads the contents of the file into the document instance

When the user chooses Save or Save As from the File menu, the document controller does the following things:

1. If needed (if the document has not been saved before, or if the user chooses Save As), displays the Save panel and gets the user's selection
2. Uses the type information from the filename that the user gave and requests the data from the application using the dataRepresentationOfType: method
3. Stores the data in the returned data object into the filesystem

In a document-based application, many of the application's menu items are already connected to the document controller. These methods are implemented by the NSDocumentController class and are listed in Table 10-1.

Table 10-1. Target/action configuration for default multidocument application

File menu command	First responder action implemented by NSDocumentController
New	newDocument:
Open	openDocument:
Save	saveDocument:
Save As	saveDocumentAs:
Save To	saveDocumentTo:

Table 10-1. Target/action configuration for default multidocument application (continued)

File menu command	First responder action implemented by NSDocumentController
Save All	`saveAllDocuments:`
Close	`closeDocument:`
Revert	`revertDocumentToSaved:`
Print	`printDocument:`
Page Layout	`runPageLayout:`

The default document-controller behavior provided by the `NSDocumentController` class is usually sufficient for most situations; you shouldn't need to subclass it unless you need to provide alternative functionality for the methods listed earlier.

The Window Controller

A *window controller*, an instance of the `NSWindowController` class, manages one window associated with a document. If a document has multiple open windows, each window has its own instance of `NSWindowController`. For example, a document might have a main data-entry window and a window that lists records for selection. Each window would have its own window controller. When a document has multiple window controllers, only one of them is considered the primary window controller. When the primary window is closed, the document and all other windows are closed.

When requested by the `NSDocument` class, a window controller loads the nib file containing a window and displays it. The window controller assumes responsibility for managing the nib file.

When a document is closed, the window controller is responsible for properly closing windows, as well as freeing any top-level objects instantiated by the nib file. This includes the window itself and any additional objects added to the nib.

Most of the time, you can use the default window controller provided by the App-Kit. Some applications may want to subclass `NSWindowController` to move the user-interface-specific logic out of the `NSDocument` subclass. The Sketch sample application in */Developer/Examples/AppKit* uses this technique. Another situation that would make subclassing desirable is if you wanted to support multiple views onto a document; for example, in a 3D modeling application you would want to present various views of the model.

Memory Management

The multiple-document architecture automates much of the memory management for documents and their associated window and document controllers. One of the document controller's responsibilities is to ensure that a document is open and using memory only if it has a window open on the screen. When a window closes, it tells its window controller that it is closing. The window controller, in turn, tells its document that it is closing. The document notes that the window controller is closing, removes the window controller from its list of window controllers, and releases it. As this is the only place the window controller is retained, the window controller gets released and deallocated as a result.

Building a Document-Based Application

It is possible to put together a document-based application without writing very much code. If your requirements are minimal, the AppKit provides you with default window-controller and document-controller instances. You are left with the task of composing the document interface, implementing a subclass of NSDocument, and adding any other custom classes or behavior required by your application.

To show how the pieces of the document-based architecture fit together in practice, we will create a very simple text editor. By the time we're finished with this example, which consists of a relatively small amount of code, we'll have created an application that—without Cocoa's help—might have taken days or weeks to construct and debug.

Document-Based Application Template

Project Builder provides a template named "Document-based Application" to expedite the development of these kinds of applications. This project type provides the following things:

The application's main nib file
> This nib contains a standard Cocoa application menu bar. The menu items in the File and Edit menus are already connected to the appropriate first responder action methods in the document controller.

A nib file for the application's document
> This nib file contains a single window to which other UI elements can be added. A subclass of NSDocument, named MyDocument, has been created, has an outlet to the document window, and has been made File's Owner of the nib file.

A skeletal NSDocument subclass implementation
> The project includes *MyDocument.h* and *MyDocument.m* files, matching the definition of the NSDocument subclass in the document's nib file. The *MyDocument. m* file contains commented starter implementations of important methods (called "stubbed-out" methods) that will help you implement the functionality needed.

A document-type entry in the application's info property list
> In the Application Settings pane of the Targets display is a simple user interface for modifying the application's *Info.plist* file. The provided file contains placeholder values for global application keys, as well as the document type array.

Create the Project

To get started working on building our text editor:

1. Launch Project Builder, and choose New Project from the File menu (File → New Project).

2. Select Cocoa Document-based Application from the application type dialog box, as shown in Figure 10-2.

Figure 10-2. Creating a document-based application

3. Name the project "Simple Text Edit", and save it into your *~/LearningCocoa* folder.

Examine the Document Interface

Double-click on the *MyDocument.nib* file (located in the Resources folder of the Groups & Files panel in Project Builder), so you can examine the interface in Interface Builder. The nib file is quite simple, as shown in Figure 10-3. There is only a single window with a default text string.

If you select the File's Owner instance and bring up the Inspector (Tools → Show Info, or Shift-⌘-I), you'll notice in the Attributes pane that File's Owner is set to correspond to an instance of MyDocument. Also, in the Connections pane, you'll see an outlet with a connection to the window.

Switch back to Project Builder, and double-click on the *MainMenu.nib* file to open it in Interface Builder. Click through the menu items with the Connections inspector open, as shown in Figure 10-4, and notice how many of the application's menu items have already been connected to appropriate first responder action methods. These methods are implemented by the application's document controller (an NSDocumentController instance).

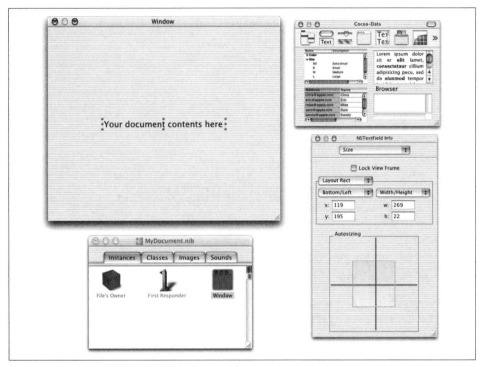

Figure 10-3. MyDocument.nib in Interface Builder

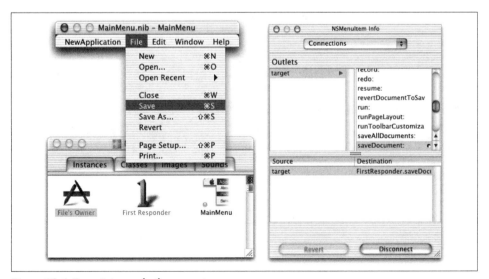

Figure 10-4. Examining prebuilt connections

Examine the Document Implementation

Return to Project Builder, and open *MyDocument.m*, located in the Classes folder of the Groups & Files pane. Examine the skeletal implementation of this NSDocument subclass, and you'll see that the four methods that must be implemented already have a skeletal implementation, as shown in Example 10-1.

Example 10-1. Skeletal NSDocument subclass implementation

```
#import "MyDocument.h"

@implementation MyDocument

- (id)init
{
    [super init];
    if (self) {

        // Add your subclass-specific initialization here.
        // If an error occurs here, send a [self dealloc] message and return nil.

    }
    return self;
}

- (NSString *)windowNibName
{
    // Override returning the nib file name of the document
    // If you need to use a subclass of NSWindowController or if your
    // document supports multiple NSWindowControllers, you should remove
    // this method and override -makeWindowControllers instead.
    return @"MyDocument";
}

- (void)windowControllerDidLoadNib:(NSWindowController *) aController
{
    [super windowControllerDidLoadNib:aController];
    // Add any code here that need to be executed once the windowController
    // has loaded the document's window.
}

- (NSData *)dataRepresentationOfType:(NSString *)aType
{
    // Insert code here to write your document from the given data.
    // You can also choose to override -fileWrapperRepresentationOfType:
    // or -writeToFile:ofType: instead.
    return nil;
}

- (BOOL)loadDataRepresentation:(NSData *)data ofType:(NSString *)aType
{
    // Insert code here to read your document from the given data.
    // You can also choose to override -loadFileWrapperRepresentation:ofType:
```

Example 10-1. Skeletal NSDocument subclass implementation (continued)

```
    // or -readFromFile:ofType: instead.
    return YES;
}

@end
```

Save the project (File → Save, or ⌘-S), and then build and run the application (Build → Build and Run, or ⌘-R).

Now you can experiment with the document-based application.

1. Create new document windows (File → New, or ⌘-N), and close them (File → Close, or ⌘-W).

2. Next, try saving a document window (File → Save, or ⌘-S). Notice that a dialog box asks you to select a location in which to save the document. Choose a location and hit OK. Another dialog box says that the file could not be saved. This is because the default dataRepresentationOfType: method returns nil instead of a valid NSData object, because no default file type has been specified.

3. Now quit the application (NewApplication → Quit, or ⌘-Q).

Next, we'll implement the functionality needed to turn this skeleton into a full-blown text editor that allows us to save and open text files.

Compose the Interface

In this section, you'll define the look and feel of the application's document. Just modify the default nib file (created by Project Builder's template) by adding a text view that will allow the user to view and edit text.

1. Open *MyDocument.nib* in Interface Builder, if it isn't already open.

2. Remove the default text object that says "Your document contents here."

3. Drag an NSTextView to the window from the Cocoa-Data views pane of the palette, as shown in Figure 10-5.

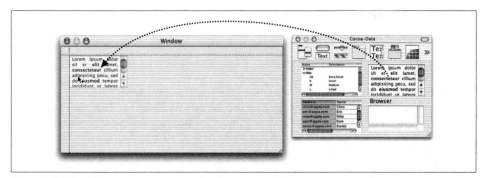

Figure 10-5. Dragging a text view onto the document window

4. Move and resize the text view so that it occupies the entire window, as shown in Figure 10-6.

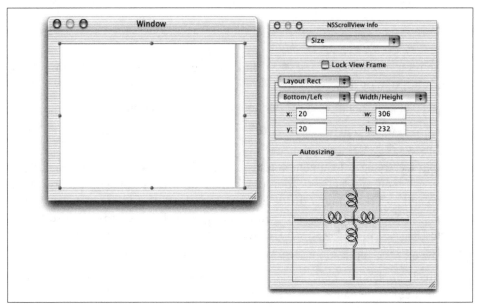

Figure 10-6. Resizing and setting the attributes of the text view

5. With the text view selected, bring up the Size pane in the Inspector. Change the Autosizing options so that the view will follow changes in the windows size.

6. Switch back to Project Builder, open *MyDocument.h*, and add a declaration for the text view's outlet by inserting the **boldface** text shown in Example 10-2.

Example 10-2. Adding the textView outlet to the NSDocument subclass

```
#import <Cocoa/Cocoa.h>

@interface MyDocument : NSDocument
{
    IBOutlet NSTextView * textView;
}
@end
```

7. Save (⌘-S) *MyDocument.h*.

8. Bring Interface Builder to the front, and drag *MyDocument.h* from Project Builder's Group & Files listing into the Instances panel of Interface Builder's *MyDocument.nib* window. This gives Interface Builder the opportunity to parse the outlet, so you can use it for connections.

9. In Interface Builder's Instances pane, Control-drag a connection from the File's Owner instance (this is a proxy for a MyDocument instance) to the text view.

10. Connect the textView outlet to the view by clicking on the Connect button in the Info window.

 Do not generate an instance of MyDocument to make this connection. The document-based application framework makes an instance automatically, which is assigned to the File's Owner object. At runtime, the File's Owner will be an instance of MyDocument.

11. Save (⌘-S) the nib file.

Modify the Info Property List

The Applications Settings pane of the target window allows you to create and modify a variety of application-wide properties. Critical values, like the name of the executable and the name of the main Cocoa class, are provided by default. Many of the other properties are important for a full-fledged application, but they can remain unset for this simple example. You'll learn more about these properties later in the book. For now, don't worry about them.

Our Simple Text Edit application will handle only one kind of data: text. It's very simple to modify the application's info property list to add support for this document type.

1. In Project Builder, select the Targets pane in the main window.
2. Select the default (and only) target named Simple Text Edit.
3. Select the Info.plist Entries → Simple View → Document Types in the outline, as shown in Figure 10-7.
4. Modify the default document type entry. Rename DocumentType to Text, and replace the quoted question marks with *txt* in the Extensions field and with *TXT* in the OS types field. Once you've entered this information, click on the Change button.

These settings allow the document architecture to recognize *.txt* files as files that can be opened by our application, instructing the system to use an instance of the MyDocument class to open those files. In addition, the system will allow only files saved from a MyDocument instance to have the extension *.txt*.

Implement the MyDocument Class

Now, we implement the MyDocument class to support reading and writing text data.

1. In Project Builder, click vertical Files tab, then select the *MyDocument.h* file from the Classes folder in the Groups & Files panel.

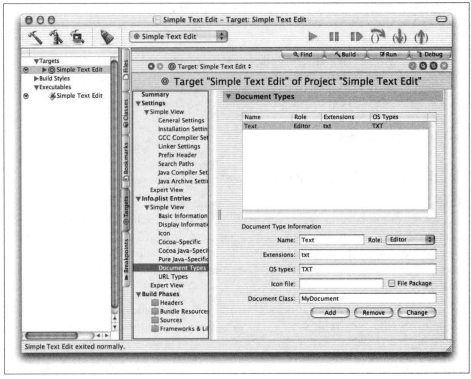

Figure 10-7. Editing a document type

2. Add the `dataFromFile` instance variable as shown:

```
#import <Cocoa/Cocoa.h>

@interface MyDocument : NSDocument
{
    IBOutlet NSTextView * textView;
    NSData * dataFromFile;
}
@end
```

This variable will hold a reference to the raw data loaded from a file.

Open *MyDocument.m*. The following steps will fill in the methods of the skeleton source file from Example 10-1. We'll fill in the stubbed methods in a different order than they appear in the file so that we can have each step build on top of the previous one. In addition, we'll show the code without the comments—it's your choice whether to leave them in your application.

1. Implement the `loadDataRepresentation:` method so that text data can be loaded from the filesystem into the document. When a new document is created, this method is called before the nib is fully loaded and all of the connections have been made. Because of this, the connection to the text view won't be made yet.

In this method, we are just going to store the data object into the `dataFromFile` variable.

```
- (BOOL)loadDataRepresentation:(NSData *)data ofType:(NSString *)aType
{
    dataFromFile = [data retain];
    return YES;
}
```

2. Implement the `dataRepresentationOfType:` method so that the document can save its contents. The NSTextView class can present its data as a string that we can encode into a data object.

```
- (NSData *)dataRepresentationOfType:(NSString *)aType
{
    NSString * text = [textView string];
    return [text dataUsingEncoding:NSUTF8StringEncoding];
}
```

3. Implement the `windowControllerDidLoadNib:` method so that text data can be loaded into the text view.

```
- (void)windowControllerDidLoadNib:(NSWindowController *) aController
{
    [super windowControllerDidLoadNib:aController];
    if (dataFromFile){
        NSString * text = [[NSString alloc]initWithData:dataFromFile      // a
                                          encoding:NSUTF8StringEncoding];
        [textView setString:text];                                        // b
        [text release];
    }
    [textView setAllowsUndo:YES];                                         // c
}
```

The code we added does the following things:

a. Creates a string from the `dataFromFile` object.

b. Sets the string that serves as the `textView`'s model to the string that we just created for the `dataFromFile` object.

c. Enables Undo and Redo functionality that is already built into the NSTextView class. With this enabled, text changes can be undone and redone. The Undo Manager can keep an unlimited number of undos in its stack. As well, the document can keep track of the edited status of the application.

4. Add a dealloc method at the end of the *MyDocument.m* file (before the @end statement) to clean up the `dataFromFile` object.

```
- (void)dealloc
{
    [dataFromFile release];
    [super dealloc];
}
```

5. Save the project (⌘-S), clean it (Build → Clean),* and then build and run the application (Build → Build and Run, or ⌘-R). Try the following:

   a. Type some text into the running application. Use Cut and Paste to edit the text.

   b. Save the document. Note the filename appears in the window's titlebar. Make sure that the "Hide Extension" checkbox is not clicked so that you can see the extension of the file in the Finder and other applications.

   c. Play with the spell checker.

   d. Close the document window (File → Close, or ⌘-W).

   e. Open the document you saved in step 2 in TextEdit (*/Applications*) to see how Mac OS X's default text editor handles the data created by the Simple Text Editor application.

   f. Quit TextEdit.

Cocoa's multiple-document architecture, as well as the capabilities built into the NSTextView class, provides the functionality that users expect Cfrom a text editing application. We've simply glued these features together by adding just a few lines of code.

Exercises

1. Read the Apple developer documentation on the NSDocumentController and NSDocument classes.

2. Add the ability for the editor to read and write Property List (*plist*) files.

3. Try to revert (File → Revert) functionality. Can you explain why it doesn't seem to work?

---

* A bug in Project Builder (up to and including version 2.0.1) requires you to clean the project so that the new *Info.plist* settings can be incorporated into the application.

CHAPTER 11

Rich-Text Handling

In the Chapter 10, we showed how Cocoa's multiple-document architecture takes care of many of the tasks involved in building a document-centric application, and we used a simple text editor as an example. Cocoa's text-handling ability goes much further by supporting multiple fonts, various paragraph styles, embedded images, undo, drag-and-drop, and even spell checking. It can handle differences in text directionality and provides sophisticated typesetting capabilities, such as the ability to control kerning between characters.

In this chapter, we are going to examine the functionality of NSTextView and the other classes that compose the text system. We'll then dive into code and add the following functionality, one step at a time, to a rich-text editor:

- Enable the font menu
- Work with attributed text
- Register undo actions
- Enable the text menu
- Handle embedded images
- Add a special feature that we'll save for last

That's a lot of ground to cover, so let's get going!

Cocoa's Text System

Cocoa's text system, which underlies the functionality we worked with in Chapter 10, consists of three API layers, as shown in Figure 11-1. You can see the same Model-View-Controller (MVC) paradigm we've talked about previously in the design of the text system. At the top layer is the NSTextView that provides the on-screen view of text.

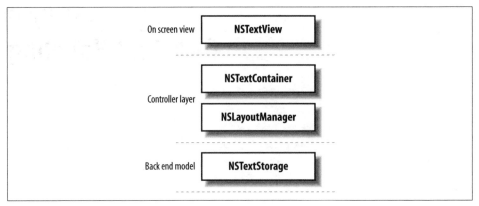

Figure 11-1. Three layers of the Cocoa text system

At the bottom layer, the NSTextStorage class gives programmatic access to the text. This allows you to search for text and manipulate paragraph and character styles without incurring the overhead of laying out the text for display.

In the middle layer are the NSLayoutManager and NSTextContainer classes, which control the way text is laid out on-screen or on the printed page. An NSTextContainer object defines a region where text can be laid out. Typically, this is a rectangular region, but subclasses can support other shapes. If a container's area is inset from the text view's bounds, a margin appears around the text. An instance of the NSLayoutManager class displays the text contained in an NSTextStorage object, rendering text in an NSTextView's display according to the areas defined by NSTextContainer objects.

For most uses, the API provided by the NSTextView class is all that you need to learn to enable rich-text functionality in your applications.

Supported Text Data Types

Cocoa's text system supports the following types of data that can be read, displayed, and saved:

A simple string
> As we saw in Chapter 10, you can set and read the contents of a text view to and from an NSString instance. This is the easiest way to deal with plain text files.

Data as rich text
> The Rich Text Format (RTF) is a standard created by Microsoft for representing text with multiple fonts and colors. RTF is supported by many word processors (including the TextEdit application that comes with Mac OS X) as an interchange format, but serves quite well as a primary document format. Files saved in RTF format will be assigned an *.rtf* extension.

Data as rich text with images

Standard RTF files can also contain attachments, such as images, audio clips, and even QuickTime movies, which are embedded in the file. These files, known as RTFD (the "D" stands for *directory*) use a type of package format, or directory, in which the embedded files of the RTF document are stored. The package will contain the RTF file (e.g., *text.rtf*), along with any associated attachments (e.g., *fuzzball.tiff*). When the file is saved, it will be assigned an *.rtfd* extension.

Working with File Wrappers

Because RTFD files are not simple files, but are composed of many files in a directory structure, the `dataRepresentationOfType:` and `loadDataRepresentation:ofType:` methods will not read them. To handle complex file types that consist of bundled directories, Cocoa provides *file wrappers*. File wrappers can be of three distinct types:

- A directory wrapper that holds a directory and all the files and subdirectories within it
- A regular file wrapper that holds the contents of a single file
- A link wrapper that represents a symbolic link, or alias, in the filesystem

The `NSDocument` class provides the following methods for loading data from, and saving data to, file wrappers:

- `(BOOL)loadFileWrapperRepresentation:(NSFileWrapper *)wrapper ofType:(NSString *)type`
  Loads the document data contained by the given file wrapper into the receiving NSDocument object

- `(NSFileWrapper *)fileWrapperRepresentationOfType:(NSString *)type`
  Returns a file wrapper object that represents the contents of the document for a given document type

In fact, the `NSDocument` implementation of these methods actually calls the `dataRepresentationOfType:` and `loadDataRepresentation:ofType:` methods that we used in the Simple Text Edit application in Chapter 10. By overloading the file wrapper load and save methods, we can support RTFD.

Creating a Rich-Text Editor

To show how to work with rich text, we're going to create a new project similar to the Simple Text Edit application. The big difference is that the application we'll build in this chapter will work with rich-text files instead of just plain text. We'll make a few changes to the recipe along the way; but not too much has changed, so we'll zip through the parts that we've already covered. Refer back to Chapter 10 if you need help with any of the steps.

To get started:

1. Launch Project Builder, and choose New Project from the File menu (File → New Project).

2. From the New Project window, select Application → Cocoa Document-based Application.

3. Name the project "RTF Edit", and save it into your *~/LearningCocoa* folder.

4. Compose the UI by opening the *MyDocument.nib* file in Interface Builder and performing the following steps:

   a. Remove the default text field.

   b. Drag an NSTextView from the Views palette to the application's window.

   c. Resize the text view so that it occupies the entire window.

   d. Change the Autosizing options so that the view will follow changes in the window's size.

5. In Project Builder, open *MyDocument.h* from the Classes directory, and add a declaration for the text view's outlet.

```
#import <Cocoa/Cocoa.h>

@interface MyDocument : NSDocument
{
    IBOutlet NSTextView * textView;
}
@end
```

6. Save (File → Save, or ⌘-S) *MyDocument.h*, and then drag it onto Interface Builder's *MyDocument.nib* window so that Interface Builder can pick up the change to the file.

7. Control-drag a connection from the File's Owner object (remember, this is a proxy for the MyDocument instance at runtime) to the NSTextView we added in step 4, and connect it to the textView outlet.

8. Save (File → Save, or ⌘-S) the nib file.

9. In Project Builder, open the active target (Project → Edit Active Target, or Option-⌘-E), and select the Info.plist Entries → Simple View → Document Types item in the outline.

10. Modify the default document type entry as shown in Figure 11-12. Simply click on the "DocumentType" entry to select it, rename "DocumentType" to "Rich Text", enter the values (*rtf* for Extension and *RTF* for OS types) into the Document Type Information area, and click Change to apply these settings.

11. Open *MyDocument.h*, and add the dataFromFile instance variable to hold the raw RTF data loaded from a file.

```
#import <Cocoa/Cocoa.h>

@interface MyDocument : NSDocument
```

```
{
    IBOutlet NSTextView * textView;
    NSAttributedString * rtfData;
}
@end
```

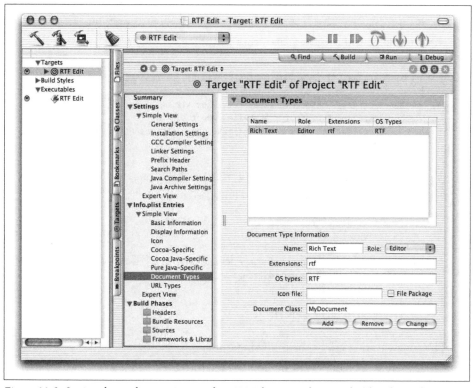

Figure 11-2. Setting the application settings for RTF Edit. Don't forget to hit the Change button!

12. Open *MyDocument.m*, and remove the loadDataRepresentation:ofType: and dataRepresentationOfType: methods. We are removing them now because later on we will load RTFD data from a directory, and we will need the functionality that the file wrapper version of these methods will give us.

13. Implement the loadFileWrapperRepresentation:ofType:.method:

```
- (BOOL)loadFileWrapperRepresentation:(NSFileWrapper *)wrapper
                               ofType:(NSString *)type
{
    rtfData = [[NSAttributedString alloc]
        initWithRTF:[wrapper regularFileContents] documentAttributes:nil];   // a
    if (textView) {                                                           // b
        [[textView textStorage]
            replaceCharactersInRange:NSMakeRange(0, [[textView string] length])];
                withAttributedString:rtfData];
        [rtfData release];
    }
```

```
    return YES;
}
```

The code we added does the following things:

a. Creates a new `NSAttributedString` based on the RTF contents of the file wrapper.

b. If there is a `textView` instead, we will load the RTF straight into it.

14. Next, implement the `fileWrapperRepresentationOfType:` method so that the document can save its contents.

```
- (NSFileWrapper *)fileWrapperRepresentationOfType:(NSString *)type
{
    NSRange range = NSMakeRange(0,[[textView string] length];
    NSFileWrapper * wrapper = [[NSFileWrapper alloc]
        initRegularFileWithContents:[textView RTFFromRange:range]];
    return [wrapper autorelease];
}
```

15. Finally, implement the `windowControllerDidLoadNib:` method.

```
- (void)windowControllerDidLoadNib:(NSWindowController *) aController
{
    [super windowControllerDidLoadNib:aController];
    if (rtfData) {                                                  // a
        [[textView textStorage]
            replaceCharactersInRange:NSMakeRange(0, [[textView string] length]);
                withAttributedString:rtfData];
        [rtfData release];
    }
    [textView setAllowsUndo:YES];                                   // b
}
```

The code we added does the following things:

a. If there is RTF data waiting, it is loaded into the text view.

b. Sets the text view to allow for undo actions to be performed.

16. Save the project (File → Save, or ⌘-S).

17. Build and run (Build → Build and Run, or ⌘-R) the application. You should see the text editor as shown in Figure 11-3. You should be able to save and open rich-text files with it.

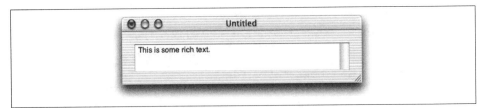

Figure 11-3. RTF Edit in action

Enabling the Font Menu

Text views are already wired to work with the AppKit's font system, which is defined by the NSFontPanel and NSFontManager classes. The font manager keeps track of the currently selected font, while the font panel lets users change the current font. When a user enters text into a text view, the view stores the text into the underlying text-storage object with attributes matching the current font.

The font manager, font panel, and an associated Font menu are set up using Interface Builder. To add font-handling functionality to our RTF Edit application, perform the following tasks:

1. Open *MainMenu.nib* in Interface Builder.

2. Open the Cocoa-Menus palette, and drag a Font menu to the MainMenu menu bar. Drop it between the Edit and Window menus, as shown in Figure 11-4.

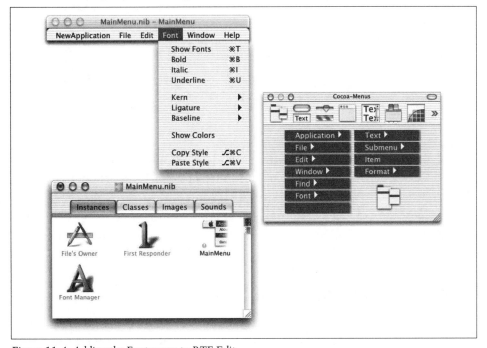

Figure 11-4. Adding the Font menu to RTF Edit

Notice that when you drop it, a Font Manager object is added to the nib. This is a reference to the Font Manager so that you can connect it to other objects in your application if needed.

3. Save (File → Save, or ⌘-S) the nib file.

4. Return to Project Builder, and Build and Run (⌘-R) the project. Try the following tasks:

   a. Type some text into the document, and select it. Open up the Font Panel (Font → Show Fonts, or ⌘-T), and change the font. Watch the selected text change, similar to what is shown in Figure 11-5.

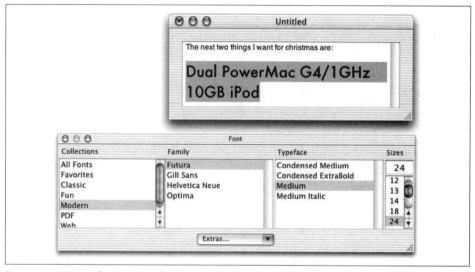

Figure 11-5. Using the Font Panel

   b. From the Extras pop-up menu at the bottom of the Font Panel, select the Color item. Change the text to a different color by selecting a color and clicking the Apply button.

   c. Close the Color and Font panels by clicking on their close window buttons.

   d. Save your file, and then open it in Text Edit to see your changes work in various applications.

Text Storage and Attributed Text

The text-storage object, an instance of `NSTextStorage`, serves as the data repository for the contents of a text view. Conceptually, each character of text in the text-storage object has an associated dictionary of keys and values that describe the characteristics, or *attributes*—such as font, color, and paragraph style—of that character. Chapter 7's String View application first introduced the notion of using attributes when drawing text. To make our text string show up in red, we set the following attribute in a dictionary (that we used when we drew the text):

```
[attribs setObject:[NSColor redColor]
        forKey:NSForegroundColorAttributeName];
```

You can associate any attribute you want with text; however, the attributes that Cocoa's text system pays attention to are listed in Table 11-1.

Table 11-1. Standard Cocoa text attributes

Attribute identifier	Class of value	Default value
NSAttachmentAttributeName	NSTextAttachment	None
NSBackgroundColorAttributeName	NSColor	None
NSBaselineOffsetAttributeName	NSNumber *(float)*	0.0
NSFontAttributeName	NSFont	Helvetica, 12pt
NSForegroundColorAttributeName	NSColor	Black
NSKernAttributeName	NSNumber *(float)*	0.0
NSLigatureAttributeName	NSNumber *(int)*	1
NSLinkAttributeName	id	None
NSParagraphStyleName	NSParagraphStyle	Default paragraph style
NSSuperScriptAttributeName	NSNumber *(int)*	0
NSUnderlineStyleAttributeName	NSNumber *(int)*	None

In Table 11-1, we refer to NSNumber *(int)* and NSNumber *(float)*. This means that the attribute should be set to an NSNumber object that was created with the type specified.

Working with Attributed Text

The text-storage class provides methods to access the various attributes of the text it contains. To show how to work with text attributes, we'll add an analyzer to RTF Edit. Our analysis will count the number of characters in the document and give the number of font changes. To do so, follow these steps:

1. In Project Builder, edit the *MyDocument.h* file, and add the following action:

   ```
   #import <Cocoa/Cocoa.h>

   @interface MyDocument : NSDocument
   {
       IBOutlet NSTextView * textView;
       NSAttributedString * rtfData;
   }
   - (IBAction)analyzeText:(id)sender;
   @end
   ```

2. Save the *MyDocument.h* file, then open *MyDocument.nib* in Interface Builder.

3. Reparse the *MyDocument.h* file in Interface Builder. To do this, drag the *MyDocument.h* file to the *MyDocument.nib* window.

4. Add a button to our document interface, and name it Analyze, as shown in Figure 11-6.

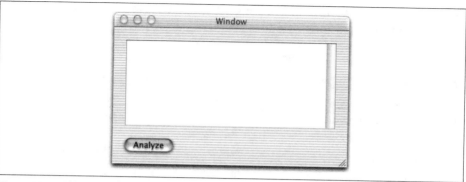

Figure 11-6. Adding an Analyze button to our interface

5. Control-drag a connection from the Analyze button to the File's Owner object, and connect the button to the analyzeText: method.

6. Save (⌘-S) the nib file, and return to Project Builder.

7. Edit the *MyDocument.m* file, and add the analyzeText: method as shown.

```
- (IBAction)analyzeText:(id)sender
{
    int count = 0;                                    // a
    int fontChanges = -1;                             // b
    id lastAttribute = nil;                           // c
    NSTextStorage * storage = [textView textStorage]; // d

    while (count < [storage length]) {                // e
        id attributeValue = [storage attribute:NSFontAttributeName
                             atIndex:count
                             effectiveRange:nil];
        if (attributeValue != lastAttribute) {        // f
            fontChanges++;
        }
        lastAttribute = attributeValue;               // g
        count++;                                      // h
    }

    NSBeginAlertSheet(@"Analysis",        // title                 // i
                @"OK",                    // default button label
                nil,                      // cancel button label
                nil,                      // other button label
                [textView window],        // document window
                nil,                      // modal delegate
                NULL,                     // selector to method
                NULL,                     // dismiss selector
                nil,                      // context info
                @"Font Changes %i",
                fontChanges);
}
```

The code we added performs the following tasks:

a. Sets up a counter to loop through all the characters in the document. This will allow us to examine the characters and notice font changes as we loop through the document.

b. Sets up a counter that will be used to keep track of the number of font changes that are found in the document.

c. Acts as a holder for the text-attribute object that was examined during a previous iteration of our loop.

d. Gets a reference to the text-storage object behind the text view.

e. Sets up a loop that will continue until we have examined every character in the document. Each time the loop is executed, the attribute value for the current character is obtained.

f. Checks to see if the font attribute of the current character is the same as the last character. If not, we record the change in font.

g. Stores this font attribute so that we can compare it to the font attribute we'll see the next time through the loop.

h. Increments our counter.

i. Creates our message and displays it to the user on a sheet attached to the window. We can pass in nil and NULL to most of the arguments since the sheet is for informative purposes only.

8. Save the project (File → Save, or ⌘-S).

9. Build and run (⌘-R) the application. Type some text, change the fonts, and then hit the Analyze button. You should see something like Figure 11-7.

Our next set of additions to the code will change the formatting of the text in our document.

1. In Project Builder, edit the *MyDocument.h* file, and add the following action:

```
#import <Cocoa/Cocoa.h>

@interface MyDocument : NSDocument
{
    IBOutlet NSTextView * textView;
    NSData * dataFromFile;
}
- (IBAction)analyzeText:(id)sender;
- (IBAction)clearFormatting:(id)sender;
@end
```

2. Save the *MyDocument.h* file; then open *MyDocument.nib* in Interface Builder.

3. Reparse the *MyDocument.h* file in Interface Builder. To do this, drag the *MyDocument.h* file to the *MyDocument.nib* window.

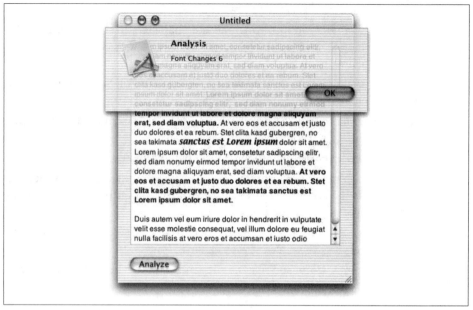

Figure 11-7. RTF Edit analyzing its text

4. Add a button to our document interface, and name it Remove Formatting, as shown in Figure 11-8.

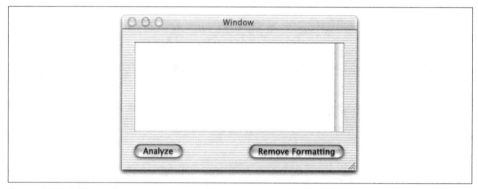

Figure 11-8. Adding a Remove Formatting button to RTF Edit

5. Control-drag a connection from the Remove Formatting button to the File's Owner object, and connect the button to the clearFormatting: method.

6. Save (⌘-S) the nib file, and return to Project Builder.

7. Edit the *MyDocument.m* file, and add the clearFormatting: method as shown.

```
- (IBAction)clearFormatting:(id)sender
{
    NSTextStorage * storage = [textView textStorage];      // a
    NSRange range = NSMakeRange(0, [storage length]);      // b
```

```
    NSMutableDictionary * attribs = [NSMutableDictionary dictionary];    // c
    [attribs setObject:[NSFont fontWithName:@"Helvetica" size:12]        // d
            forKey:NSFontAttributeName];
    [storage setAttributes:attribs range:range];                        // e
}
```

The code that we added performs the following tasks:

  a. Gets a reference to the text-storage object behind the text view

  b. Creates a range structure that will encompass all of the text in the storage object

  c. Creates a new mutable dictionary for the attributes to which we will set the text

  d. Adds an attribute to the dictionary to format the text with the Helvetica font in size 12

  e. Tells the storage to apply the new attributes to all characters

8. Save the project (File → Save, or ⌘-S).

9. Build and run (⌘-R) the application. Type some text, change the fonts, and then hit the Remove Formatting button. You should see all of your changes disappear.

Registering Undo Actions

There's one small problem with our method to remove formatting. When you make changes after removing the formatting and then want to undo changes to a point in time before you cleared the formatting, things don't work as expected. This is because we need to register the change with the *undo manager*.

The undo manager, implemented by the NSUndoManager class, is a general-purpose recorder of operations that can be undone or redone. An undoable operation is registered with the undo manager by specifying an object and a method to call on that object, along with an argument to pass to that method.

To allow the RTF Edit application to undo the removal of formatting, perform the following steps:

1. Edit the removeFormatting: method in *MyDocuments.m*, adding the code indicated in boldface:

```
- (IBAction)clearFormatting:(id)sender
{
    NSTextStorage * storage = [textView textStorage];
    NSRange range = NSMakeRange(0, [storage length]);
    NSMutableDictionary * attribs = [NSMutableDictionary dictionary];

    NSUndoManager * undoManager = [self undoManager];            // a
    [undoManager registerUndoWithTarget:storage                  // b
                        selector:@selector(setAttributedString:)
                        object:[storage copy]];
```

```
        [attribs setObject:[NSFont fontWithName:@"Helvetica"
                                          size:12]
                  forKey:NSFontAttributeName];
        [storage setAttributes:attribs range:range];
}
```

The code we added performs the following tasks:

   a. Gets the undoManager from the document. Each document has an associated
      undoManager.

   b. Registers an undo action with the undoManager. This action calls the underly-
      ing text-storage object's setAttributedString: method with a copy of the
      current storage—effectively resetting the contents of the storage to the same
      state as before the change.

2. Save the project (File → Save, ⌘-S).

3. Build and run (⌘-R) the application. Undo should now work correctly.

Enabling the Text Menu

Not only do text views come wired to work with the AppKit's font system, they are
also prewired to work with paragraph-formatting rulers. These rulers let a user specify paragraph formatting for his documents. The easiest way to enable this functionality is to use Interface Builder. Perform the following steps:

1. Open *MainMenu.nib* in Interface Builder.

2. Open the Cocoa Menus palette, and drag a Text menu to the MainMenu menu
   bar. Drop it between the Font and Window menus, as shown in Figure 11-9.

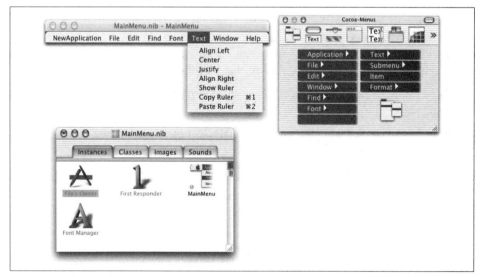

Figure 11-9. Adding the Text Menu to RTF Edit's main menu bar

---

3. Save (File → Save, or ⌘-S) the nib file.

4. Return to Project Builder, and Build and run (⌘-R) the project. Try the following:

    a. Select the Show Ruler menu item (Text → Show Ruler). A ruler will appear on the text view, as shown in Figure 11-10. The ruler displays margin and tab markers similar to those used in full-blown word processors.

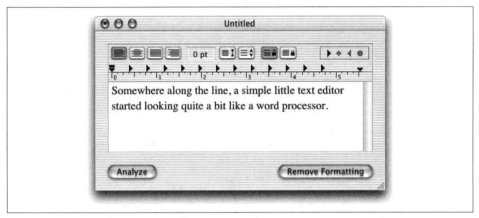

Figure 11-10. RTF Edit sporting a ruler

    b. Type some text, and change the paragraph alignment using the four buttons along the top-left hand side of the ruler.

    c. Create another paragraph, and change its indentation settings using the controls provided by the ruler.

Handling Embedded Images

The next piece of functionality we will add to RTF Edit is the ability to handle embedded images. To do this, we tell the text view that we want it place graphics into documents, and we add methods to support the loading and saving of RTFD files.

1. In Project Builder, open the RTF Edit target (Project → Edit Active Target, or Option-⌘-E), and select the Application Settings tab.

2. Add a new document type entry as shown in Figure 11-11. Fill out the Document Type Information fields with the fields shown, and click Add. Don't forget to set the Document Class field to MyDocument.

3. Open *MyDocument.m*, and change the loadFileWrapperRepresentation:ofType: method as shown. This will allow RTF edit to open either RTF or RTFD files. Note that we use the name of the document type we set previously in step 2.

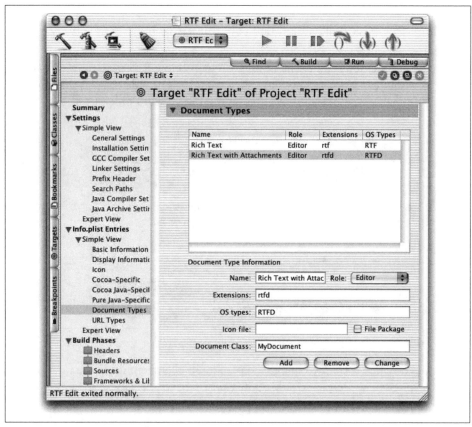

Figure 11-11. Adding the rtfd file type to the RTF Edit application

```
- (BOOL)loadFileWrapperRepresentation:(NSFileWrapper *) ofType:(NSString *)type
{
    if ([type isEqualToString:@"Rich Text with Attachments"]) {
        rtfData = [[NSAttributedString alloc]
            initWithRTFDFileWrapper:wrapper documentAttributes:nil];
    } else {
        rtfData = [[NSAttributedString alloc]
            initWithRTF:[wrapper regularFileContents] documentAttributes:nil];
    }
    if (textView) {
        [[textView textStorage]
            replaceCharactersInRange:NSMakeRange(0, [[textView string] length])
                withAttributedString:rtfData];
        [rtfData release];
    }
    return YES;
}
```

4. Next, change the `fileWrapperRepresentationOfType:` method so that the document can save its contents according to the type of data requested.

```
- (NSFileWrapper *)fileWrapperRepresentationOfType:(NSString *)type
{
    NSRange range = NSMakeRange(0, [[textView string] length]);
    if ([type isEqualToString:@"Rich Text with Attachments"]) {
        return [[textView textStorage] RTFDFileWrapperFromRange:range
                                            documentAttributes:nil];
    } else {
        NSFileWrapper * wrapper = [[NSFileWrapper alloc]
            initRegularFileWithContents:[textView RTFFromRange:range]];
        return [wrapper autorelease];
    }
}
```

5. Finally, change the `windowControllerDidLoadNib:` method so that graphics can be added to the documents.

```
- (void)windowControllerDidLoadNib:(NSWindowController *) aController
{
    [super windowControllerDidLoadNib:aController];
    if (rtfData) {
        [[textView textStorage]
            replaceCharactersInRange:NSMakeRange(0, [[textView string] length]);
                withAttributedString:rtfData];
        [rtfData release];
    }
    [textView setAllowsUndo:YES];
    [textView setImportsGraphics:YES];
}
```

6. Save the project (File → Save, or ⌘-S).

7. Clean the project (Build → Clean, or Shift-⌘-K).[*]

8. Build and run (⌘-R) the application. Create a document, and drag an image into it. When you save the document, the Save panel will have a pull-down menu to select what kind of file you are saving, as shown in Figure 11-12. Be sure to select Rich Text with Attachments in order to save your image information.

The Spoken Word

The last thing we will add to our application has very little to do with rich text, but it's fun and shows off one of the ways that Cocoa is integrated with other Mac OS X technologies. We'll add a button that, when pressed, will speak the contents of a document to us using Mac OS X's built-in Text-To-Speech engine.

1. In Project Builder, edit *MyDocument.h*, and add the following action declaration:

```
#import <Cocoa/Cocoa.h>

@interface MyDocument : NSDocument
```

---

[*] In some of the versions of Project Builder that we worked with while writing this book, there was a problem with adding document types unless you forced this cleaning step.

```
{
    IBOutlet NSTextView * textView;
    NSData * dataFromFile;
    NSString * dataType;
}
- (IBAction)analyzeText:(id)sender;
- (IBAction)removeFormatting:(id)sender;
- (IBAction)speakText:(id)sender;
@end
```

2. Save the *MyDocument.h* file; then open *MyDocument.nib* in Interface Builder.

3. Reparse the *MyDocument.h* file by dragging the *MyDocument.h* file from Project
   Builder to Interface Builder's *MyDocument.nib* window.

4. Add a button to our document interface, and name it Speak, as shown in
   Figure 11-13.

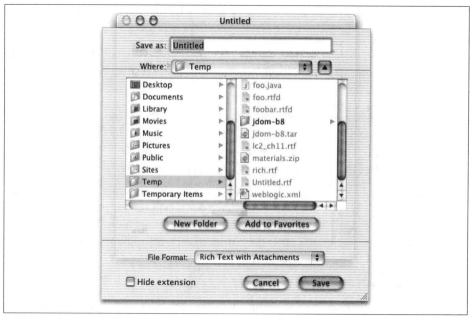

Figure 11-12. Saving a file with attachments

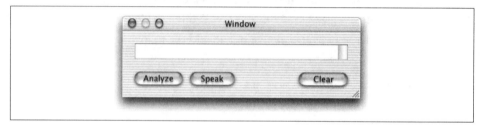

Figure 11-13. Adding the Speak button to RTF Edit

5. Control-drag a connection from the Speak button to the File's Owner object, and connect it to the speakText: method.

6. Save (⌘-S) the nib file, and return to Project Builder.

7. In Project Builder, edit the *MyDocument.m* file, and add the speakText: method as shown:
   ```
   - (IBAction)speakText:(id)sender
   {
       [textView startSpeaking:sender];
   }
   ```

8. Save the project (File → Save, or ⌘-S).

9. Build and run (⌘-R) the application. Type some text, then click on the Speak button. The built-in Text-to-Speech engine will start reading off what you typed.

Exercises

1. Using Interface Builder, turn on image attachments and undo by removing the two lines of code in the awakeFromNib method that perform this duty.

2. Set the ruler to appear automatically when a document window opens.

3. Replace the Speak buttons with menu items.

4. Add a number of characters line to the Analyze sheet.

PART IV

Miscellaneous Topics

This part covers a variety of Mac OS X and Cocoa features that are important to delivering finished applications and giving them their finishing touches. The chapters in this part of the book cover diverse topics and can be read in any order.

Chapters in this part of the book include the following:

CHAPTER 12

Printing

In the past, code to handle printing has been difficult to write. Many factors, such as margins, page orientation, and paper size, come into play. The differences in drawing models (between screen drawing and drawing to the printer) have made things even more challenging. Cocoa provides a clean printing interface that uses the same drawing model used to draw to the screen. In addition, just as Cocoa supports the use of calibrated color when drawing to the screen, ColorSync provides advanced color management when printing to paper.

As we saw in Chapter 7, when a view object receives a `drawRect:` message, it responds by drawing itself into the current graphics context. Usually, this context is a frame buffer, and the `drawRect:` message results in the view drawing its contents to the screen. The same machinery is used during printing, but the current graphics context is set to be the printer.

Remember (as discussed in Chapter 7) that the `drawRect:` method is never called directly to make a view appear on the screen; it is called only when the display message is sent to the view. The same methodology applies to printing; the `drawRect:` method is called when a `print:` message is sent to the view. Calling `print:` on a view causes the AppKit to display a print panel that asks the user which printer she wishes to use (along with page setup information). When the user clicks the Print button of the print panel, a sequence of `drawRect:` messages—one for each page—is sent to the view.

This chapter focuses on enabling basic printing from Cocoa applications. As with most things, once you have mastered the basics, you can make printing fairly complex—such as adding UI elements to the print panel and using alternate text views to reflow text—to satisfy special needs.

Printing a View

Since Cocoa makes it so easy to print a view, we're not going to waste any time. The following steps guide you through creating your first print job.

1. Create a new Cocoa Application project in Project Builder (File → New Project → Application → Cocoa Application) named "View Print", and save it in your *~/LearningCocoa* folder.

2. Use the Finder to locate the *Ripples Blue.jpg* file (*/Library/Desktop Pictures*), and drag it to the Resources group of your project.

3. Open the *MainMenu.nib* file in Interface Builder. Click the Images tab on the MainMenu.nib window, and notice that the image we just added is present.

4. Drag an Image View (NSImageView) from the Other Cocoa Views palette onto the main window, and then resize it to be larger, as shown in Figure 12-1.

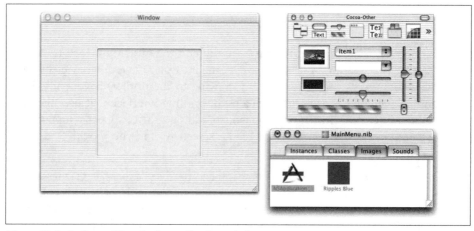

Figure 12-1. An Image View in the application window

5. Drag the Ripples Blue image from the MainMenu.nib window to the Image View that we just added. When you drop the image onto the view, you should see the image appear there.

6. Control-drag a connection from the File → Print menu item to the Image View. The inspector will pop up, if it's not already open, and indicate that the menu item is connected to FirstResponder.print:. Disconnect this connection, and connect the File → Print menu item to the print: action of the view, as shown in Figure 12-2. Be careful when dragging the connection, as it's easy to select the window as the target of the action.

7. Save (⌘-S) the nib file, and return to Project Builder.

8. Build and run the project (⌘-R).

9. Select Print (File → Print, or ⌘-P) in the running application. The print dialog box will open, as shown in Figure 12-3.

10. Click the Preview button. The application prints to a PDF file that will be displayed in the Preview application. Repeat the process, and click Print if you want to see the results printed on your printer.

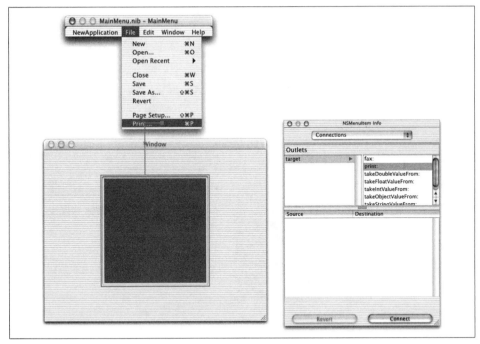

Figure 12-2. Creating a connection from the print menu item

Now that you have printed the view, notice that the entire image view drew itself onto the printer—border and all—and appears just as it did onscreen. If you just wanted to draw the image itself to the printer, you'd need to add a little code to control what gets printed. In the next section, we'll do just that with text.

Using Print Operations

Usually, you'll want more control over your printing than was available in our View Print application. This control is provided in Cocoa by creating print operations (instances of the NSPrintOperation class) and running them. You can think of a print operation as a controller object that mediates between the underlying print machinery of Mac OS X and the view being printed. Print operations use a helper object of type NSPrintInfo to help them determine how the page should be printed. If the print operation is constructed without a print info object, a default print info object for the application will be used.

We'll show you how to use print operations and print info objects in conjunction with printing using the document architecture, as covered in Chapter 10 and Chapter 11.

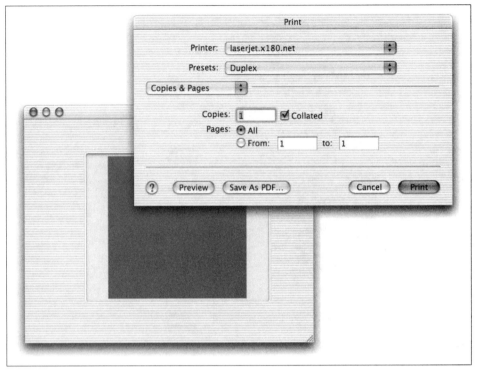

Figure 12-3. The print dialog panel in action

Printing Using the Document Architecture

To enable simple printing from a document-based application simply requires that a printShowingPrintPanel: method be implemented in the document class. This method is called by the document architecture on the active document when a user selects File → Print or presses ⌘-P.

To show this in action, we will create a simple editor that just prints the contents of the text document. So we can just focus on the printing-related code, we're going to create a new editor rather than using the one we just built. The following steps will guide you:

1. Create a new Document-Based Application in Project Builder (File → New Project → Application → Cocoa Document-based Application) named "Document Print", and save it in your *~/LearningCocoa* folder.

2. Design the GUI by opening the *MyDocument.nib* file in Interface Builder and performing the following steps:

   a. Remove the default text field.

   b. Drag an NSTextView from the Cocoa Data Views palette to the application's window.

   c. Resize the text view so that it occupies the entire window.

d. Change the Autosizing options so that the view will follow changes in the window's size.

3. In Project Builder, open *MyDocument.h*, and add a declaration as follows for the text view's outlet:

```
#import <Cocoa/Cocoa.h>

@interface MyDocument : NSDocument
{
    IBOutlet NSTextView * textView;
}
@end
```

4. Save (File → Save, or ⌘-S) *MyDocument.h*; then drag it onto Interface Builder's MyDocument.nib window so that Interface Builder can pick up the change to the file.

5. Control-drag a connection from the File's Owner object (remember, this is a proxy for the MyDocument instance at runtime), and connect it to the textView outlet.

6. Save (File → , or ⌘-S) the nib file.

7. In Project Builder, open *MyDocument.m* and add the printShowingPrintPanel: method as shown here:

```
- (void)printShowingPrintPanel:(BOOL)flag
{
    NSPrintInfo * printInfo = [self printInfo];          // a
    NSPrintOperation * printOp;                          // b
    printOp = [NSPrintOperation printOperationWithView:textView    // c
                                 printInfo:printInfo];
    [printOp runOperation];                              // d
}
```

The code we added performs the following tasks:

a. Obtains a reference to the printInfo object used by the document. This object is created automatically by Cocoa's document architecture for each document.

b. Declares a printOp variable of type NSPrintOperation.

c. Creates a new print operation that will print the contents of our text view using the print information that we obtained in line a.

d. Calls the runOperation method on the print operation object. This puts the printing machinery into play.

8. Save the project (File → Save, or ⌘-S).

9. Build and run (⌘-R) the application.

a. Create some text and then print it (File → Print, or ⌘-P). A print dialog box will appear, as shown in Figure 12-4.

b. Click either the Print button (to send the print job to your printer) or the Preview button (to send the print information to the Preview application, as shown in Figure 12-5). We recommend that you use the Preview button as you work through this chapter so that a few sheets of paper can be saved.

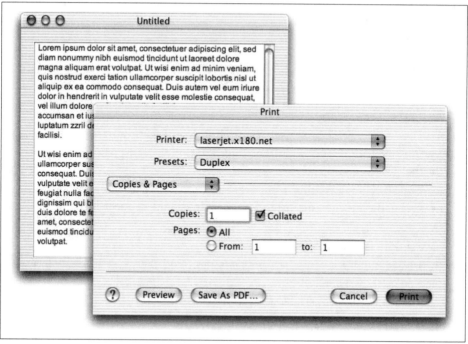

Figure 12-4. Printing from a document-based application

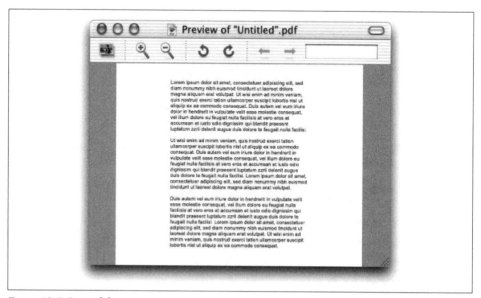

Figure 12-5. Printed document in Preview.app

c. Use the Page Setup (File → Page Setup, or Shift-⌘-P) functionality to change the paper size and the orientation used.

Setting Margins

When printing text documents, we don't usually want the text centered on the page; we'd rather have it printed from the top-lefthand corner with some given margin.

1. Modify our printShowingPanel: method as follows:

```
- (void)printShowingPrintPanel:(BOOL)flag
{
    NSPrintInfo * printInfo = [self printInfo];
    NSPrintOperation * printOp;

    [printInfo setTopMargin:36.0];                          // a
    [printInfo setLeftMargin:36.0];                         // b

    [printInfo setHorizontallyCentered:NO];                 // c
    [printInfo setVerticallyCentered:NO];                   // d

    printOp = [NSPrintOperation printOperationWithView:textView
                                             printInfo:printInfo];
    [printOp runOperation];
}
```

The code we added performs the following tasks:

a. Sets the top margin of the printed page to 36 points (1/2 inch). Points are a unit of measure used in page layout and typography, based on a scale of 72 points per inch. See Table 12-1 for a quick reference.

Table 12-1. Points to inches conversion chart

Point Size	Measurement in Inches
9	1/8
18	1/4
27	3/8
36	1/2
45	5/8
54	3/4
63	7/8
72	1

b. Sets the left margin of the printed page to 36 points.

c. Indicates that the printed view should not be horizontally centered on the page.

d. Indicates that the printed view should not be vertically centered on the page

2. Save the project (File → Save, or ⌘-S).

3. Build and run (⌘-R) the application. Now, when you print out a block of text, it will be printed starting at the upper-left corner, as shown in Figure 12-6.

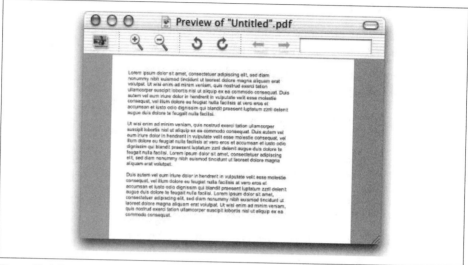

Figure 12-6. Printing at the top-left corner

Complete information on the settings for a print info object can be found in the */Developer/Documentation/Cocoa/TasksAndConcepts/ProgrammingTopics/Printing/index.html* file installed on your hard drive with the Developer Tools.

Exercises

1. Add a Font menu to the application, and print out files with various fonts.

2. Add printing to the Dot View application that we created in Chapter 8.

3. Resize the image view in View Print to occupy the entire window (don't forget to set the Autosizing attributes!), and experiment with printing other images.

CHAPTER 13

Bundles and Resources

Even though it may look like a single file in the Finder, a Cocoa application is actually a collection of files in a special directory structure known as a *bundle*. Bundle directories in the filesystem have a special significance that the Finder understands and that allows users to treat applications, as well as other types of bundles, as a single entity. This allows users to install an application simply by dragging it from a CD image and relocate it by dragging it around the filesystem.

There are three general types of bundles:

Application bundles
> Application bundles contain an executable and all its related resources, such as nib files, image files, and localized strings. For example, most of the applications installed in the */Applications* folder are application bundles.

Plug-in bundles
> Plug-in bundles provide code that extends or enhances the functionality of a host application in some way. They plug into some kind of architecture provided by the host application. An example of a plug-in bundle is the screensaver modules installed in the */System/Library/Screen Savers* folder. Each of these bundles is used by the screensaver system (whose control panel is in the System Preferences).

Framework bundles
> Framework bundles contain dynamic shared libraries, as well as header files, images, and documentation. For example, the two Cocoa frameworks, Foundation and AppKit, are packaged as framework bundles in the */System/Library/Frameworks* folder. Framework bundles differ from other bundles in that the Finder allows you to browse their contents. This allows you to browse the contents of a framework easily.

The essence of a bundle is that it pulls together a set of resources into a single package. This mechanism works on a variety of filesystems, from the dual fork–based HFS+ filesystem that Mac OS X prefers to single-fork SMB and NFS volumes that might be mounted from Windows or Unix servers. In this chapter, we take a look at application and other bundles and how to manage and obtain resources from them.

Peeking Inside Bundles

To get a better idea of how bundles go together, let's take a look inside a bundle that is already on your system.

1. Use the Finder to browse to the iPhoto application, located in the */Applications* folder.

2. Control-click on iPhoto. Select Show Package Contents from the context menu. A Finder window rooted at the directory in which iPhoto is located will open. You can use this Finder window to browse around the internals of the application. Figure 13-1 shows a column view of the application.

Figure 13-1. Looking inside an application bundle

All of the contents of a bundle exist in the aptly named *Contents* directory. At a very minimum, a bundle consists of two files—*Info.plist* and *PkgInfo*—located in the *Contents* directory, as shown in Figure 13-2.

The *Info.plist* file is an XML-based property list file that specifies the following:

- The name of the main executable for the bundle
- Version info
- Type and creator codes

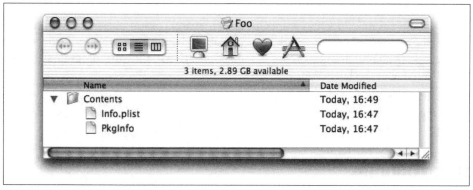

Figure 13-2. A minimal bundle

- Document types that the application handles and what role (*editor* or *view*) the application plays for a document type
- Application and document icons
- The kinds of data that the application can handle via the pasteboard
- Application-specific attribute information

When we used Project Builder in Chapter 11 to manipulate the document-type application settings for Simple Edit and RTF Edit, those settings were automatically made into the *Info.plist* file.

PkgInfo contains only the type and creator codes for the application. This info is redundant with that in the *Info.plist*, but it is held separately so the Finder can use this information more efficiently.

Bundle Directories

In addition to the *Info.plist* and *PkgInfo* files, the following directories can appear in the *Contents* directory:

MacOS
Contains the actual executable code for an application or plug-in.

Resources
Contains the various resources an application uses. These resources include nib files, images, localized strings, and icon files. Older Mac OS applications stored these resources in the resource fork of the application's executable file.

Frameworks
Contains frameworks on which the application depends. These frameworks will always be used by an application, even if newer versions exist on the users' system. This ensures that a specific version of a framework, which you need for your application, is always used.

Shared Frameworks

Contains frameworks that will be used by the application unless a newer version of the framework exists on the local system. These frameworks can be superceded by shared frameworks in other applications, allowing programs to take advantage of the latest code.

Shared Support

Contains helper applications, assistants, and other tools that may be used by an application.

Using Bundles

You can obtain the contents of bundles, even the application bundle from which your application is running, by using the NSBundle class. This class provides methods to obtain the paths to resources within your application, as well as methods to load and link executable code that is located in a bundle.

To demonstrate working with bundles, we will build a simple application that loads an image into an image view.

1. Create a new Cocoa Application project in Project Builder (File → New Project → Application → Cocoa Application) named "Image Bundle", and save it in your *~/LearningCocoa* folder.

2. Add some image files to the project using the Add Files command (Project → Add Files). Navigate to the */Library/Desktop Pictures/Abstract* folder, select all the JPEG images (named *Abstract 1-8.jpg*), and click the Add button.

 To select multiple files, as required in step 2, you can ⌘-click each image file and then click the Add button to load all of the images at once. This method of selecting files is particularly helpful when you want to pick and choose the files, rather than selecting them all.

When adding files, Project Builder also allows you to select a directory and click the Add button.

3. In the next sheet that drops down, make sure that the Copy items checkbox is clicked, as shown in Figure 13-3, and click the Add button.

4. Save the project (File → Save, or ⌘-S).

5. Next, open the *MainMenu.nib* file in Interface Builder.

6. Drag an image view (NSImageView) object from the Cocoa-Other views palette into the main application window, and resize it so that it occupies the entire window, as shown as Figure 13-4. Set the Autosizing attributes so that the view will expand and contract if the user resizes the window.

7. Create a subclass of NSObject in Interface Builder. To do this, click on the Classes tab of the MainMenu.nib window, find and Control-click on NSObject, and then select Subclass NSObject from the pop-up menu. Name the subclass "Controller".

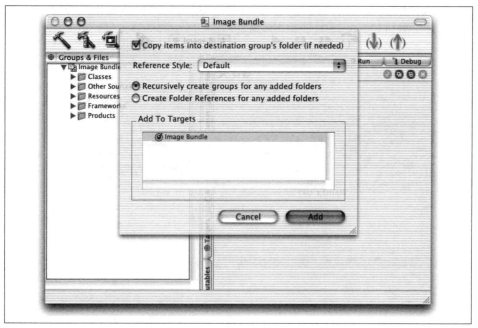

Figure 13-3. Adding files to the project

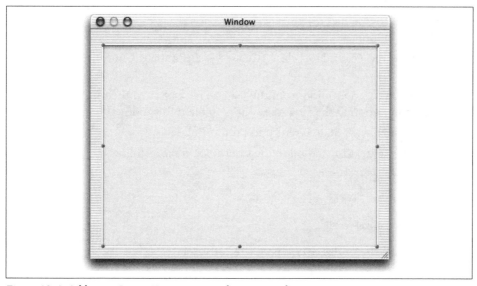

Figure 13-4. Adding an Image View to our application window

 You can also create a subclass by locating NSObject in the Classes pane and hitting the Return key. A new subclass will be created, and all you need to do is enter a new name for the subclass.

8. Create an outlet named `imageView` on the Controller object using the Inspector, as shown in Figure 13-5. Type the outlet as `NSImageView`.

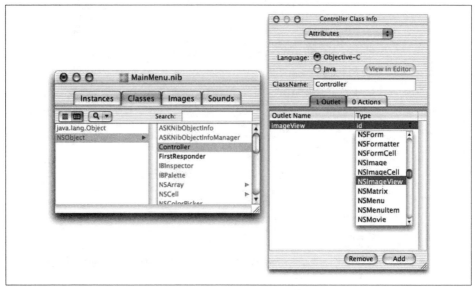

Figure 13-5. Adding an imageView outlet to the Controller class

9. Create the source files for the `Controller` class (Classes → Create Files for Controller, or Option-⌘-F).

10. Instantiate the `Controller` class (Classes → Instantiate Controller, or Option-⌘-I).

11. Control-drag a connection from the `Controller` object to the image view. Hook up the connection to the `imageView` outlet in the Info window.

12. Save the nib file (⌘-S), and return to Project Builder.

13. Add an `awakeFromNib` method to the *Controller.m* file as follows:

```
#import "Controller.h"

@implementation Controller

- (void)awakeFromNib
{
    NSBundle * mainBundle = [NSBundle mainBundle];                   // a
    NSString * path = [mainBundle pathForResource:@"Abstract 1"      // b
                                    ofType:@"jpg"];
    NSImage * image = [[NSImage alloc]initWithContentsOfFile:path];  // c
    [imageView setImage:image];                                     // d
    [image release];                                                // e
}
@end
```

The code we added performs the following tasks:

a. Gets a reference to the bundle object from which this application was loaded.

b. Uses the `pathForResource:ofType:` method of the `NSBundle` class to look up the path of the *Abstract 1.jpg* file in the application bundle. If we were to print out the path that results, it would be as follows:

```
~/LearningCocoa/Image Bundle/build/Image Bundle.app/Contents/Resources/
Abstract 1.jpg
```

c. Creates an `NSImage` object using the file in our application bundle.

d. Tells the `imageView` of our application interface to display the image.

e. Releases the image, now that we are done with it and the image view has it.

14. Build and run (⌘-R) the application. The application should look like Figure 13-6.

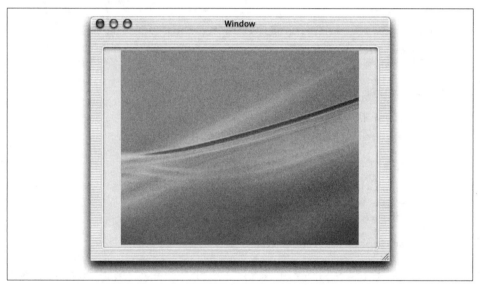

Figure 13-6. Image Bundle running and showing Abstract 1.jpg

15. Open the Products group in the Groups & Files pane, and examine the *Image Bundle.app* item, shown in Figure 13-7. This is the built application bundle and all of the resources inside of it. During the build process, Project Builder automatically moves the image files that we added to the project into the Resources directory of the application bundle.

Instead of just obtaining specific files from the application bundle, we can get all of the resources of a particular type. To illustrate this, we'll add a Next button to the application, which will iterate over the set of images in our application.

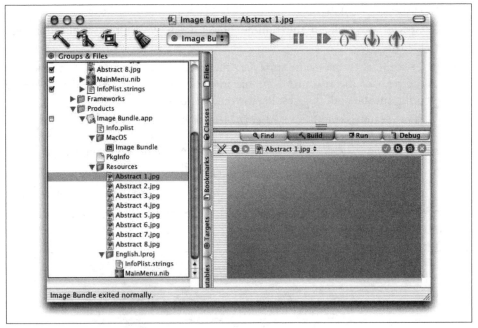

Figure 13-7. Examining the built application bundle for Image Bundle

1. Edit the *Controller.h* file, and add the following code:

```
#import <Cocoa/Cocoa.h>

@interface Controller : NSObject
{
    IBOutlet NSImageView *imageView;
    NSArray * imagePaths;
    int currentImage;
}
- (IBAction)nextImage:(id)sender;
@end
```

This allows us to keep track of the paths to all the images in the bundle, as well as keep a count of what image we're showing. In addition, it adds the method declaration for the action method.

2. Save (⌘-S) the *Controller.h* file.

3. Open the *MainMenu.nib* file in Interface Builder.

4. Click on the Classes tab of the MainMenu.nib window; find the Controller class, and then reread the source file (Classes → Read Controller.h) so that Interface Builder can pick up the new action method.

5. Add a new button, named Next, to our interface, as shown in Figure 13-8.

6. Connect the Next button to the nextImage: action method on the Controller instance object.

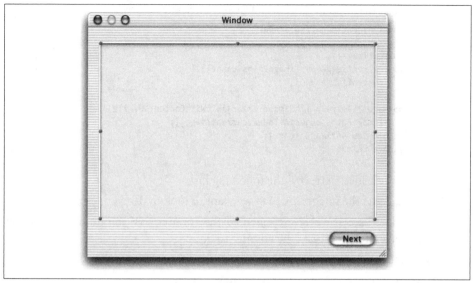

Figure 13-8. Adding a Next button to our interface

7. Save the nib, and return to Project Builder.

8. Modify the awakeFromNib method in *Controller.m* to match the following code. Note that we have changed lines b and c from the previous implementation of this method.

```
- (void)awakeFromNib
{
    NSBundle * mainBundle = [NSBundle mainBundle];
    imagePaths = [mainBundle pathsForResourcesOfType:@"jpg"        // a
                              inDirectory:nil];
    [imagePaths retain];                                            // b
    currentImage = 0;                                              // c
    NSImage * image = [[NSImage alloc]initWithContentsOfFile:      // d
        [imagePaths objectAtIndex:currentImage]];
    [imageView setImage:image];
    [image release];
}
```

This code performs the following tasks:

a. Obtains an array of paths for all the JPEG files in our application. The nil argument tells the method to look in the default Resources directory. If the images were located in a subdirectory of the bundle, we could specify that subdirectory here as well.

b. Retains the reference to the imagePaths array so that it doesn't disappear out from under us.

c. Sets the currentImage counter to 0.

d. Creates a new NSImage object using the first path of the array of paths we obtained in line a.

9. Add the nextImage: action method to *Controller.m* as follows:

```
- (IBAction)nextImage:(id)sender
{
    currentImage++;                                              // a
    if (currentImage == [imagePaths count]) {                    // b
        currentImage = 0;
    }
    NSImage * image = [[NSImage alloc]initWithContentsOfFile:     // c
        [imagePaths objectAtIndex:currentImage]];
    [imageView setImage:image];                                  // d
    [image release];
}
```

The code we added performs the following tasks:

a. Increments the image at which we want to look by 1.

b. Checks to see if we've incremented the counter past the number of images we have. If so, we reset the counter to 0.

c. Creates an NSImage object using the path at the current index.

d. Sets the image view to display the new image.

10. Save the project (File → Save, or ⌘-S).

11. Build and run (⌘-R) the application. You should now be able to step through the sequence of images in the bundle.

A Performance Diversion

When you run the Image Bundle application, you'll notice that loading the next image isn't exactly snappy. Even on a PowerBook G4, there is a notable lag as each image loads into the window. This is because we are going back to the filesystem and forcing Cocoa to reload the image each time we click on the Next button. We can fix this performance problem by preloading the images. The following steps will modify the code:

1. Modify the *Controller.h* file to match the following code:

```
#import <Cocoa/Cocoa.h>

@interface Controller : NSObject
{
    IBOutlet NSImageView *imageView;
    NSMutableArray * images;
    int currentImage;
}
- (IBAction)nextImage:(id)sender;
@end
```

Here, we've changed the name of the array to indicate that we will hold references to images, not to the paths at which the images are located.

2. Modify the `awakeFromNib` method in *Controller.m* to match the following code. We are changing almost every line of code, so be careful here.

```
- (void)awakeFromNib
{
    NSBundle * mainBundle = [NSBundle mainBundle];
    NSArray * imagePaths = [mainBundle pathsForResourcesOfType:@"jpg"    // a
                                              inDirectory:nil];
    images = [[NSMutableArray alloc] init];                              // b
    int count = [imagePaths count];
    int i;
    for (i = 0; i < count; i++) {                                        // c
        NSImage * image = [[NSImage alloc] initWithContentsOfFile:
            [imagePaths objectAtIndex:i]];
        [images addObject:image];
        [image release]
    }
    currentImage = 0;
    [imageView setImage:[images objectAtIndex:currentImage]];           // d
}
```

This code does the following things:

a. Loads the paths to all the JPEG images in the bundle into an array

b. Creates a mutable array to the location where the images will be stored

c. Loops through the image paths and creates a new `NSImage` object with each path

d. Sets the image view to display the first image

3. Now, modify the `nextImage:` method in *Controller.m* to match the following code. This method actually gets simpler as a result of the work that we did in the `awakeFromNib` method.

```
- (IBAction)nextImage:(id)sender
{
    currentImage++;
    if (currentImage == [images count]) {                               // a
        currentImage = 0;
    }
    [imageView setImage:[images objectAtIndex:currentImage]];           // b
}
```

The code we added does the following things:

a. Checks to see if we have incremented the counter past the number of images loaded. If so, it resets the counter to 0.

b. Sets the image displayed into the image view to the next image.

4. Save the project (File → Save, or ⌘-S).

5. Build and run (⌘-R) the project. You'll notice that it takes longer for the application to launch than it did before, but switching between images is now much quicker. As with most performance optimizations, the price of loading the images has to be paid somewhere; it's just a matter of when the price is paid.

The real answer to our performance problem is a background thread that loads the images after the first image is loaded and displayed. Doing this would move the price of loading the images to after the application was already displayed, when the user wouldn't care. However, using threads is not easy and is an advanced topic beyond the scope of this book.

Exercises

1. Add a Previous button to the Image Bundle application.
2. Add keyboard shortcuts for both the Next and Previous buttons.

CHAPTER 14

Localization

If an application will be used in more than one part of the world, its resources should be customized, or *localized*, for the language, country, or cultural region. Cocoa provides a group of conventions and services, known as an *internationalization architecture*, that are flexible enough to enable multiple localizations of character strings, icons, user interfaces, and even context help packaged into your application. The localized resources appropriate to the user's preferences are dynamically loaded as needed.

The aim of Cocoa's localization architecture is to enable multilingual applications to be created without generating any new Objective-C code for each supported locale. Even if you don't have an immediate need for multilingual support in your application, it is always a good idea to keep the localization abilities of a Cocoa application in mind, so you can enable it when the need arises. With proper design, your application's source code won't have to be touched if and when it does need to be localized—minimizing the risk of introducing problems by modifying the code.

In this chapter, we'll take a look at how Cocoa's localization system works, how it depends on the user's language preferences, and how to structure your application's nib files and use of strings to take advantage of it.

Mac OS X Language Preferences

To see how Mac OS X supports different languages, try the following process:

1. Open the TextEdit application (*/Applications/TextEdit*), and take a look at its user interface.

2. Close TextEdit, and open the System Preferences application. Select the International preferences panel.

3. Reorder your preferred language order by dragging Français to the top of the list, as shown in Figure 14-1.

Figure 14-1. Changing language preferences

4. Open TextEdit again, and notice how the menu items are now in French rather than English, as shown in Figure 14-2.

5. Quit TextEdit (File → Quit, or ⌘-Q), and then reset your language preferences to English.

What just happened here? By changing the System Preferences, TextEdit uses Mac OS X's and Cocoa's internationalization system to display the correct interface for the locale we specified. Under the hood, the system is using localized interface components stored within separate files and directories within the application's bundle.

Localizing Resources

In Chapter 13, we took a look at how Cocoa applications are packaged into application bundles. These bundles can contain multiple sets of resources, each set contained in a directory with an *.lproj* extension and identified by a combination of language and locale. The ability for bundles to hold all of the localized resources for an application, combined the ability for with bundle resource look-up routines to be aware of a user's language preferences, is what enables one version of an application to support multiple languages.

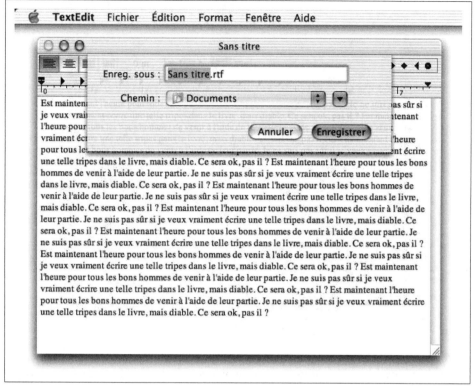

Figure 14-2. TextEdit running in French

To get a feel for how localized resources are stored inside an application bundle, take a look at the contents of the Clock application.

1. Use the Finder to locate the Clock application (*/Applications/Clock*).

2. Control-click on the Clock application icon, and select Show Package Contents from the pop-up menu.

3. Select View → List from the Finder menus, browse through the application as shown in Figure 14-3, and notice the files shown.

As you can see, the same files, *Clock2.nib* and *InfoPlist.strings*, exist in various sub-folders of the *Resources* folder. These subfolders, which have a language name or country code and a *.lproj* extension, contain the language-support files for the project.

Mac OS X defines localizations using three different conventions. Each convention allows a different degree of specificity.

A language name

Languages supported by Mac OS X include English, French, German, Japanese, Chinese, Spanish, Italian, Swedish, and Portuguese.

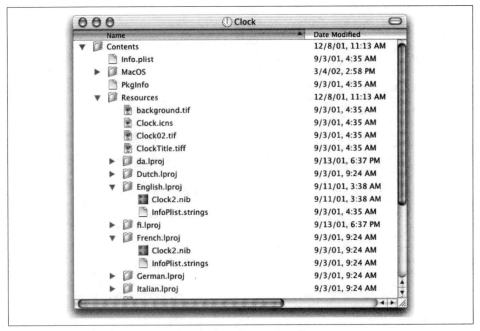

Figure 14-3. Localized resources in the Clock application bundle

A language abbreviation

The language abbreviations, some of which are shown in Table 14-1, conform to the ISO 639 specification.

Table 14-1. Some common language abbreviations supported by Mac OS X

Language	Country code or abbreviation
Chinese	zh
Danish	da
Dutch	nl
English	en
French	Fr
Korean	Ko
Polish	Pl

 You can easily find language abbreviations on the Web by searching for "iso 639". One resource is OASIS-OPEN (*http://www.oasis-open. org/cover/iso639a.html*).

A locale abbreviation

The locale abbreviations consist of a language abbreviation (see Table 14-1), followed by an underscore and a two letter code. These codes, some of which are shown in Table 14-2, conform to the ISO 3166 specification that can identify a regional variant of a language.

Table 14-2. Some regional language codes

Region	Locale abbreviation
British English	en_UK
American English	en_US
Canadian French	fr_CA
Tawainese Chinese	zh_TW
Mainland China Chinese	zh_CN

 Again, you can easily find country abbreviates on the web by searching for "iso 3166". OASIS-OPEN has a resource at *http://www.oasis-open.org/cover/country3166.html*.

A common practice of developers is to use the traditional language name for those that exist, then to use the language abbreviation, and then—only when necessary—the regional variant abbreviation.

Localized Resource Search Algorithm

Cocoa's various resource-handling methods in the NSBundle class automatically return the filesystem location of the resource that best matches the user's language and regional preferences. These methods look for resources of the following types until a matching resource is found:

Global Resource
   Files that are stored at the top level of the *Resources* directory in the bundle

User Region Specific Resource
   Files that are stored in a regional directory (such as *en_UK.lproj*) under the Resources directory, as specified by the user's preferences

User Language Specific Resources
   Files that are stored in a regional directory (such as *English.lproj*, *da.lproj*, or *French.lproj*), as specified by the user's preferences

Developer Region Specific Resource
   Files that are in a regional directory (such as *en_UK.lproj*), as specified by the region in which the application was developed

Developer Language Specific Resource
   Files that are in a language directory (such as *English.lproj*, *da.lproj*, or *French. lproj*), as specified by the region in which the application was developed

Note that global resources take precedence over localized resources. This allows a quick return of resources that never change between locales, without going through the rest of the search process. You shouldn't have a global version of a resource if you have localized versions, as the localized versions will always be masked by a global version.

Localizing Nib Files

Nib files are typically localized all at once. A person performing localization takes a nib file, translates all the user-visible strings, and makes any adjustments that are necessary, such as resizing controls so that the translated strings appear correctly.

To illustrate how to localize nib files, we will create an application interface that isn't hooked up to anything, but which contains various controls that we can localize. The following steps will guide you:

1. Create a new Cocoa Application project in Project Builder (File → New Project → Application → Cocoa Application) named "Localization", and save it in your *~/LearningCocoa* folder.

2. Open the *MainMenu.nib* file in Interface Builder by double-clicking on its icon in the Resources folder of the Groups & Files pane in Project Builder.

3. Using the various controls available on Interface Builder's palettes, lay out an interface that looks like Figure 14-4.

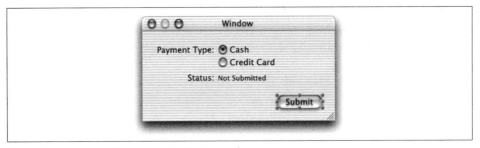

Figure 14-4. Our Localization application's interface

4. Create a subclass of NSObject. Click on the Classes tab of the MainMenu.nib window, find NSObject, Control-click it, and select Subclass NSObject from the pop-up menu; name the subclass Controller.

5. Create an outlet named statusField on the Controller object, using the Info window (Tools → Show Info, or Shift-⌘-I).

6. Create an action for the Controller subclass, named submit:.

7. Create the files for the Controller subclass (Classes → Create Files for Controller).

8. Instantiate the Controller subclass (Classes → Instantiate Controller).

9. Control-drag a connection between the Controller object and the Not Submitted text field, and connect it to the statusField outlet in the Info window.

10. Connect the Submit button to the `submit:` method of the `Controller` by Control-dragging a connection from the Submit button to the Controller object.

11. Save the nib file (⌘-S), close the MainMenu.nib window in Interface Builder, and then return to Project Builder.

12. In Project Builder's Groups & Files panel, click the disclosure triangle beside the MainMenu.nib file, and select the English entry underneath it, as shown in Figure 14-5.

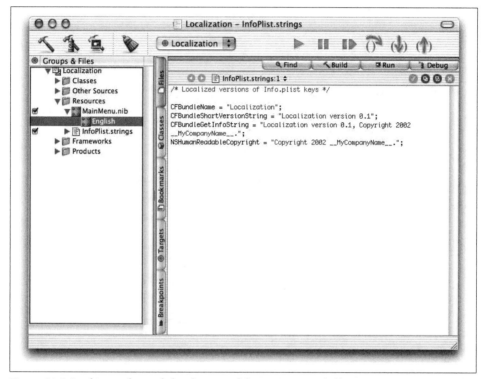

Figure 14-5. Looking at the single localization of the MainMenu.nib file

13. Bring up the Info panel (Project → Show Info, or ⌘-I).

14. Select Add Localized Variant from the Localization & Platforms pop-up menu. You will be prompted for a locale. Enter French, as shown in Figure 14-6.

15. Close the Info window by clicking on the red close window button.

16. You should see two localizations of the MainMenu.nib file in Project Builder.

17. Double-click the French variant to open it in Interface Builder.

18. Modify the various strings in the interface to match Figure 14-7. To type in the é character, type **Option-e**, then **e** again (without the Option key). Notice that you'll have to resize the window and move things around to accommodate the longer text fields.

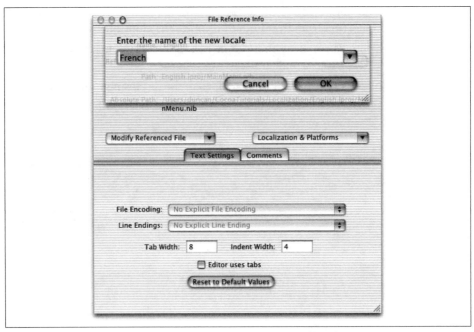

Figure 14-6. Adding a French localization of the MainMenu.nib file

Figure 14-7. Our interface in French

19. Save the nib file (⌘-S), and return to Project Builder.

20. Build and run the application (⌘-R) to verify that everything works.

21. Quit the application (⌘-Q).

22. Launch the System Preferences application in the Dock, and click on the International button to open its preferences panel.

23. Change your language preferences from English to Français by clicking on Français and dragging it to the top of the list in the Languages window.

24. Run the application again to see the French interface run.

25. Quit and return to the System Preferences; reset your preferred language to English by dragging it to the top of the list.

Localizing Strings

Not all strings used by a program are located in a nib file. Many strings, such as those that appear in dialog boxes, are usually encoded directly in source code. To localize these strings without requiring changes to the source, Cocoa provides a function to look up strings against a strings file directly from code. This function has the following signature:

```
NSLocalizedString(NSString *key, NSString *comment);
```

This function uses the localizedStringForKey:value:table: method of the NSBundle class to look up the strings out of the main application bundle. We will add a couple of *.strings* files (and a bit of code that uses them) in our project to illustrate how this works.

1. Add a new file, named *Localizable.strings*, to the project in Project Builder (File → New File → Empty File). Save it to the *~/LearningCocoa/Localization/English. lproj* folder. Make sure that it is in the Resources group, as shown in Figure 14-8.

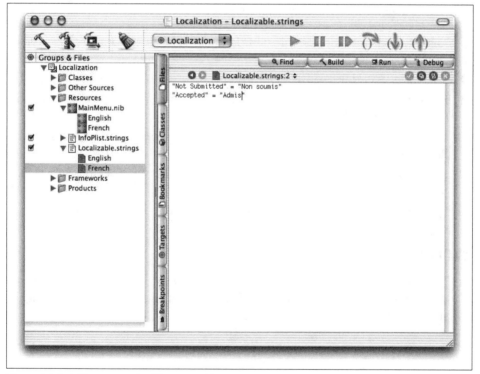

Figure 14-8. Adding a Localizable.strings file

2. Edit the new file to have the following text:

```
"Not Submitted" = "Not Submitted";
"Accepted" = "Accepted";
```

3. Bring up the Info panel (Project → Show Info, or ⌘-I).

4. Select Add Localized Variant from the Localization & Platforms pop-up menu. You will be prompted for a localization. Enter French, and then close the Info window.

5. Click on the disclosure triangle next to the *Localizable.strings* file. Beneath that, you will see two files: *English*, which we created in steps 1 and 2; and *French*, which we created in the previous step.

6. Edit the French variant of the file to match the following text:

```
"Not Submitted" = "Non soumis";
"Accepted" = "Admis";
```

7. Edit the submit: method of the *Controller.m* file.

```
- (IBAction)submit:(id)sender
{
    [statusField setStringValue:NSLocalizedString(@"Accepted", nil)];
}
```

This code sets the value of our status field to the localized form of the Accepted string.

8. Save the project (File → Save, or ⌘-S).

9. Build and run (⌘-R) the application. Test out the Submit button, and make sure that the status field changes.

10. Quit the application, and set Français as your preferred language using System Preferences.

11. Run the application again to see the French interface run. Click the Submit button.

12. Quit and return your preferred language to English.

Exercises

1. Localize the Currency Converter project from Chapter 5 into the language of your choice. Use the Translation channel of Sherlock 3 if you need help translating the strings.

CHAPTER 15

Defaults and Preferences

Most applications need to store and retrieve *preferences* that allow for user customization of an application's behavior and keep track of configuration settings. Mac OS X provides, as part of its Core Foundation framework, a preferences system that provides a simple and standard way to maintain these preferences. Cocoa calls these preferences *defaults*.

If you go to the *~/Library/Preferences* folder, you will see the user-preferences database used by the applications you run on your system. In fact, many of the applications we have created in this book have written preferences to this database. Take a look, and you'll see that you probably have *Dot View.plist*, *Menu.plist*, and *RTF Edit. plist* files. These contain preferences used by some of the various Cocoa base classes used in the sample applications we've built throughout the book.

In this chapter we'll show you how to take advantage of the user-preferences system from your applications using Cocoa.

How Preferences Work

The preference system in Mac OS X allows you to store values associated with a key—the name of a property—that can later be used to look up the preference value when you need it. These key-value pairs are scoped using a combination of username and application ID. All of the preferences for a user are stored in his *~/Library /Preferences* folder.

There are multiple domains—or different scopes of coverage—in which a preference can exist. When you request a preference, the following resources are searched—in order—until a match is found:

1. The list of arguments that were passed to an application. This lets an application start up with a preference setting to override all other values for that preference's key.

2. The users preferences stored in the *~/Library/Preferences* folder. This is where preferences that are unique to a user and that need to last between invocations of an application are kept.

3. A set of global preferences used across all applications that a user may use. For example, rulers in text views will obtain a user's preferred unit of measurement. These preferences are stored in the *~/Library/Preferences/GlobalPreferences.plist* file. Many of these preferences are set using the System Preferences application.

4. The set of preferences that your application registers as the defaults for your application. If a value for a preference is not found anywhere else, then this allows your application to provide a default value.

Preferences in the *~/Library/Preferences* folder are stored in the same property-list file format used by the *Info.plist* file included with application bundles. Preference value objects can be of any of the following types:

- NSString for storing string values
- NSNumber for storing number values derived from integers, floats, and other numeric types
- NSBoolean for storing YES or NO values
- NSDate for storing date information
- NSData for storing arbitrary data
- NSArray for storing arrays that consists of any of the previously listed types
- NSDictionary for storing name/value dictionaries that have values of any of the previously listed types

 While it is possible to edit the files in your *~/Library/Preferences* folder yourself using any text editor, you probably should not. You might introduce accidental errors into the XML syntax of the files. We'll see some other ways to edit these files in just a bit.

Using Defaults

To show how to use the NSUserDefaults class, the mechanism by which Cocoa provides access to Mac OS X's preference system, we'll build a simple application to keep track of a few of our favorite things.

1. Create a new Cocoa application project in Project Builder (File → New Project → Application → Cocoa Application) named "Favorites", and save it in your *~/LearningCocoa* folder.

2. Open the *MainMenu.nib* file in Interface Builder.

3. Lay out the user interface as shown in Figure 15-1.

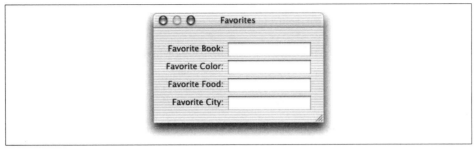

Figure 15-1. Favorites application interface

4. Create a subclass of NSObject in Interface Builder. Click on the Classes tab of the MainMenu.nib window, find NSObject, Control-click it, and select Subclass NSObject from the pop-up menu. Name the subclass "Controller".

5. Create the following outlets on the Controller class:

   - bookField

   - colorField

   - foodField

   - cityField

6. Create an action named textFieldChanged:. This action will tell the preferences database when an item has changed.

7. Generate the source-code files for the Controller class (Classes → Create Files for Controller).

8. Instantiate the Controller class (Classes → Instantiate Controller).

9. Connect the four text fields on the user interface to their respective outlets by control-dragging a connection from the Controller instance to each of the fields in turn.

10. Connect each of the four text fields to the Controller's textFieldChanged action method by control-dragging a connection from the text field to the Controller instance.

11. Save (File → Save, or ⌘-S) the nib file, and return to Project Builder.

12. Edit the *Controller.h* file as shown, adding an instance variable that will hold a reference to a NSUserDefaults object.

    ```
    #import <Cocoa/Cocoa.h>

    @interface Controller : NSObject
    {
        IBOutlet id bookField;
        IBOutlet id cityField;
        IBOutlet id colorField;
        IBOutlet id foodField;
        NSUserDefaults * prefs;
    ```

```
}
- (IBAction)textFieldChanged:(id)sender;
@end
```

13. Add an init method to the *Controller.m* file. This will set the prefs instance variable.

```
- (id)init
{
    [super init];
    NSMutableDictionary * defaultPrefs = [NSMutableDictionary dictionary];      // a

    [defaultPrefs setObject:@"Learning Cocoa" forKey:@"FavBook"];               // b
    [defaultPrefs setObject:@"San Francisco" forKey:@"FavCity"];
    [defaultPrefs setObject:@"Red" forKey:@"FavColor"];
    [defaultPrefs setObject:@"Mexican" forKey:@"FavFood"];

    prefs = [[NSUserDefaults standardUserDefaults] retain];                     // c
    [prefs registerDefaults:defaultPrefs];                                      // d

    return self;
}
```

This code does the following things:

a. Creates a new mutable dictionary that will serve as the container for the default values the application will use

b. Sets four key/value pairs that correspond to the default values we want to store in the preferences system

c. Obtains a reference to the preferences system

d. Indicates to the prefs object that we want to use the defaultPrefs dictionary as the set of default preferences

14. Add a dealloc method so that the class cleans up after itself properly.

```
- (void)dealloc
{
    [prefs release];
    [super dealloc];
}
```

15. Add an awakeFromNib method to populate the user interface from any settings that are in the prefs object.

```
- (void)awakeFromNib
{
    [bookField setStringValue:[prefs stringForKey:@"FavBook"]];
    [cityField setStringValue:[prefs stringForKey:@"FavCity"]];
    [colorField setStringValue:[prefs stringForKey:@"FavColor"]];
    [foodField setStringValue:[prefs stringForKey:@"FavFood"]];
}
```

16. Implement the textFieldChanged: action method so that the key values are saved as they change to the prefs object.

```
- (IBAction)textFieldChanged:(id)sender
{
```

```
    if (sender == bookField) {
        [prefs setObject:[bookField stringValue] forKey:@"FavBook"];
    } else if (sender == cityField) {
        [prefs setObject:[cityField stringValue] forKey:@"FavCity"];
    } else if (sender == colorField) {
        [prefs setObject:[colorField stringValue] forKey:@"FavColor"];
    } else if (sender == foodField ){
        [prefs setObject:[foodField stringValue] forKey:@"FavFood"];
    }
}
```

17. Build and run (⌘-R) the application. You should see the interface launch as shown in Figure 15-2.

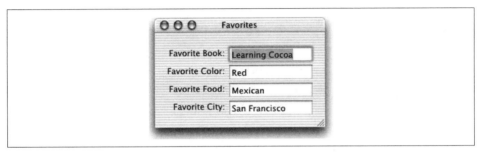

Figure 15-2. Our application running

18. Change some of the values. Quit the application, then restart to see if the values were saved.

19. Find the *Favorites.plist* file in your *~/Library/Preferences* folder. Double-click the file to launch the Property List Editor (*/Applications/Utilities*), which allows you to see the values that you changed in the file, as shown in Figure 15-3. To see the XML representation of the *plist* file, click the Dump button. You can also, if needed, edit the property list here, save the changes, and then launch the application we built to see the changes.

Command-Line Preferences Access

You can access your preferences from the Terminal by using the *defaults* command. For example, to see the defaults for the Favorites application we just built, type the following into a Terminal window:

```
defaults read Favorites
```

Something like the following should print:

```
{
    FavBook = "Stranger in a Strange Land";
    FavCity = "Dallas Texas";
    FavColor = Black;
    FavFood = Thai;
}
```

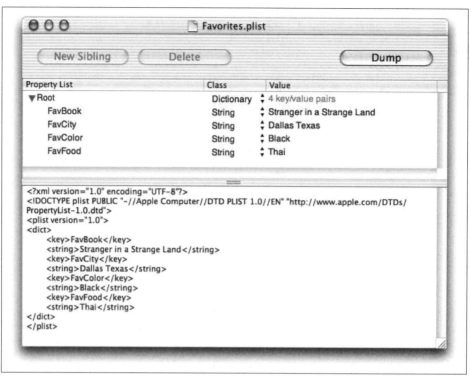

Figure 15-3. The preferences file under the hood

Overriding Preferences Using Launch Arguments

Sometimes, when you are developing an application, it is useful to override preference settings for a particular run of an application. To do this, simply specify the preference key names and values as launch arguments when you launch your application from the Terminal. These arguments are given following the pattern:

```
Application -[Key name] [Value name] ...
```

For example, to override the favorite city when we launch the Favorites application, enter the following command into a Terminal window:

```
open ~/LearningCocoa/Favorites/build/Favorites.app - FavCity "New Orleans"
```

Of course, you can apply this concept to any application on your system as long as you know the name of the preference to use. The best way to find out preference names is to look in the *plist* files that they leave in the *~/Library/Preferences* folder.

If you want to modify a preference from the command line, you can use the *defaults* command's *write* option. For example, to change our favorite city to Sedona, Arizona, issue the following command (the quotes are needed to accommodate the comma in the value string we are using):

```
defaults write Favorites FavCity "Sedona, Arizona"
```

Now go back to Project Builder, and build and run (⌘-R) the Favorites application again to see the changes.

Using Unique Application Identifiers

As we said before, preferences are stored in files using an application's ID. So far, our sample applications haven't specified a particular application ID, so the system has used the name of the application as its ID.

However, when you browse through your *~/Library/Preferences* folder, you'll see that quite a few of the files have long names like *com.apple.iPhoto.plist*. When Apple created the iPhoto application, they assigned it an application ID of *com.apple.iPhoto*— Apple's domain name followed by the application name—to reduce the possibility of somebody else's application named iPhoto interfering with the preferences used by the system. Obviously, for an application like iPhoto, there probably won't be a collision. But for applications with more common names—like the ones that we have been creating in this book—this level of namespace protection is valuable.

For example, all of the Mac OS X applications created by O'Reilly & Associates should have application IDs that start with *com.oreilly*. Following this logic, our Favorites application should have an application ID of *com.oreilly.Favorites*. To specify this application ID:

1. Open up the main target of the application, navigate the outline view to Info. plist Entries → Simple View → Basic information, and change the Identifier field, as shown in Figure 15-4.

2. Build and run (⌘-R) the application, change the values, and quit the application.

3. Using the Finder, you can see that there is now a *com.oreilly.Favorites.plist* file in your *~/Library/Preferences* folder. If you wanted to read this file from the command line, you could use the following command:

```
defaults read com.oreilly.Favorites
```

Exercises

1. Take a look at the contents of the Favorites preference list file using Property List Editor.

2. Add a reset button to the Favorites application that will reset the values to their original state.

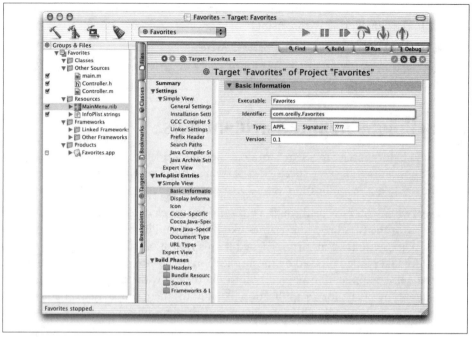

Figure 15-4. Setting the application identifier

3. Modify the Favorites application so that it reads its application defaults from a *.plist* file contained as a resource in its application bundle.

4. Modify the Currency Converter application from Chapter 5 to remember the exchange rate between invocations of the application.

CHAPTER 16

Accessory Windows

When a Cocoa-based application starts up, it loads all of the objects in the main nib file, then initializes, connects, and displays them. This can take some time, and the more objects you have in your interface, the longer it will take. While this process is happening, nothing else can happen in your application, and the user gets to watch the application icon bounce.

To shorten load time, lower initial memory consumption, and help organize your application better, Cocoa lets you use multiple nib files and load them on demand. For example, you can have separate nib files for info panels, toolbars, and dialog boxes. This chapter shows you how to use auxiliary windows with your application, explaining how to load them and how to manipulate their contents to create inspectors.

The Role of File's Owner

So far, we haven't paid much attention to the special File's Owner object that shows up in Interface Builder—other than to say that it is a proxy object that "owns" the objects in a nib file. However, when working with multiple nib files, it is crucial to understand the role that the File's Owner plays as the object that loads—and thus "owns"—the nib file. When working with a single nib file, it is easy enough to create connections between your code and controls in the nib file. However, when working with multiple nib files, it becomes more difficult to make clear connections between controls in an auxiliary nib file and those of the main application. To make these connections, you use the File's Owner object proxy.

In the applications that we've put together so far, File's Owner has been assigned to the main object (an instance of NSApplication) of the application or, in the case of a document-based application, a document object (a subclass of NSDocument). You can see this connection in Interface Builder by selecting the File's Owner and looking at the Attribute's inspector, as shown in Figure 16-1.

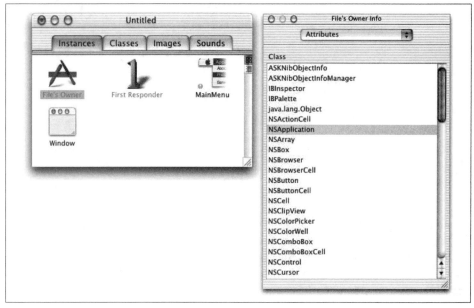

Figure 16-1. The default File's Owner object

As you can see from Figure 16-1, you can assign the File's Owner object to any class. When creating an auxiliary nib file, you will need to assign the File's Owner proxy to the class that will load the nib and be responsible for mediating between the functionality of the secondary window and the rest of the application.

Making an Info Window

To illustrate how to use auxiliary windows and how the File's Owner proxy enables the various parts of an application to communicate, we will create a simple inspector to tell us how many characters are in a text view.

Create the Main Interface

1. Create a new Cocoa Application project in Project Builder (File → New Project → Application → Cocoa Application) named "Simple Inspector", and save it in your *~/LearningCocoa* folder.

2. Open the *MainMenu.nib* file in Interface Builder.

3. Create a subclass of NSObject in Interface Builder, named Controller. (Click on the Classes tab of the MainMenu.nib window, find NSObject, Control-click it, and select Subclass NSObject).

4. Create an action method on the Controller class, named showInfoPanel:.

5. Create four outlets on the Controller class, named `infoPanel`, `infoPanelController`, `textLengthField`, and `textView`, and assign their types as shown in Table 16-1 and Figure 16-2.

Table 16-1. Assigning the types for the outlets of the Simple Inspector application

Outlet	Type
infoPanel	NSPanel
infoPanelController	NSWindowController
textLengthField	NSTextField
textView	NSTextView

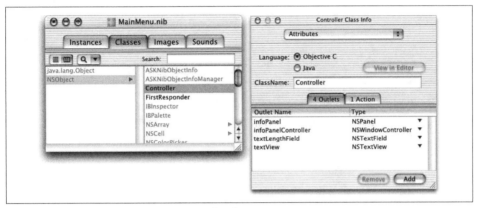

Figure 16-2. Creating outlets on the Controller class

The `infoPanel` outlet will hold a reference to our inspector panel. The `infoPanelController` will serve as the window controller for the panel. The `textFieldLength` outlet will point to a text field in our inspector panel that will display the total number of characters in the `textView`.

6. Generate the source-code files for the `Controller` class (Classes → Create Files for Controller).

7. Instantiate the `Controller` class (Classes → Instantiate Controller).

8. Drag a text view out to the application's main window, and set its Autosizing attributes so that it will resize along with the window that contains it.

9. Control-drag a connection from the Controller instance object to the text view, as shown in Figure 16-3, and connect it to the `textView` outlet.

10. Add a Show Info menu item to the MainMenu's Window menu, as shown in Figure 16-4. Give it a key equivalent of ⌘-I. This will let the user of our application get the info panel either by using the menu item or by just using the Command-key equivalent.

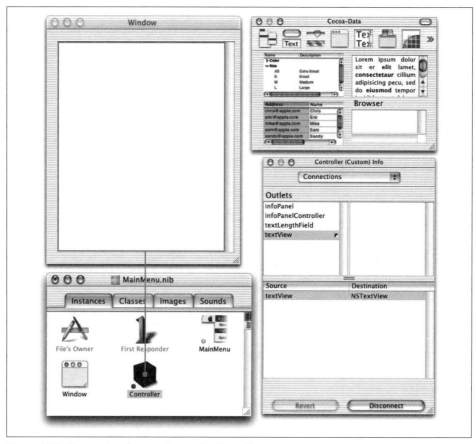

Figure 16-3. Connecting the text view to the Controller

From the Cocoa-Menus palette:

    a. Drag an Item to the menu, and place it as shown in Figure 16-4.

    b. Use the Info panel to change its name and assign a Command-key equivalent.

11. Connect the Show Info menu item to the Controller's `showInfoPanel:` action method by Control-dragging a connection from the menu item to the `Controller` object, as shown in Figure 16-5.

12. Save (⌘-S) and close (⌘-W) the nib file.

Create the Inspector Panel

Now that we've created the controller object for the application, the application's main window with a text view, and the menu item for the user to request the info panel, we need to create a new nib file to contain the user interface for the info panel.

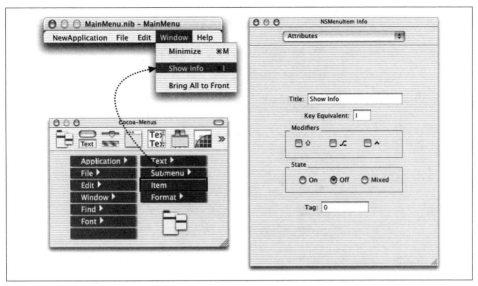

Figure 16-4. Adding a Show Info window to the application's menu bar

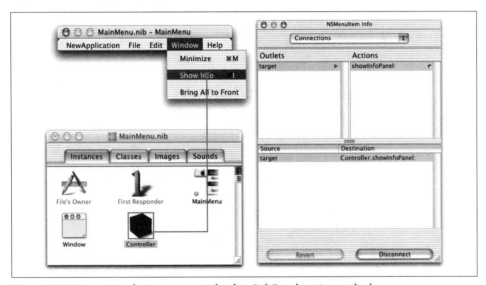

Figure 16-5. Connecting the menu item to the showInfoPanel: action method

1. Create a new nib file in Interface Builder (File → New). Interface builder will show a dialog box similar to that in Figure 16-6. Select Empty and click New.

2. Save the file as *InfoPanel.nib* in your *~/LearningCocoa/Simple Inspector /English.lproj* folder, as shown in Figure 16-7. You will be prompted to add the nib file to the Simple Inspector target; click the Add button to do so.

Figure 16-6. Interface Builder's starting point

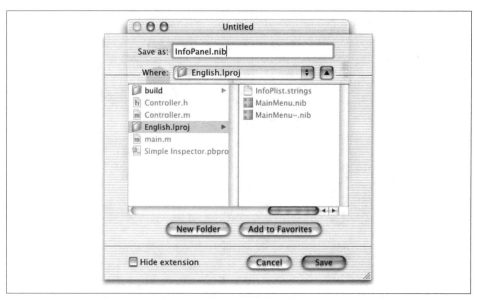

Figure 16-7. Saving the InfoPanel.nib file

3. Now, we need to designate our Controller class as the object that will be the File's Owner for this nib file at runtime. To let Interface Builder know that the Controller class exists, drag the *Controller.h* file from Project Builder onto the InfoPanel.nib window.

4. Select the File's Owner proxy object in the InfoPanel.nib window, and, using the File's Owner Info inspector as shown in Figure 16-8, set the File's Owner class to Controller.

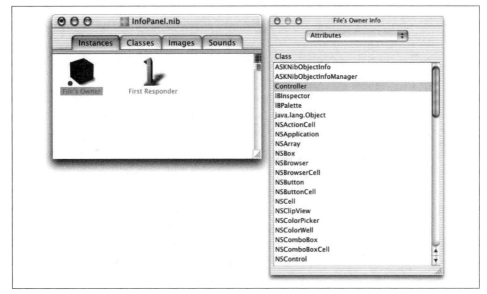

Figure 16-8. Setting the File's Owner class

This tells Interface Builder that the class responsible for loading this nib file will be of type Controller. By setting this class as the File's Owner, we can designate that various interface components in this nib file should be connected to the outlets of the Controller class.

5. Drag out a panel from the Windows palette. Name the panel Info by using the NSPanel Info inspector, as shown in Figure 16-9. Also, make sure that the Hide on deactivate and Utility window (Panel only) options are checked. These options will make our panel look like an Info panel and ensure that it disappears when our application is not active.

6. Drag two text fields onto the panel; name them "Length of Text View:" and "Number". Control-drag a connection from the File's Owner proxy object (remember, this is a stand-in for our Controller class) to the Number field, and set the textLengthField outlet, as shown in Figure 16-10.

7. Control-drag a connection from the File's Owner object to the Panel object in the InfoPanel.nib window, as shown in Figure 16-11, and connect it to the infoPanel outlet.

8. Save the nib file (⌘-S), and return to Project Builder.

Implement the Code

Now that we have our two nib files designed, it's time to implement the code that ties all the pieces together.

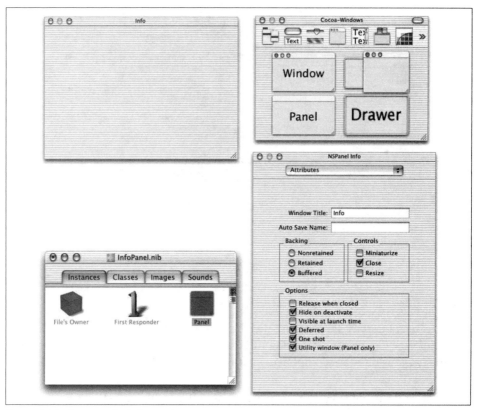

Figure 16-9. Creating the Info panel

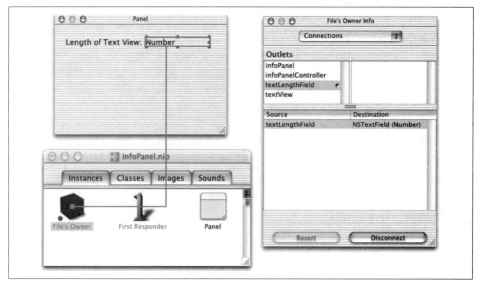

Figure 16-10. Connecting the textLengthField

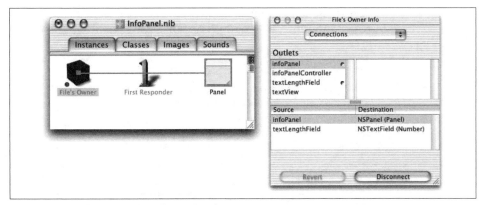

Figure 16-11. Connecting the infoPanel outlet

1. Edit the *Controller.m* file as follows:

```
#import "Controller.h"

@implementation Controller

- (IBAction)showInfoPanel:(id)sender
{
    if (!infoPanelController) {                                    // a
        [NSBundle loadNibNamed:@"InfoPanel" owner:self];          // b
        infoPanelController = [[NSWindowController alloc]         // c
            initWithWindow:infoPanel];
    }
    [textLengthField setIntValue:[[textView textStorage] length]]; // d
    [infoPanelController showWindow:self];                         // e
}

@end
```

The code we added performs the following tasks:

a. Checks to see if we have a reference to a window controller for the Info panel. If we don't, it means that we need to load the nib file that contains the panel. On the other hand, if we have a reference, then we don't need to load it.

b. Loads the InfoPanel nib file. Notice that we don't use the *.nib* extension here. When the nib is loaded, the connections assigned to the File's Owner will be made to the Controller object.

c. Creates a new window controller, assigns it to the infoPanelController variable, and initializes it to use the panel loaded from the nib.

d. Sets the textLengthField to the length of the textStorage object.

e. Shows the Info panel.

2. Build and run (⌘-R) the application. Enter some text into the text view, then show the Info panel (Window → Show Info or ⌘-I). You should see something like Figure 16-12.

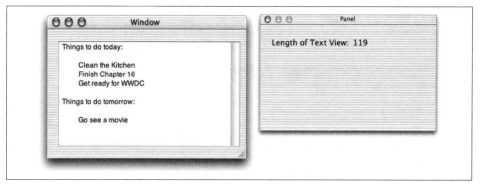

Figure 16-12. Our inspector in action

Obviously, we could add all sorts of information to our inspector window, such as the number of words in the file, number of paragraphs, etc. We'll leave these tasks as exercises at the end of the chapter.

Tracking Changes with Notifications

Notice that we have a problem with our application. When you show the Info panel, you see the number of characters in the text view, but when you change the text in the text view, the info panel becomes out of date. The information only updates when you close the Info panel and select Show Info again. We see this behavior because we are only setting the information in the panel when the user tells the application to show the panel. We probably want this information to be updated dynamically as the text view's contents change.

To get this functionality, we'll use a notification that the text-view object will post to the notification center whenever its contents change. For more information about notifications, see Chapter 8.

1. Add the following code to the *Controller.m* file:

```
#import "Controller.h"

@implementation Controller

- (void)awakeFromNib                                               // a
{
    NSNotificationCenter * center = [NSNotificationCenter defaultCenter];
    [center addObserver:self
                selector:@selector(textDidChange:)
                    name:NSTextDidChangeNotification
                  object:textView];
```

```
    }

-   (void)textDidChange:(NSNotification *)notification                      // b
    {
        [textLengthField setIntValue:[[textView textStorage] length]];
    }

-   (IBAction)showInfoPanel:(id)sender
    {
        if (!infoPanelController) {
            [NSBundle loadNibNamed:@"InfoPanel" owner:self];
            infoPanelController = [[NSWindowController alloc]
                initWithWindow:infoPanel];
        }
        [textLengthField setIntValue:[[textView textStorage] length]];
        [infoPanelController showWindow:self];
    }

    @end
```

The code we added performs the following tasks:

a. Adds an `awakeFromNib` method that will add the Controller instance as an observer to the default notification center interested in `NSTextDidChangeNotification` events on the `textView` object.

b. Implements the callback method that the notification center will call whenever text changes in the text view. We simply update the `textLengthField` in our inspector panel.

2. Build and run (⌘-R) the application. Show the Info panel (Window → Show Info or ⌘-I), then type text into the text view. The info panel will now keep up with the correct number of characters in the text view as you type.

Exercises

1. Add a field to the Simple Inspector application that will display the number of words in a document.

2. Add a field to the Simple Inspector application that will display the number of paragraphs in a document.

3. Add an Info window to Dot View (see Chapter 8) that will let the user know the current diameter of the dot.

CHAPTER 17

Finishing Touches

Over the last 16 chapters, we've covered quite a bit of material and laid a decent foundation on which you can build your Cocoa programming abilities. Before we leave you at the end of the book, let's take a look at the various finishing touches that you should put on your application before sending it out into the world. In this chapter, we explore the following topics:

- Tidying up the user interface
- Providing an icon
- Providing help
- Customizing the About box
- Tweaking compiler settings
- Packaging for distribution

Tidying Up the User Interface

You've no doubt noticed that when running the applications we've built throughout the book, the menu items refer to a "NewApplication" instead of the name of the application you created. An example of this is shown in Figure 17-1, where we see the application menu of Dot View.

Thankfully, this is easy to fix. Instead of creating a new application, as we've done to introduce most of the topics in the book, we'll add all of these finishing touches to the Dot View application we built in Chapter 8.

1. Open the Dot View project from your ~/*LearningCocoa/DotView* folder.
2. Open the MainMenu.nib file in Interface Builder.
3. Click on the NewApplication menu, as shown in Figure 17-2, and change the menu text "NewApplication" in the various menu items to read "Dot View". You can do this either by modifying the title of the menu item using the inspector, as shown in Figure 17-2, or by editing the menu items from the MainMenu. nib window.

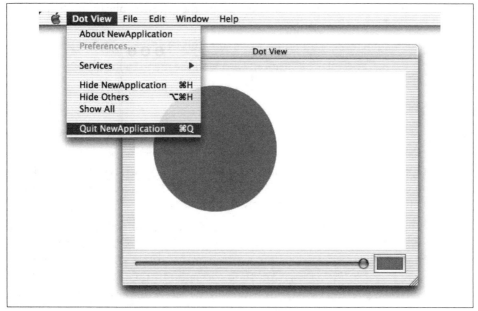

Figure 17-1. Dot View's application menu

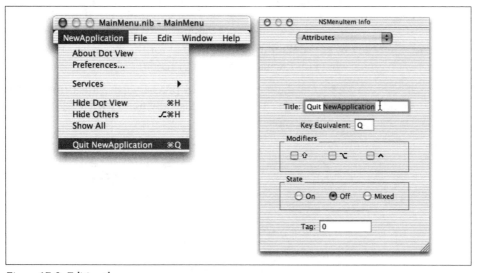

Figure 17-2. Editing the menu

If you choose to edit the menu items from the MainMenu.nib window, click once on the applicable menu, and then double-click on an item (for example, "Quit NewApplication") to highlight it. Next, double-click again on "NewApplication" to highlight just that word, and type in the name of the application—in this case, Dot View.

4. Click on the Help menu item, and change the "NewApplication" help menu item to read "Dot View Help".

5. Save the nib file (⌘-S), and return to Project Builder.

6. Build and run (⌘-R) the application. Check all the menu items.

Providing an Icon

All Mac OS X applications should provide an icon for their application. In fact, icons are probably the single most visible attribute of your application, so investing a bit of time and effort into them is warranted. Application icons are typically stored in a *.icns* file in the application's bundle. These *.icns* files contain several images to use as the application's icons, in various sizes and bit depths.

The Developer Tools package contains a very simple utility called IconComposer (*/Developer/Applications*) that will convert images into Mac OS X–style icon files. Using a standard graphics application, you can create art for your icon, save it as a 32-bit image in TIFF, PICT, or Photoshop format, and then import it into Icon-Composer. Once the image has been imported, IconComposer can create icon masks for icons sizes that require one.

If you are comfortable working with Adobe Photoshop, use this section learn how to create source art for an icon in just a few seconds. If you don't use Photoshop, you can adapt these instructions to other graphics applications; or, you can just grab the *DotViewIcon.psd* file out of the sample-code download for this book (see the Preface for information about where to download the example code).

1. Launch Photoshop, and make a new 128×128 pixel image with a transparent background, as shown in Figure 17-3. It doesn't really matter what DPI you use, but 72 DPI is traditional for screen work.

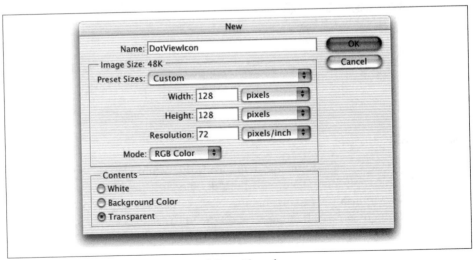

Figure 17-3. Creating the DotViewIcon.psd file in Photoshop

2. Create your icon. The icon that we designed (and which you can get from the example download package) is shown in Figure 17-4.

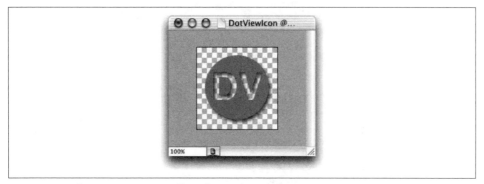

Figure 17-4. The Dot View icon in Photoshop

3. Save the file as a Photoshop document. Be sure to save with transparency.

4. Launch IconComposer.

5. Chose File → Import Image. IconComposer's dialog box will have a pop-up menu that lets you specify what kind of icon to make from the imported data. Select Thumbnail 32 bit data, and open the document saved in step 4.

6. The image will appear in the Thumbnail slot of IconComposer. Drag and drop the image from the Thumbnail row to the Huge, Large, and Small rows, as shown in Figure 17-5. Each time you do this, you'll be asked whether you want to use a scaled version (say yes) and whether you want to extract a 1-bit mask from the data (also say yes).

7. Save the file as ~/LearningCocoa/DotView.icns.

8. Return to Project Builder, and add the *DotView.icns* file to the project (Project → Add Files). It doesn't need to be copied into the project directory, since we saved it there, but make sure that it is added to the Dot View target.

9. Edit the main target (Project → Edit Active Target), navigate the outline view to Info.plist Entries → Simple View → Icon, and enter *DotView.icns* into the Icon file field, as shown in Figure 17-6.

10. Build and run (⌘-R) the application. When the application launches, you probably won't see the new icon in the Dock; but, when you try to close the window, you will see it in the sheet, as shown in Figure 17-7.

When you run the Dot View application from Project Builder or out of the build directory, you won't always see the icon used in the Dock or in the Finder. However, as soon as you drag the built application to another directory (e.g., ~/*Applications*), the icon will *probably* work correctly. Sometimes logging out and back into your machine is required. This behavior is due to the Finder caching the icons for display on screen.

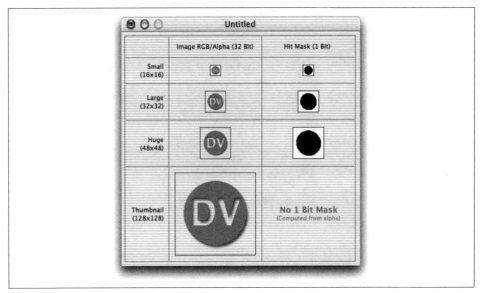

Figure 17-5. The Dot View icon in Icon Composer

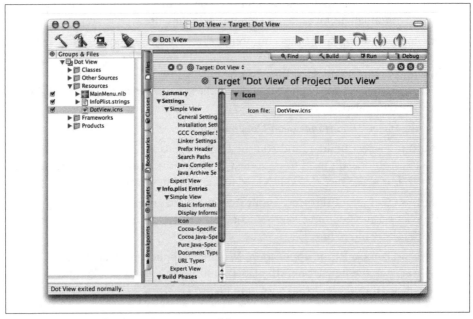

Figure 17-6. Setting the Icon using Project Builder

Chapter 10 of Apple's *Inside Mac OS X: Human Interface Guidelines* contains quite a bit of information about icon design. You can find this book on your system in the */Developer/Documentation/Essentials/AquaHIGuidelines* folder.

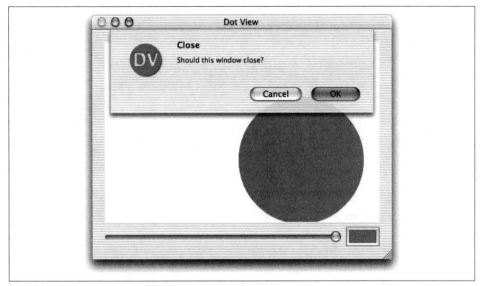

Figure 17-7. The icon file in use by the application

Providing Help

Among the other features of Mac OS X is an integrated help system known as Apple Help. Introduced as part of Mac OS 8.5 as part of Carbon, Apple Help is an integral part of Mac OS X, displaying help content authored in the HTML format in the industry standard HTML 3.2 specification. Using HTML for the help file format is a big win and means that you can create help files using a text editor or your favorite web page authoring tools, such as BBEdit, Dreamweaver, or GoLive. In addition, Apple Help can display any media supported by QuickTime. This means that most of the major image formats, as well as Flash content, are supported for display.

The following steps guide you through adding help to the Dot View application:

1. Create a subfolder in your *~/LearningCocoa/Dot View* folder, named *Help*, as shown in Figure 17-8.

2. Add the *Help* folder to Project Builder (Project → Add Files). Select the *Help* folder created in step 1, and click the Add button. On the next sheet that appears, click the Create Folder References for any added folders radio button, as shown in Figure 17-9. This instructs Project Builder to copy all of the contents of the built application's Resources folder.

3. Create a new file (File → New File → Empty File) named *index.html* in the Help directory.

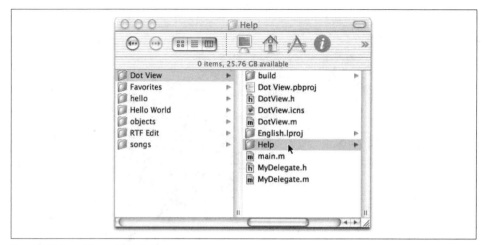

Figure 17-8. Adding a Help folder

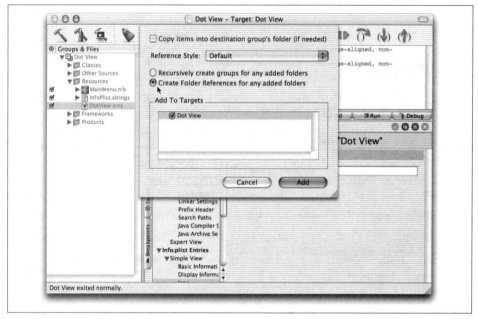

Figure 17-9. Adding the help folder as a Folder Reference to our project

4. Edit the *index.html* file as follows:

```
<html>
<head>
<meta name="AppleTitle" content="Dot View Help">
<title>Dot View Help</title>
</head>
<body>
<h1>Dot View</h1>
<p>Click the Dot. Change its color. Have Fun.</p>
```

```
</body>
</html>
```

This is a standard HTML file with the addition of a `meta` tag that names its attribute set to `AppleTitle`. This `meta` tag is used by Apple Help.

You can find much more 0information about Apple Help, including all the special tags that you can add to your HTML files, in the Carbon documentation installed with the Developer Tools. Start with */Developer/Documentation/Carbon/HumanInterfaceToolbox/AppleHelp /ProvidingUserAssitAppleHelp/index.html*.

5. The last step is to add two keys to the application's property list. Unlike setting the icon file, Project Builder doesn't yet provide a GUI for setting these properties, so use the following directions:

   a. Open the main target of the application (Project → Edit Active Target).

   b. Navigate the outline view to Info.plist Entries → Expert View, as shown in Figure 17-10.

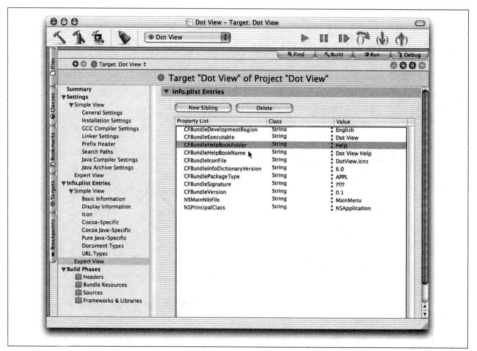

Figure 17-10. Adding properties to the target in the Expert View

   c. Click the New Sibling button. Name the new key `CFBundleHelpBookFolder`, and give it a string value of `Help`.

   d. Click the New Sibling button again. Name the new key `CFBundleHelpBookName`, and give it a string value of `Dot View Help`.

6. Build and run (⌘-R) the application. When the application launches, ask for Help (Help → Dot View Help, or use the ⌘-? keyboard shortcut). The Apple Help application will launch and display your help, as shown in Figure 17-11.

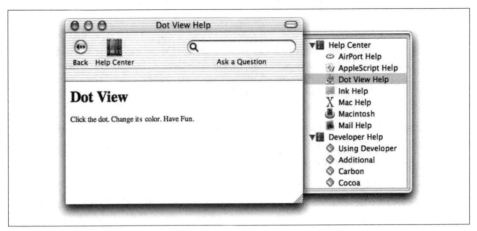

Figure 17-11. Dot View Help

Customizing the About Box

Cocoa applications get a "free" About Box by default. When you run the Dot View application and select the Dot View → About Dot View menu item, you'll see an About Box that looks like Figure 17-12.

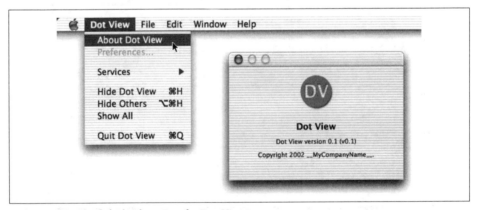

Figure 17-12. The default About Box for Dot View

This default about box displays the application icon—in our case, the icon we added earlier in the chapter—the application name, and a couple of strings obtained from the application bundle. To set these strings to something a bit more sensible, use the following steps.

1. Open the *InfoPlist.strings* file in the Resources folder of the Groups & Files panel, as shown in Figure 17-13.

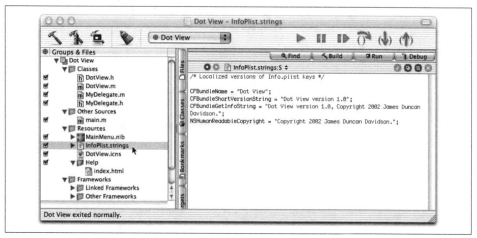

Figure 17-13. Editing the InfoPlist.strings file

2. Edit the `CFBundleGetInfoString` and `NSHumanReadableCopyright` strings to whatever you choose. These strings are what the default about box uses.

3. Build and run (⌘-R) the application. When you open the About Box, you'll see the strings that we just edited.

You'll notice that one part of the about box still refers to a "v0.1". You can change this string in the Info.plist Entries → Simple View → Basic Information area of the Dot View target.

Giving Some Credit

It's not obvious, but if you provide a *Credits.rtf* file in your application's bundle, the default about box will display it as part of its content. To see this in action:

1. Use Text Edit (or the Simple RTF Edit application we made in Chapter 11) to create a *Credits.rtf* file. You can say anything you'd like here. We chose to create the text you see in Figure 17-14.

2. Save this file to *~/LearningCocoa/Dot View/Credits.rtf*.

3. Return to Project Builder, and add the *Credits.rtf* file to the project (Project → Add Files). Be sure that it is added to the Dot View target.

4. Build and run (⌘-R) the application. When you open the about box, you should see something like Figure 17-15.

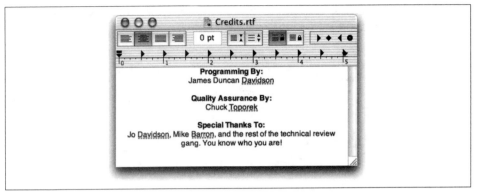

Figure 17-14. Creating the Credits.rtf file

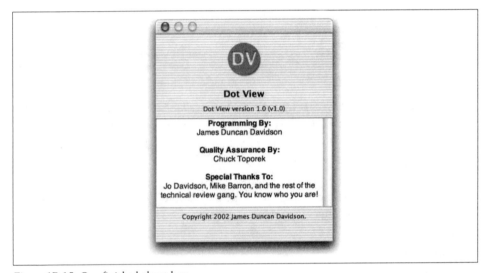

Figure 17-15. Our finished about box

Once you create an RTF file and add it to Project Builder, you can edit it directly in Project Builder. However, we couldn't start by creating the RTF file directly in Project Builder. Hopefully, the Project Builder team will add this functionality in future revisions to the Developer Tools.

Tweaking Compiler Settings

The last step before shipping an application is to build an optimized version of it with no debugging information. To set up the compiler for this:

1. Open the active target settings (Project → Edit Active Target), and navigate to the Settings → Simple View → GCC Compiler Settings panel, as shown in Figure 17-16.

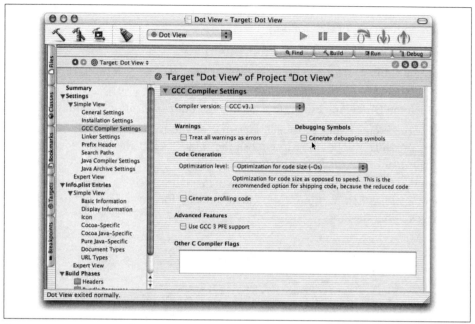

Figure 17-16. GCC Compiler Settings

2. Uncheck the Generate debugging symbols box.

A setting that you will be tempted to tweak, but probably shouldn't until you have quite a bit of experience, is the optimization level box. Project Builder ships with many possible settings for this, but in general the default setting of -0s (optimize for code size) is the best to use, as it makes the resulting binary as small as possible, both on disk and in memory. The number one performance problem of applications, according to Apple engineers, is that a large application memory footprint will cause Mac OS X's virtual memory system to work overtime. Using the -0s setting helps prevent your application from large amounts of memory swapping to and from disk, thus increasing your user's experience.

Packaging for Distribution

The last thing you do when developing an application—packing it up for distribution—is the first experience most users will have with your software. Unfortunately, too many applications out there come with installers that make their users jump through hoops. Since Cocoa applications are bundles that can be drag-and-dropped anywhere on your system with ease, it makes sense to distribute your applications in the simplest way possible: using compressed disk images. Compressed disk images download easily, most browsers will automatically mount the drives contained in them, and, best of all, they don't require the purchase of an expensive installer that your user probably won't appreciate.

Making a compressed disk image is simple. The following steps will bundle up our Dot View application for distribution:

1. Create a new folder on your desktop, named *Dist*.

2. Drag the built Dot View application from the *~/LearningCocoa/Dot View/build* folder to the *Dist* folder on your desktop.

3. Launch the Disk Copy utility. It is located in your */Applications/Utilities* folder.

4. Select the New → Image from Folder or Volume menu from Disk Copy. Disk Copy presents a dialog box to choose the folder. Select the *Dist* folder on your desktop, and click the Image button.

5. Another dialog box will open, as shown in Figure 17-17, asking you to select some options. Select compressed for the image format, and save the resulting image to your desktop.

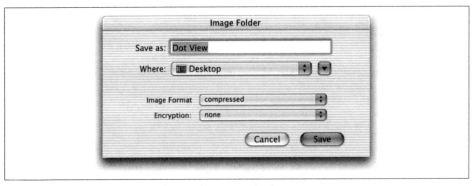

Figure 17-17. Making a compressed disk image using Disk Copy

6. Click the Save button. After a few status boxes go by, you should have a *Dot View.dmg* file ready for distribution. Double click on the *.dmg* file, and mount it as a disk drive.

Closure

After 17 chapters, you should now have a working foundation of how to build simple Cocoa applications. (And it is quite likely that you have finished the book in a much shorter time than it took to write!) To be sure, we haven't covered every topic in depth, but we have given you enough knowledge to be dangerous. These are the next steps you should take in your quest to become a great Cocoa programmer:

- Read more about Cocoa. We noted a few books on Cocoa in the Preface, which you should check out.

- Write applications. There's no substitute for experience.

There's still a lot you will need to learn to master Cocoa programming, but you should now be over the initial "huh?" stage and ready to dive in deep.

Good luck!

Exercises

1. Provide an icon, "help", and customize the about box for the Simple RTF Edit application from Chapter 11.
2. Package up for distribution the Simple RTF Edit application.
3. Write a complete application from scratch, utilizing the knowledge that you've gained from this book.

PART V

Appendixes

The appendixes include quick-reference material for learning more about Cocoa's Objective-C classes. In addition, they list resources beyond the scope of this book, to expand your Cocoa development horizon.

This section includes the following appendixes:

Appendix A, *Exercise Solutions*

Appendix B, *Additional Resources*

Appendix C, *Using the Foundation and Application Kit API References*

Exercise Solutions

This appendix gives some tips, hints, and answers to the exercises found at the end of each chapter.

Chapter 2, *Cocoa Development Tools*

1. Open a Finder window, and navigate to the */Developer/Applications* folder. Drag the Project Builder and Interface Builder icons to your Dock.

2. Open a Finder window and navigate to the */Developer/Documentation/Cocoa* folder. Drag the *CocoaTopics.html* file to your Dock.

Chapter 3, *Object-Oriented Programming with Objective-C*

1. One way to access the documentation:

   Open the */Developer/Documentation/Cocoa/CocoaTopics.html* file in your web browser of choice, click on the Foundation link in the Objective-C Framework Reference section, and then follow the NSObject and NSString links.

2. One way to find the documentation:

   In the Foundation reference document that the NSObject and NSString links are on, go to the bottom of the page, and click on the Functions link. You'll find the NSLog documentation on this page.

    Use the Find functionality of your browser (Edit → Find, or ⌘-F on most browsers) to search for the NSLog documentation on this rather large page.

3. One way to do it is to add the following line to the initWithName:artist: method of the Song class:

   ```
   NSLog(@"isa: %@ self %@", isa, self);
   ```
   This will print the name of the class as well as the description.

Chapter 4, *The Cocoa Foundation Kit*

1. Here's one way to do it:

   Open the strings project we created, and place a breakpoint before the [artist release] statement. Debug the application, and enter in the following commands into the *gdb* console:

   ```
   (gdb) print-object [artist lowercaseString]
   (gdb) print-object [artist uppercaseString]
   ```

2. One possible solution is to create a project named "fileprinter" with the following *main.m* file:

   ```
   #import <Foundation/Foundation.h>

   int main(int argc, const char * argv[]) {
       NSAutoreleasePool * pool = [[NSAutoreleasePool alloc] init];
       if (argc > 1) {
           NSString * filename = [NSString stringWithCString:argv[1]];
           NSString * file = [NSString stringWithContentsOfFile:filename];
           printf("%s\n", [file UTF8String]);
       }
       [pool release];
       return 0;
   }
   ```

   When executed from Project Builder, nothing will happen, but if you go to the terminal and issue the following commands, you will see the contents of the *main.m* file printed:

   ```
   [titanium:~] duncan% cd ~/LearningCocoa/fileprinter
   [titanium:~/LearningCocoa/fileprinter] duncan% build/fileprinter main.m
   ```

   Try this with a few other files.

3. One way to look up this documentation:

   Open the */Developer/Documentation/Cocoa/CocoaTopics.html* file in your web browser of choice, click on the Foundation link in the Objective-C Framework Reference section, and then follow the NSArray, NSSet and NSDictionary links.

4. One solution is to add the following line of code to the main method:

   ```
   [array writeToFile:@"foo.plist" atomically:YES];
   ```

   When you run the arrays program with this additional line, a *foo.plist* file will be written into *~/LearningCocoa/arrays/build* containing the elements of the array.

5. One possible solution is to create a project named "dictionarysaver" with the following *main.m* file:

   ```
   #import <Foundation/Foundation.h>

   int main(int argc, const char * argv[]) {
       NSAutoreleasePool * pool = [[NSAutoreleasePool alloc] init];
       NSMutableDictionary * dict = [NSMutableDictionary dictionary];
       [dict setObject:@"The Meaning of Life" forKey:@"A String"];
   ```

```
    [dict setObject:[NSNumber numberWithInt:42] forKey:@"An Integer"];
    [dict writeToFile:@"dict.plist" atomically:YES];
    [pool release];
    return 0;
}
```

When you run this program, the dictionary will be written to the *dict.plist* file in the *~/LearningCocoa/dictionarysaver* folder. This file will look as follows:

```
<?xml version="1.0" encoding="UTF-8"?>
<!DOCTYPE plist PUBLIC "-//Apple Computer//DTD PLIST 1.0//EN" "http://www.apple.
com/DTDs/PropertyList-1.0.dtd">
<plist version="1.0">
<dict>
        <key>A String</key>
        <string>The Meaning of Life</string>
        <key>An Integer</key>
        <integer>42</integer>
</dict>
</plist>
```

6. The dictionaries example application doesn't release the dict object. The following line of code is needed after the printf statement:

   [dict release];

Chapter 5, *Graphical User Interfaces*

1. One way to do this is to select the text labels, then change the font using the
   Font Panel (Format → Show Fonts, or ⌘-T).

2. One way to do this is to select the totalField, then change the font color using
   the Font Panel. To access the color picker, use the Extras... pull-down menu on
   the Font Panel.

Chapter 6, *Windows, Views, and Controls*

1. The documentation can be found in the */Developer/Documentation/Cocoa
   /CocoaTopics.html* folder. Click on the Application Kit link in the Objective-C
   Framework Reference section, and then follow the NSWindow and NSView links.

2. The easiest way to do this is to select the window in Interface Builder and change
   the title using the Attributes inspector. You can bring the inspector up by hitting
   Shift-⌘-I.

3. One way to do this is to edit the *Controller.h* file directly to match the following
   code:

```
@interface Controller : NSObject
{
    IBOutlet id converter;
    IBOutlet NSTextField dollarField;
    IBOutlet NSTextField rateField;
```

```
    IBOutlet NSTextField totalField;
}
- (IBAction)convert:(id)sender;
@end
```

Chapter 7, *Custom Views*

1. One way to do this is to edit the drawRect: method as follows:

```
- (void)drawRect:(NSRect)rect
{
    [[NSColor colorWithCalibratedRed:1.0 green:0.0 blue:0.0 alpha:1.0] set];
    NSRectFill([self bounds]);
}
```

2. The easiest way to do this is to add the drawing code from the String View appli-cation into the Line View drawRect: method as follows:

```
- (void)drawRect:(NSRect)rect
{
    NSRect bounds = [self bounds];
    NSPoint bottom = NSMakePoint((bounds.size.width/2.0), 0);
    NSPoint top = NSMakePoint((bounds.size.width/2.0), bounds.size.height);
    NSPoint left = NSMakePoint(0, (bounds.size.height/2.0));
    NSPoint right = NSMakePoint(bounds.size.width, (bounds.size.height/2.0));

    [[NSColor whiteColor] set];
    [NSBezierPath fillRect:bounds];

    [[NSColor blackColor] set];
    [NSBezierPath strokeRect:bounds];

    [NSBezierPath strokeLineFromPoint:top toPoint:bottom];
    [NSBezierPath strokeLineFromPoint:right toPoint:left];

    [[NSBezierPath bezierPathWithOvalInRect:bounds] stroke];

    NSString * hello = @"Hello World!";
    NSMutableDictionary * attribs = [NSMutableDictionary dictionary];
    [attribs setObject:[NSFont fontWithName:@"Times" size:24]
                forKey:NSFontAttributeName];
    [attribs setObject:[NSColor redColor]
                forKey:NSForegroundColorAttributeName];
    [hello drawAtPoint:NSMakePoint((bounds.size.width/2.0),
                                    (bounds.size.height/2.0))
        withAttributes:attribs];

}
@end
```

3. One way to do this is to insert the following line of code before drawing any of the lines in Line View:

```
[NSBezierPath setDefaultLineWidth:3.0];
```

This will cause all paths to be drawn with 3-point-wide strokes. Try some other values.

4. One way of finding the NSBezierPath documentation is to click the Find tab in Project Builder (or use the menu Find → Show Batch Find). Enter NSBezierPath into the Find box, and hit Return. After a few moments, Project Builder will show you all the occurrences of the NSBezierPath string, both in your project and in the frameworks against which it's linked. To limit the search to just your project, adjust the "This Project" pull-down to "This Project, no frameworks."

Chapter 8, *Event Handling*

1. The easiest way to accomplish this is to rename the mouseDown: method to mouseDragged:.

2. One way to do this is to modify the initWithFrame: method as follows:

```
- (id)initWithFrame:(NSRect)frame
{
    self = [super initWithFrame:frame];
    center.x = frame.size.width / 2.0;
    center.y = frame.size.height / 2.0;
    radius = 20.0;
    color = [[NSColor redColor] retain];
    return self;
}
```

3. One way of changing the setRadius: method is as follows:

```
- (IBAction)setRadius:(id)sender
{
    float newRadius = [sender floatValue];
    if (newRadius != radius) {
        radius = newRadius;
        [self setNeedsDisplay:YES];
    }
}
```

This will ensure that a redraw of the interface only occurs when it is needed.

4. One way to do this is to make the MyDelegate object instance a delegate of NSApplication and implement the applicationShouldTerminate: method. To do this, Control-drag a connection from File's Owner to MyDelegate in Interface Builder, then add the following method to the MyDelegate class:

```
- (NSTerminationReply)applicationShouldTerminate:(NSApplication *)sender
{
    int answer = NSRunAlertPanel(@"Quit", @"Are you sure?",
                                 @"Quit", @"Cancel", nil);
    if (answer == NSAlertDefaultReturn) {
        return NSTerminateNow;
    } else {
        return NSTerminateCancel;
    }
}
```

5. We suggest changing it to blue by modifying the `initWithFrame:` method as follows:

```
- (id)initWithFrame:(NSRect)frame
{
    self = [super initWithFrame:frame];
    center.x = frame.size.width / 2;
    center.y = frame.size.height / 2;
    radius = 20.0;
    color = [[NSColor blueColor] retain];
    return self;
}
```

Of course you can change it to whatever color you please.

6. To do this requires setting the springs appropriately in Interface Builder.

   a. Set the springs for the Dot View as shown in Figure A-1.

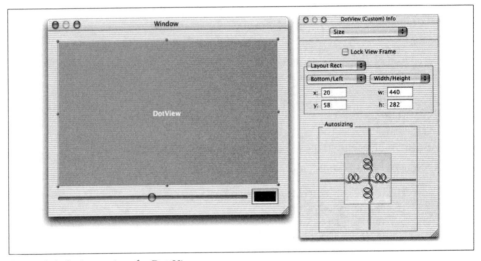

Figure A-1. Spring settings for Dot View

   b. Set the springs for the slider as shown in Figure A-3.

   c. Set the springs for the color well as shown in Figure A-2.

Chapter 9, *Models and Data Functionality*

1. Go into Interface Builder, and either edit the column header, either directly or using the inspector.

2. One way to do it is to make the `MyDataSource` object instance a delegate of `NSApplication` and implement the `applicationShouldTerminate:` method. To do this, Control-drag a connection from File's Owner to MyDataSource in Interface Builder, then add the following method to the `MyDataSource` class:

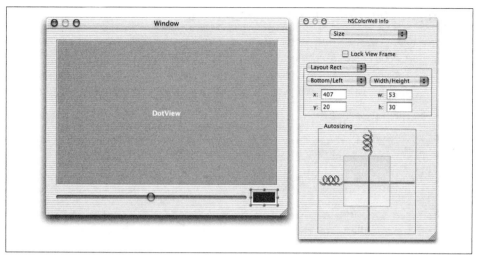

Figure A-2. Spring settings for Dot View's color well

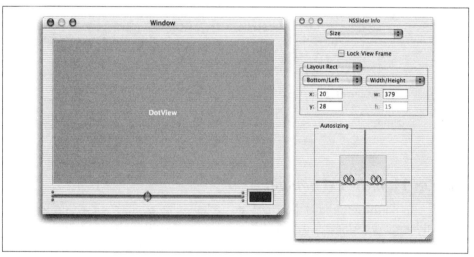

Figure A-3. Spring settings for Dot View's slider

```
- (NSTerminationReply)applicationShouldTerminate:(NSApplication *)sender
{
    int answer = NSRunAlertPanel(@"Quit", @"Are you sure?",
                                 @"Quit", @"Cancel", nil);
    if (answer == NSAlertDefaultReturn) {
        return NSTerminateNow;
    } else {
        return NSTerminateCancel;
    }
}
```

3. The FoodItem class needs a dealloc method to release the name and price variables.

Chapter 10, *Multiple Document Architecture*

1. Once again, the documentation can be found in the */Developer/Documentation /Cocoa/CocoaTopics.html* file.

2. In the active target panel of Project Builder (Project → Edit Active Target), add a document type with the following settings:

   - Name: Property List
   - Extensions: plist
   - Document Class: MyDocument

   Build and run (⌘-R) the application. You should be able to read and write *plist* files now.

3. The revert functionality doesn't work because the `windowControllerDidLoadNib` method isn't called, and that is where we turn the contents of a file into a string to use. To fix this, edit the `loadDataRepresentation:ofType:` method as follows:

   ```
   - (BOOL)loadDataRepresentation:(NSData *)data ofType:(NSString *)type
   {
       if (textView){
           NSString * text = [[NSString alloc]initWithData:dataFromFile
                                               encoding:NSUTF8StringEncoding];
           [textView setString:text];
           [text release];
       } else {
           dataFromFile = [data retain];
       }
       return YES;
   }
   ```

Chapter 11, *Rich-Text Handling*

1. To turn on the ability for the TextView to handle graphics from within Interface Builder, simply click on the TextView, and bring up the Attributes inspector, as shown in Figure A-4. Simply click on the radio buttons, and then remove the corresponding lines of code from *MyDocument.m*.

2. Add the following line to the `awakeFromNib:` method:

   ```
   [textView setRulerVisible:YES];
   ```

3. One solution:

   Add a menu item named "Speak" to the File menu of the *MainMenu.nib* file. Connect the menu item to `FirstResponder.startSpeaking` by Control-dragging a connection from the menu item to the First Responder icon. This makes our speakText method obsolete, so it can be removed.

4. One way to do this is to modify the `analyzeText:` method, as shown here:

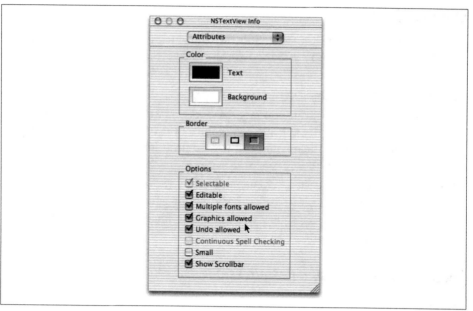

Figure A-4. TextView attribute inspector

```
- (IBAction)analyzeText:(id)sender
{
    int count = 0;
    int fontChanges = -1;
    id lastAttribute = nil;
    NSTextStorage * storage = [textView textStorage];

    while (count < [storage length]) {
        id attributeValue = [storage attribute:NSFontAttributeName
                                    atIndex:count
                                effectiveRange:nil];
        if (attributeValue != lastAttribute) {
            fontChanges++;
        }
        lastAttribute = attributeValue;
        count++;
    }

    NSBeginAlertSheet(@"Analysis",        // title              // i
                      @"OK",              // default button label
                      nil,                // cancel button label
                      nil,                // other button label
                      [textView window],  // document window
                      nil,                // modal delegate
                      NULL,               // selector to method
                      NULL,               // dismiss selector
                      nil,                // context info
                      @"Font Changes %i\nCharacter Count %i",
                      fontChanges, [storage length]);
}
```

Chapter 12, *Printing*

1. The easiest way to do this is to add the Font menu to the *MainMenu.nib* file. Then, in your application, use the Font menu to bring up the Font Panel (or hit ⌘-T).

2. This is almost a trick question.

   By default, the File → Print command works and will print out the Dot View window. To print just the Dot View, disconnect the File → Print menu item from `FirstResponder.print`, then connect it (by Control-dragging) to the `DotView` area and the `print:` action.

3. Simply drag the image view to encompass the entire window. You may even want to turn the border off so that only the image contained by the view will print. Try setting the image view to some of the images in the */Library/Desktop Pictures* folder for printing.

Chapter 13, *Bundles and Resources*

1. One way to do this:

   Add the following method to *Controller.m*, and connect it to a "Previous Image" button:

   ```
   - (IBAction)prevousImage:(id)sender
   {
       if (currentImage == 0) {
           currentImage = [images count] - 1;
       } else {
           currentImage--;
       }
       [imageView setImage objectAtIndex:currentImage];
   }
   ```

2. One way to do this is in Interface Builder. In the inspector, set the key equivalent of the next button to "n" and of the previous button to "p".

    Be sure to hit Return after entering in the key equivalent so that it is stored in the nib file. We had a few problems with this feature on some builds of Interface Builder until we discovered this.

Chapter 14, *Localization*

1. The best way to do this is to follow the procedure that we detailed in the chapter:

   a. Create a localized nib file variant.

   b. Modify the various strings in the UI for their new language.

If you don't know another language, or if you just want to check your translations, use the Translation channel of Sherlock 3.

Chapter 15, *Defaults and Preferences*

1. Find the *~/Library/Preferences/com.oreilly.Favorites* file, and double-click it to open it in the Property List Editor (*/Developer/Applications*).

2. Create a button on the interface for the Favorites application, and have it call the following action method:

```
- (IBAction)reset:(id)sender
{
    [prefs removeObjectForKey:@"FavBook"];
    [prefs removeObjectForKey:@"FavCity"];
    [prefs removeObjectForKey:@"FavColor"];
    [prefs removeObjectForKey:@"FavFood"];
}
```

3. One way to do this:

    a. Create a *default.plist* file using Property List Editor. The root key should be of type Dictionary, and it should have four children. The file should look as follows when you are done with it:

```
<?xml version="1.0" encoding="UTF-8"?>
<!DOCTYPE plist SYSTEM "file://localhost/System/Library/DTDs/PropertyList.dtd">
<plist version="0.9">
<dict>
    <key>FavBook</key>
    <string>Learning Cocoa</string>
    <key>FavCity</key>
    <string>San Francisco </string>
    <key>FavColor</key>
    <string>Red</string>
    <key>FavFood</key>
    <string>Mexican</string>
</dict>
</plist>
```

    b. Add the *default.plist* file as a resource to your project.

    c. Change the init method as follows:

```
- (id)init
{
    [super init];
    NSString file = [[NSBundle mainBundle]
        pathForResource:@"default" ofType:@"plist"];
    NSDictionary * defaultPrefs = [NSDictionary
        dictionaryWithContentsOfFile:file];
    prefs = [[NSUserDefaults standardUserDefaults] retain];
    [prefs registerDefaults:defaultPrefs];
    return self;
}
```

4. One way to do this:

Create a new action method in the *Controller.h* file as follows:

```
- (IBAction)rateUpdated:(id)sender
{
    [[NSUserDefaults standardUserDefaults] setFloatValue:[sender floatValue]
                                       forKey:@"rate"];
}
```

Hook the rateField text field to the rateUpdated: action method so that it is called whenever the contents of the field are changed. Next, add an awakeFromNib method to the *Controller.h* file as follows:

```
- (void)awakeFromNib
{
    [rateField setFloatValue:[[NSUserDefaults standardUserDefaults]
        floatForKey:@"rate"];
}
```

Chapter 16, *Accessory Windows*

1. One way to do this:

    a. Add an outlet named wordCountField to the Controller class.

    b. Add two text labels to the utility panel: the first named "Number of Words" and the second being a place holder. Connect the place holder to the wordCountField outlet in the File's Owner object proxy.

    c. Add the following code to the showInfoPanel: method:

```
#import "Controller.h"

@implementation Controller

- (IBAction)showInfoPanel:(id)sender
{
    if (!infoPanelController) {
        [NSBundle loadNibNamed:@"InfoPanel" owner:self];
        infoPanelController = [[NSWindowController alloc]
            initWithWindow:infoPanel];
    }
    [textLengthField setIntValue:[[textView textStorage] length]];

    [wordCountField setIntValue:[[textStorage
        componentsSeparatedByString:@" "] count];
    [infoPanelController showWindow:self];
}
@end
```

2. Follow the same process as listed earlier with a new paraCountField, and separate the string based on the \n character.

3. Use the following process to guide you:

   a. Add a `radiusTextField` outlet and a `showInfoPanel:` action method to the DotView class.

   b. Create a new nib file named *InfoPanel.nib*.

   c. Lay out a user interface that allows the radius to be displayed via a `radiusTextField` outlet.

   d. Set the File's Owner of *InfoPanel.nib* to the DotView class.

   e. Add a menu item to the menu bar to show the Info panel, and connect it to the `showInfoPanel:` action method.

Chapter 17, *Finishing Touches*

We're going to leave the final exercises up to you to complete on your own. By now you should be able to tackle them without any help from us. However, here are a couple of ideas for an application to write:

- A home inventory keeper that can keep a list of all the items in your house, complete with serial numbers and date of purchase

- An application that is like Dot View, but can draw shapes with a variable number of sides

Good luck!

Additional Resources

If your mission is to produce commercial-quality software for Mac OS X, *Learning Cocoa with Objective-C* has provided a great liftoff, but your journey to market still has a fair distance to go. This appendix lists information about the documents referred to in this book and points you to other resources that can further help you in your Cocoa application development. These resources include the following:

- Cocoa and Mac OS X books aimed at the general programmer audience
- Articles and postings about particular Cocoa programming topics
- Sample code
- Cocoa developer mailing lists and newsgroups
- Partnership programs with Apple Computer

Your first source of additional information pertaining to the material presented in this book is the book's own web site, located at the following URL:

> *http://www.oreilly.com/catalog/learncocoa2/*

At this site, you'll find the book's sample code available for downloading, as well as any errata and plans for future editions.

Documentation on Your Hard Drive

Many of the best resources on Cocoa development are installed on your hard drive:

Mac OS X Release Notes
> Updated with every release of Mac OS X, these notes are typically one step ahead of the rest of Apple's documentation. You should read through these every time you update your system so that you can stay on top of the latest and greatest trends.
>
> */Developer/Documentation/ReleaseNotes*

Cocoa Developer Documentation

The one-stop shop to get access to all the nitty-gritty documentation about Cocoa installed onto your hard drive.

/Developer/Documentation/Cocoa/CocoaTopics.html

Inside Mac OS X: System Overview

This overview of Mac OS X is valuable for anyone doing software development with Cocoa. You should read *Inside Mac OS X: System Overview* to familiarize yourself with the architecture of Mac OS X and how to take best advantage of its design. This guide not only describes the features and capabilities of the operating system, but also describes concepts, facilities, and conventions common to the system's Carbon, Cocoa, Java, and BSD application environments.

/Developer/Documentation/Essentials/SystemOverview/SystemOverview.pdf

Inside Mac OS X: The Objective-C Programming Language

This book fully documents the Objective-C language and provides a foundation for understanding how Cocoa works.

/Developer/Documentation/Cocoa/ObjectiveC/ObjC.pdf

Inside Mac OS X: Aqua Human Interface Guidelines

This book describes how to design your application for the Mac OS X user interface, known as Aqua. This guide provides examples of how to use such Aqua interface elements as windows, controls, dialogs, and icons so that the users of your Cocoa application will be familiar and comfortable with your product the moment they double-click its icon.

/Developer/Documentation/Essentials/AquaHIGuidelines/AquaHIGuidelines.pdf

Inside Mac OS X: Performance

This book tells you how to enhance your program to achieve maximum performance and how to use development tools to analyze and tune your code. Topics include: managing virtual memory; accessing files efficiently; optimizing Carbon applications; building efficient C, C++, and Java code; using the Mac OS X performance measurement and analysis tools; and optimizing the in-memory layout of your program.

/Developer/Documentation/Essentials/Performance/performance.pdf

Core Foundation Developer Documentation

Cocoa is built upon the Core Foundation framework. Occasionally, you will need to use functionality that is at the Core Foundation level and isn't exposed via the Cocoa APIs.

/Developer/Documentation/CoreFoundation/corefoundation_carbon.html

Printed Documentation

If you prefer print over PDF, you can order printed, bound copies of many selected documents, including the full Cocoa API reference, from Apple's print-on-demand provider, Vervante:

http://www.vervante.com/apple

Getting Sample Code

Sometimes there is no better way to learn how to write code than to see working code written by someone else. Apple provides software development kits (SDKs) free of charge for most of Apple's key technologies. You'll find header files, libraries, sample code, and other useful tools and resources in each SDK. You can access a link to Apple's SDKs from this web site:

http://developer.apple.com/cocoa/index.html

You'll also find links to *Cocoa Development Tips & Tricks*, a page dedicated to sharing Cocoa development, debugging, and porting information.

Web Sites

The Web provides a cornucopia of information about Cocoa (as it does everything else). We've found it useful to use Google (*http://www.google.com/*) to provide help for the most arcane of issues, including odd compiler error messages. Just type it into the search field and go.

These are the sites that we browse most often for Cocoa information:

Apple Developer Connection
Apple uses the Developer Documentation area of this web site to post new documents, and update existing ones, on a frequent basis. In addition, being a member of the ADC (basic online membership is free) gives you access to the latest Developer Tools releases.

http://developer.apple.com/

O'Reilly's Mac DevCenter
Affiliated with O'Reilly & Associates, Inc., the O'Reilly Network is home to the Mac DevCenter, a hub site that offers news, FAQs, original articles, and other technical information for Mac OS X developers.

http://www.macdevcenter.com/

MacTech Magazine
This *MacTech* web site also contains a lot of downloadable source code and a web version of *MacTech Online*, a monthly column from the magazine that pro-

vides online technologies and resources. These resources include links to web pages, shareware archives, newsgroups, mailing lists, and castanet channels aimed at Macintosh programmers.

http://www.mactech.com/

Stepwise

One of the original Cocoa sites, Stepwise was created as a resource for NeXT-STEP developers and serves as an excellent resource for Cocoa and WebObjects programming.

http://www.stepwise.com/

The Vermont Recipes

Published on Stepwise, this group of articles written by Bill Cheeseman serves as a cookbook for developing Mac OS X applications with Cocoa using a no-nonsense, hands-on, step-by-step approach.

http://www.stepwise.com/Articles/VermontRecipes/index.html

Cocoa Dev Central

This site is updated fairly frequently with tips, tricks, and tutorials for the novice Cocoa developer.

http://www.cocoadevcentral.com/

CocoaDev Wiki

This user-editable web site is by and for the Mac OS X developer community. If you've never used a WikiWeb before, this style of site gives literally anyone capable of viewing the page the ability to add information.

http://www.cocoadev.com/

Mailing Lists

Many programmers find online mailing lists to be the best way to stay on top of what's fresh and new in the Cocoa community. In addition, they can be an excellent place to get help for a problem; just be sure to search the archives first before asking!

Apple's cocoa-dev mailing list

Apple's moderated email list focused exclusively on Cocoa development issues.

http://lists.apple.com/mailman/listinfo/cocoa-dev

Apple's projectbuilder-users mailing list

Apple's moderated email list focused on Project Builder issues.

http://lists.apple.com/mailman/listinfo/projectbuilder-users

The OmniGroup's MacOSX-dev mailing list

A mailing list set up by one of the premier Cocoa development houses for developers to assist each other.

http://www.omnigroup.com/developer/mailinglists/macosx-dev/

The MacDev-1 mailing list
> A source of news, information, updates, and special offers for the Mac programmer community.

> *http://www.mactech.com/macdev-1/index.html*

Mamasam's Cocoa List Archive
> A browsable, searchable archive of Apple's *cocoa-dev* and The OmniGroup's *MacOSX-dev* mailing lists.

> *http://cocoa.mamasam.com/*

Partnering with Apple

Apple knows that your success is Apple's success. Apple wants developers like you to create successful applications that make customers clamor for Apple computers.

You should tap into some of the programs, products, and services offered by Apple Developer Connection (ADC). Aimed at both large and small developers, the stated purpose of ADC is "to help you successfully develop, test, market, and distribute software and hardware products for Apple platforms and technologies."

In addition to publishing the Developer web site at *developer.apple.com* (which includes the Cocoa Developer Documentation suite), hosting an annual Apple Worldwide Developers Conference (WWDC), and championing developer needs to Apple's own development engineers, ADC offers several program packages useful to you and other developers.

You should become a member of one of these programs. At minimum, sign up for the Online program … it's free! The Online program allows you to download up-to-date development tools, gain access to certain early software releases, and receive weekly technical updates via email.

If you'd rather have this type of information mailed to you, you can pay to become an ADC Mailing customer. You'll then receive the latest in development tools, system software, development kits, and reference materials via a CD series delivered to you monthly via snail mail.

A low-cost ADC Student Program is targeted at university students around the world. ADC Student developers receive special introductory tools, access to a student community of Mac programmers, and other educational opportunities, including the chance to win scholarships to the Worldwide Developers Conference.

The priciest ADC programs are called Select and Premier. These programs offer a multitude of plush products and services, including fat discounts on Apple hardware and third-party products and services, as well as access to Apple's technical-support engineers.

For information on signing up for any of these programs, go to the following URL:

> *http://developer.apple.com/membership/*

Using the Foundation and Application Kit API References

When you install Apple's developer tools on your system, a set of reference documents is installed with them into the */Developer/Documentation* folder on your hard drive. This documentation covers all aspects of Mac OS X development, from building kernel extensions to Carbon and Cocoa development. For Cocoa development, the place to start looking is in the */Developer/Documentation/Cocoa* folder, as shown in Figure C-1.

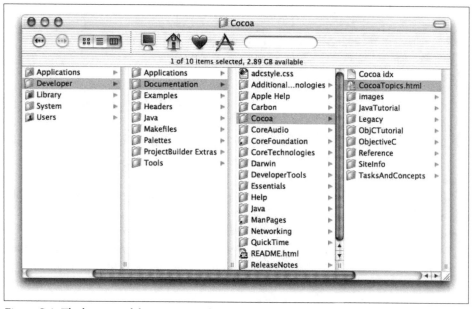

Figure C-1. The location of the Cocoa Developer Documentation

Simply double-click the *CocoaTopics.html* file, and your browser will open it, showing you the complete set of Cocoa documentation. While using this book, one of the most important parts of this documentation set will be the Objective-C Framework Reference, highlighted in Figure C-2.

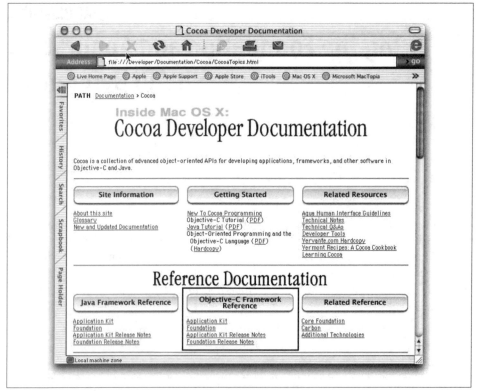

Figure C-2. Cocoa Developer Documentation index page

The Objective-C Framework Reference consists of four primary sections:

Application Kit Reference
>   The authoritative and comprehensive reference to all of the classes, protocols, functions, and types in the Application Kit.

Foundation Reference
>   The authoritative and comprehensive reference to all of the classes, protocols, functions, and types in the Foundation Kit.

Application Kit Release Notes
>   An overview of the changes to the Application Kit in the last release. With each release of Mac OS X comes new features and functionality. This document details the changes in the AppKit that will affect you. You should read these to keep on top of new developments.

Foundation Release Notes
>   An overview of the changes to the Foundation Kit in the latest release.

The benefit to this reference set is that it will always be there, even if you are hacking Cocoa on your PowerBook at 38,000 feet above the Atlantic Ocean. However, the shear mass of documentation on the system can be intimidating to use.

Cocoa Browser

When writing this book, we were planning on putting in quick references to the Foundation and Application Kit APIs as a couple of long appendixes. We thought a bit about the best way to organize the information and came up with a few solutions that might have worked. Then we stumbled across Cocoa Browser, an Open Source documentation viewer written by Hoshi Takanori and Max Horn. It was good enough, even at version 0.4, to recommend as a replacement for the 50 or more pages of reference that would quickly become dated in this book (not to mention that including that many pages would probably drive up the price of the book).

Cocoa Browser presents an effective column-based interface—similar to the Finder's column view—to the documentation installed in your */Developer/Documentation /Cocoa* folder. This column view allows quick access to the information you need. In Figure C-3, we've drilled through to the init method of NSObject and can view the documentation for this method directly.

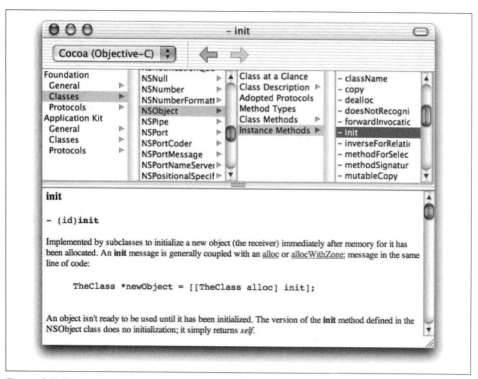

Figure C-3. Using Cocoa Browser to access API reference documentation

Cocoa Browser is also invaluable for seeing which methods a particular class supports and which arguments can be used. For example, we find ourselves looking at all the methods that NSResponder and its subclasses support on a frequent basis. In addition, the Cocoa functions and data types from both the AppKit and the Foundation Kit are easily browsable, as shown in Figure C-4.

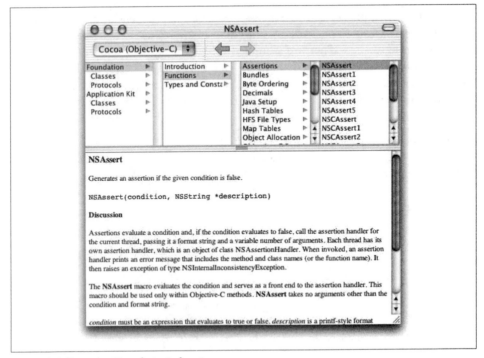

Figure C-4. Browsing Foundation's functions

You can find Cocoa Browser at the following URL:

http://homepage2.nifty.com/hoshi-takanori/cocoa-browser

Since the tool is Open Source and licensed under the GPL, it will always be available for use and can't just disappear. If, for some reason, this site goes away, we'll be sure to link to where you can pick up this tool from the web site for this book:

http://www.oreilly.com/catalog/learncocoa2

Index

We'd like to hear your suggestions for improving our indexes. Send email to *index@oreilly.com*.

initialFirstResponder method (NSWindow class), 169
initializers, 64–67
initWithCoder: method (NSCoding protocol), 210
initWithContentsOfFile: method (NSString class), 92
initWithFrame: method (NSView class), 151
    implementing, 174
input/output (see entries at I/O)
insertObject:atIndex: method (NSMutableArray class), 85
insertString:atIndex: method (NSMutableString class), 78
Inspector panel, creating, 300–303
inspector, sample application for, 298–300
instance, creating for Controller and Model classes, 119
instance methods, 51
integration of graphical elements, Foundation framework and, 17
interface, 45
    vs. graphical user interface, 55
    sample definition of, 57
Interface Builder, 35–40
    adding to the Dock, 23
    application main window, setting size and location of, 39
    File's Owner object and, 297
    parts of, 38
internationalization (see localization)
introspection, 70
I/O management, Foundation framework and, 15
IOKit drivers, 26
isa variable, 53
isOpaque method (NSView), implementing for Dot View, 177

J

Jaguar release of Mac OS X, xi
Java environment, 4
Java programming language, 9, 10
java.lang.StringBuffer, NSMutableString class analogous to, 78

K

kernel extensions, as project type, 26
key-value coding, 195–199

key-value pairs, 89
key window, 129
    panels and, 130
keyboard events, 167
keys, 195
keystrokes, 166
    (see also events)
key-value pairs, 289

L

labels, 52
language conventions, 281
language preferences in Mac OS X, 279
lastPathComponent method (NSString class), 80, 82
Layout menu, 116
layout rectangles, displaying, 116
length method (NSString class), 72
lines, adding for decoration, 115
link wrappers, 239
loadDataRepresentation:ofType: method (NSDocument class), 224
loadFileWrapperRepresentation:ofType: method (NSDocument class), 239
localization, 7, 279–288
    architecture for, 279
    functionality of, Foundation framework and, 16
localizedStringForKey:value:table: method (NSBundle class), 287
lockFocus method (NSView class), 157
locks, 14
loops, 14, 167
.lproj directory extension, 280

M

.m files (Objective-C source code), 37, 54
    for Dot View, 173
    for Currency Converter, 124
Mac OS X
    development documentation for, 343–346
    key environments of, 3–5
    language preferences for, 279
    Release 10.2 (Jaguar), xi
    Software Update tool, Developer Tools and, 22
MacOS bundle directory, 269
mailing lists, 341

NSNumber class, 195
NSObject class, 126
NSPrintInfo helper object, 261
NSPrintOperation class, 261
NSResponder class, 126, 128, 168
NSSet class, 89
NSString class, 72
NSTextContainer class, 238
NSTextStorage class, 238, 244
NSTextView class, 237
NSUndoManager class, 249
NSUserDefaults class, 290
NSView class, 126, 128
    custom views and, 151
    defining subclass of, 152
NSWindow class, 126, 128
    event handling and, 170
    notifications and, 189
NSWindowController class, 222, 226
numbers, comparing, 92

O

object composition, 48
objectAtIndex: method (NSArray class), 83
objectForKey: method (NSDictionary
        class), 90
Objective-C programming language, 9,
        43–70
    categories and, 194
    defined types of (list), 54
    protocols and, 193
Objective-C++ programming language, 10
object-oriented programming (OOP) with
        Objective-C, 43–70
objects, 43–51
    aligning, 116
    allocating, 50
    arrays and, 95
    classes of, 44
    creating, 48–51, 62–67
    deallocating, 67–69, 95
    duplicating, 111
    functionality of, Foundation framework
        and, 15
    initializing, 50, 95
    sending to another application, 210
    working with multiple, 50
onscreen/offscreen windows, 129
opacity, 157
OpenStep, 5
operating systems, Foundation framework
        and, 13

optimization level box, 319
-Os setting, 319
Other Sources group, 37
outlets, 103
    for Controller class, defining, 118
    delegate, 182
    for formatted cell example, creating, 138
    making connections and, 149
    typing, 141
oval paths, 164
overriding methods, 61–69

P

packaging applications for distribution, 319
panels, 17, 130
paragraphs, formatting, 250
pasteboards, 18
pathExtension method (NSString class), 80,
        82
paths
    drawing into views, 161–164
    oval, 164
PDF (Portable Document Format), 7
performance
    improving image load time, 276–278
    multiple nib files for, 297
periodic events, 167
Photoshop, designing icons with, 310
PID (process ID number), 31, 32
PkgInfo file, 268, 269
plist files (property lists), 92
plug-in bundles, 267
plus (+) sign in method definitions, 58
polymorphism, 61
Portable Document Format (PDF), 7
ports, 14
preferences, 289–295
    accessing from the command line, 293
    functionality of, Foundation framework
        and, 16
    language, in Mac OS X, 279
    overriding, 294
Preferences folder, caution when editing files
        in, 290
preloading images, 276–278
Preview application, 263
primitive types, 195
print command, 75, 76
print info objects, 261
print: message, 259
print-object command, 74, 76
printf (C programming language), 29

substringWithRange: method (NSString class), 77
superclasses, 46
  methods for, calling, 62
support classes, 16

T

Tab key, 117
tabbing between text fields, 115
table columns, configuring, 201
table entries, allowing modification of, 206
table views, 199–210
tables, sorting data in, 215–218
Takanori, Hoshi, 345
takeValueForKey: method (NSKeyValueCoding protocol), 195
target/action relationship, 143–150
tasks, 14
Terminal (the), 33
  accessing preferences and, 293
Terminal window, 31
text, 7, 18
  data types of, 238
  rich, 237–255
  storing, 244–249
text attributes, 244–249
  (see also string attributes)
"text editor" application, 227–236
text fields, 110–112
  adding to formatted cell example, 137
  changing attributes of, 112
  first, 115
text labels, adding to text fields, 112
Text menu, 250
text views, 231–235, 238–251
  inspector for viewing contents of, 298–307
thread stack viewer (debugger), 34
threads, 14
  image loading performance and, 278
time (see date and time)
timers, 14
timestamp, 31, 32
titles
  of columns, 201
  setting for windows, 109
tokens (string format), 49
tools (see development tools)
tracking-rectangle events, 167
transparency, 157
troubleshooting, 30

U

undo manager, 249
undo/redo, Foundation framework and, 16
unlockFocus method (NSView class), 157
URL handling, 16
URLs
  Apple Developer Connection (ADC), 340
  Apple documentation for developers, xiv
  Apple software development kits, 340
  Cocoa Browser, 346
  country abbreviations, 283
  language abbreviations, 282
  Mac DevCenter, 340
  sample code for this book, xv
  web sites about Cocoa, 340
user events (see events)
user interface
  Apple Computer guidelines for, 17
  for formatted cell example, creating, 136
  functionality of, Foundation framework and, 17
  (see also GUIs)
user language-specific resources, 283
user preferences (see preferences)
user region-specific resource, 283
UTF8String method (NSString class), 72, 75
utilities
  Disk Copy, 320
  Software Update, 22

V

valueForKey: method (NSKeyValueCoding protocol), 195
variable viewer (debugger), 34
Vervante, 340
view coordinate system, 133
"View Print" application, 260
views, 17, 105, 128
  content, 130
  custom, 151–165
  hierarchy of, 130
  printing, 259–261
voice functionality, 253–255

W

web sites (see URLs)
whatis command, 76
widgets, 17
width of table columns, adjusting, 201
window controllers, 226
window coordinate system, 133

Window Environment configuration option
(Project Builder), 24
Window menu, 129
window objects, 102
window server, 126
windowControllerDidLoadNib: method
(NSDocument class), 224
windowNibName method (NSDocument
class), 224
windows, 17, 102, 126–130
auxiliary, 297–307
key/main, 129

onscreen/offscreen, 129
resizing, 108
window controllers for, 226
windowShouldClose: method, 184, 186
writeToFile: method (NSString class), 80, 92

Z

zero-based indexing, 13

About the Authors

James Duncan Davidson. Duncan is a freelance author, speaker, and software consultant, focusing on Mac OS X, Java, and XML technologies. He regularly presents at conferences all over the world on topics ranging from Open Source to programming Java effectively. He was the original author of Apache Tomcat and Apache Ant and was instrumental in their donation to the Apache Software Foundation by Sun Microsystems. While working at Sun, he authored two versions of the Java Servlet API specification, as well as the Java API for XML Processing specification. He currently resides in San Francisco, California, and can be found on the Net at *http://www.x180.net/*.

Apple Computer, Inc. The first edition of *Learning Cocoa*, from which this new edition was derived, was created by the technical writers, engineers, support specialists, and other professionals at Apple Computer who are committed to making Mac OS X a superior platform for innovation, productivity, and enjoyment. These professionals have diligently collected, compiled, and edited the information in this book to ensure that it is a useful resource for all Mac OS X developers.

Colophon

Our look is the result of reader comments, our own experimentation, and feedback from distribution channels. Distinctive covers complement our distinctive approach to technical topics, breathing personality and life into potentially dry subjects.

The animal on the cover of *Learning Cocoa with Objective-C*, Second Edition, is an Irish setter. Bred as a sporting dog in the 19th century, the Irish setter's agility and energy made it a prime companion for pheasant and quail hunters. By the 1890s, the dog's attractive, silky red coat and elegant build boosted its popularity as a show dog. For the past century, breeders have created a larger dog with a longer coat, with deep chestnut red or patches of red and white hair. The dog is also popular as a family dog. Described as loyal, gentle, energetic, and happy, the Irish setter gets along well with children. Some hospitals, nursing homes, and rehabilitation centers also adopt the Irish setter as a therapy dog.

Brian Sawyer was the production editor and proofreader for *Learning Cocoa with Objective-C*, Second Edition. Jeff Holcomb was the copyeditor. Claire Cloutier and Sheryl Avruch provided quality control. Brenda Miller wrote the index.

Emma Colby designed the cover of this book, based on a series design by Edie Freedman. The cover image is a 19th-century engraving from the Dover Pictorial Archive. Emma Colby produced the cover layout with QuarkXPress 4.1 using Adobe's ITC Garamond font. Robert Romano and Emma Colby designed the quick reference card using Adobe's Myriad Condensed and ITC Garamond fonts.

David Futato designed the interior layout. This book was converted to FrameMaker 5.5.6 with a format conversion tool created by Erik Ray, Jason McIntosh, Neil Walls, and Mike Sierra that uses Perl and XML technologies. The text font is Linotype Birka; the heading font is Adobe Myriad Condensed; and the code font is Lucas-Font's TheSans Mono Condensed. The illustrations that appear in the book were produced by Robert Romano and Jessamyn Read using Macromedia FreeHand 9 and Adobe Photoshop 6. The tip and warning icons were drawn by Christopher Bing. This colophon was written by Ann Schirmer and Brian Sawyer.

How to stay in touch with O'Reilly

1. Visit our award-winning web site

http://www.oreilly.com/

★ "Top 100 Sites on the Web"—PC Magazine
★ CIO Magazine's Web Business 50 Awards

Our web site contains a library of comprehensive product information (including book excerpts and tables of contents), downloadable software, background articles, interviews with technology leaders, links to relevant sites, book cover art, and more. File us in your bookmarks or favorites!

2. Join our email mailing lists

Sign up to get email announcements of new books and conferences, special offers, and O'Reilly Network technology newsletters at:

http://elists.oreilly.com

It's easy to customize your free elists subscription so you'll get exactly the O'Reilly news you want.

3. Get examples from our books

To find example files for a book, go to:

http://www.oreilly.com/catalog

select the book, and follow the "Examples" link.

4. Work with us

Check out our web site for current employment opportunities:

http://jobs.oreilly.com/

5. Register your book

Register your book at:

http://register.oreilly.com

6. Contact us

O'Reilly & Associates, Inc.
1005 Gravenstein Hwy North
Sebastopol, CA 95472 USA
TEL: 707-827-7000 or 800-998-9938
      (6am to 5pm PST)
FAX: 707-829-0104

order@oreilly.com
For answers to problems regarding your order or our products. To place a book order online visit:

http://www.oreilly.com/order_new/

catalog@oreilly.com
To request a copy of our latest catalog.

booktech@oreilly.com
For book content technical questions or corrections.

corporate@oreilly.com
For educational, library, government, and corporate sales.

proposals@oreilly.com
To submit new book proposals to our editors and product managers.

international@oreilly.com
For information about our international distributors or translation queries. For a list of our distributors outside of North America check out:

http://international.oreilly.com/distributors.html

adoption@oreilly.com
For information about academic use of O'Reilly books, visit:

http://academic.oreilly.com

O'REILLY®

To order: 800-998-9938 • *order@oreilly.com* • *www.oreilly.com*
Online editions of most O'Reilly titles are available by subscription at *safari.oreilly.com*
Also available at most retail and online bookstores.